I shall pass through this world but once. Any good therefore that *I* can do or any kindness that *I* can show to any human being, let me do it now. *L*et me not defer or neglect it for *I* shall not pass this way again.

EX LIBRIS

Joe Kotcka

Ask me anything
OUR ADVENTURES WITH KHRUSHCHEV

Ask me anything

OUR ADVENTURES WITH KHRUSHCHEV

WILLIAM RANDOLPH **HEARST**, JR.
FRANK **CONNIFF**
BOB **CONSIDINE**

McGraw-Hill Book Company, Inc.
NEW YORK
TORONTO
LONDON

ASK ME ANYTHING

CHAPTERS

Prologue

by William Randolph Hearst, Jr.

Let me admit here and now that luck played a great part in putting my associates and myself on the scene in Moscow in February, 1955, when the Khrushchev era of Communist history began.

A fortunate combination of circumstances made it possible for us to be present in the Supreme Soviet when Premier Georgi Malenkov stepped down in a historic speech, and Nikolai Bulganin came forth as the front man for the new regime.

The pressing need to spread the news that a new age was dawning enabled us to obtain a rapid series of interviews with Bulganin, V. M. Molotov, and Marshal Georgi Zhukov, three members of the quadrumvirate which composed the new "collective leadership." The same urgent necessity made us the agents for introducing to the world the fourth member of the quadrumvirate, a virtual unknown who was thereafter to dominate the headlines with his exuberant personality and dynamic brand of power politics : a squat, bald, unprepossessing little man from the Ukraine named Nikita Sergeyevitch Khrushchev.

1

When we proceeded to become familiar visitors at the Kremlin and conversational partners with the highest Communist leaders, quite a few Americans were more than a little surprised. I can understand their feelings. I was more than a little surprised myself. Somehow Hearst and the Kremlin didn't seem to go together. The idea that the son of William Randolph Hearst should break the news that Communist policy was switching to a new direction didn't seem to add up.

And what about this new man that Hearst and his two associates kept talking and writing about? Zhukov and Molotov and Malenkov were well known to the American public, but who was this Nikita Khrushchev?

It is largely the desire to answer these questions that has produced this book. We hope that reading it will give you a better idea of the foe we face: a tough, cunning, and resourceful man who guides the Communist empire with skill and intelligence. We hope you will come to understand the circumstances and the environment that have shaped his character, and have fashioned his fanatical belief in communism as the future social system of the world.

The world has long since discarded the comforting thought that Khrushchev was nothing but a tosspot bully-boy who would soon be put in his place. Most people today have a more valid appreciation of his abilities, especially since his dramatic visit to America in the fall of 1959.

To penetrate such a diverse personality is difficult, but it is of vital importance that we Americans study the origins, the triumphs and defeats, the current problems of the man who told me in the Kremlin:

"In forty years, the Communist Party never gave me a task I turned down. And in forty years the Communist Party never found a single thing wrong in the way I did things."

On one hand, he is a smiling, ingratiating politician; on the other, a ruthless barbarian who gave the order for the massacre of Budapest. He is personable and even likeable at times; a sharp-witted opponent in debate whose thrusts cut to the heart of the matter under discussion; a wheel-horse politician who yet hopes to lift his country to the broad, sunlit uplands of true prosperity. His personality is evidently complex, and yet he seems to possess the simple wisdom of a peasant. Well along in years, he is still full of the bounce and snap of the younger generation; a man who remembers the horrors of the Great Russian Revolution, he dreams of a world at peace—on Communist terms, of course.

Nikita Khrushchev is all these things, and even more. We sat across the conference table from him on two separate occasions at crucial turning points in world history—in 1955, when the Malenkov upheaval first brought him to international prominence, and in November, 1957, when the first Sputnik and the ouster of Marshal Zhukov again made Moscow the news capital of the world. We have seen him in London, when the touring Soviet team of "B. and K."—Bulganin and Khrushchev—failed to break down the chilly wall of British reserve. We saw him at Geneva in 1955, when protocol forced him to remain in the wings, and we have chatted with him at embassy gatherings while he was engaged in "cocktail diplomacy." We saw him in Moscow in the summer of 1959, when his verbal jousts with Vice-President Nixon captured world headlines, and we saw him on several occasions during his tour of the United States.

Through these many contacts, an odd relationship has developed between the Premier of the U.S.S.R. and the editor-in-chief of the Hearst Newspapers. May the good Lord and my esteemed father forgive me, but we seem to get along. He calls me his "capitalist-monopolist" friend, and no protest on my part seems to rid him of the notion that I own all the newspapers in America. Many times, I have told him I wished we did have a monopoly; in several cities where we publish, our competition gives us a hard time. But Khrushchev goes on blithely insisting that I own the American press.

My own belief is that we get along because we recognize each other for what we are. To me, he is a dedicated Communist who believes world domination by his system lies somewhere in the future, and for whom no tactic is too brutal if it advances his cause. To him, I am a dedicated capitalist, sincere (but misguided, he is sure) in my allegiance to the Western democratic system. I think Khrushchev sometimes pities me because I am unable to grasp the full charm of communism, and I likewise pity him for his ignorance of the American way of life.

As I say, luck played a big role in putting us squarely in Khrushchev's path just as he was about to make his entrance on the global stage. But luck alone would never have placed us in Moscow at the exactly right moment; many other factors helped prepare the way.

For my part, I was ready when opportunity tapped at the door. For several years, I have studied intensively the career of my late father, in the hope that some of his journalistic wisdom might rub off on a less gifted son. Pop had a stormy and controversial career, and he lived it so fully and vividly that he seemed to create either fervent enemies or devoted adherents. He attacked every issue with all guns blazing, leaving many a wound and gaining some scars of his own in return. During the last years of his life, even when he more or less retired to his San Simeon castle, he was nevertheless still active, taking punishment as well as handing it out, and as usual, enjoying the struggle immensely.

But it wasn't Pop's public career, so to speak, that has particularly interested me, nor his political battles and controversies. I have concentrated most on his actual newspaper work, the technical and practical ideas of news coverage that helped him

build his huge journalistic empire. And in particular, I have concentrated on the "old days," the early years, when he was first
shaping his newspaper style. Permit me a personal aside. I know
my father was a controversial figure whose activities stirred
deep passions both for and against him. But I am convinced that
as the fires of controversy flicker out, and passions subside, Pop
will come to be recognized for what he truly was: a great newspaperman. Future students of journalism will acknowledge him
as the source of many techniques and improvements that have
come to be standard operating procedure in the modern newspaper. In the early days of his career, it was possible to attempt
projects which the complexity of modern publishing make difficult or impossible. Nonetheless, it is exactly these original ideas
and pet projects of Pop's which have always most attracted me.
His achievements seem to imply that a newspaper should develop an intimacy between itself and its readers. It is not enough
to sit in the office and record events as they are brought in by
telephone, telegraph, radio, and other impersonal instruments.
The newspaper that wishes to appeal to readers in large numbers
—always a prime objective of Hearst Newspapers—should establish a link with the reader by bringing him the news in familiar,
first-person, eyewitness style. The reader can't be there in person
when great events are happening, but a newspaper can serve as
his agent and give him personal contact with history.

I have always been especially impressed by Pop's striking
coverage of the Spanish-American war, when he chartered a
ship and took a whole crew of reporters and cartoonists with
him to Cuba. During the San Francisco earthquake and fire of
1906, he chartered one train to rush supplies and medicine to
the stricken city, and chartered another to bring a printing press
from Salt Lake City so he could continue to publish his beloved
Examiner without interruption. He always seemed to be doing
something; he appeared on the scene himself whenever possible

and made a determined attempt to give his readers a sense of personal participation in newsworthy events.

With my father's example before me, I was immediately receptive when the possibility of a fact-finding trip to Russia was broached to me by David Sentner, chief of our Washington bureau. Actually, I had long nourished a hope of one day going behind the Iron Curtain to take a look at Stalin's Russia. During the war, in fact, I almost pulled it off. Averell Harriman, a long-time neighbor of mine on Long Island, was then serving as Ambassador to Russia—and issuing warnings about Stalin's real intentions which were not heeded by the State Department—and Maj. Gen. Fred Anderson, a good friend who was then head of the Eighth Air Force Bomber Command in England, used to fly to Russia once in a while. I figured that I might hitch a ride to Moscow with him for a first-hand view of the Soviet Union.

But I figured without my Pop—the man whose early exploits were to influence my later actions so strongly. He wisely pointed out that Stalin had just caused the entire Polish underground leadership to "disappear," and nobody was making much of a fuss about it. "There won't be much sympathy for you either," he told me, "if you suddenly get lost in those Russian spaces." His logic was convincing, and I abandoned the thought of visiting Russia. But the idea never completely left me.

Dave Sentner revived my interest when he brought up the matter again at the annual Gridiron dinner in Washington in mid-December, 1954. Dave, a capable and trusted correspondent who has been with our organization for years, said later that he had received no prompting from official sources, American or Russian, in making his proposal. "I had one of those hunches that comes once in a lifetime," he said. "My instinct told me that the time was ripe for someone to go to Russia and see what had been going on since Stalin's death." Dave further reasoned that the long record of the Hearst Newspapers in opposing communism and all its works might have the perverse effect of making a visit by William Randolph Hearst, Jr., appealing to the Soviet leaders. This was a shrewd deduction on Dave's part, because later, when we published the news that the new Communist line was something called "peaceful coexistence," no one accused us of being soft on communism or of peddling the party line.

The combination of Dave's reasoning and my own predeliction for personal journalism, brought me around to a quick and positive decision. Frank Conniff, national editor of the Hearst Newspapers, also though the idea was well worth a try and gave it his support. My mother, my wife, and several of my other business associates, however, were negative about the subject. Mom and Austine feared for my safety, while R. E. "Dick" Berlin, J. D. Gortatowsky, and the late E. D. Coblentz, and other company executives whose counsel I valued, feared I might somehow make a fool of myself, not only damaging my own personal reputation, but also harming the prestige of the Newspapers.

Gorty had visions of Frank and me burning the Communist flag in Red Square after too much sampling of the vodka bottle. Cobbie, Pop's senior editor, who had practically raised me in the business, felt so strongly about the matter he summoned Frank to a conference in New York early in January. For more than an hour and a half he pleaded with him to use any influence he could to cancel the project. Frank, who respected Cobbie's judgment and loved him dearly, declined to yield. He passed Cobbie's objections on to me, but let it go at that.

These disagreements are mentioned because they help to recapture the somber tone of the cold war early in 1955, and how hard it was to believe that Russian policy had switched to a softer line. Now, thousands of tourists enter the Soviet Union,

and no one thinks there is anything remarkable about it. But
only a few years ago, our proposed visit provoked great soul-
searching and serious warnings from many of our closest friends.
We had misgivings of our own as well, and more than once
during the trip we wondered why we had left the blessed free-
doms of the U.S.A. for the journalistic enticements of Communist Russia.

It was now up to Sentner to try to get me a visa from the
Russians. I stipulated only one condition: I wanted to take
Frank and Joseph Kingsbury Smith with me. I instructed Dave
that a visa for me alone was not enough, nor even a visa for
me and one of the other two. Visas for all three, or none at all.
This almost brought Dave to despair, because, after all, who
were we to set conditions for visas when they were being denied
to all who applied? C. L. "Cy" Sulzberger, the able correspondent for *The New York Times,* told me his application had been
on file for seven years when we received ours.

But I had good reasons for my stubbornness. I had chosen
these two men not only because of our close personal relationship
and my admiration for them as journalists, but because in many
ways they supplemented and complemented one another. Joe
Kingsbury Smith had covered Europe since the war, and before
that his beat had been the State Department. He was thoroughly
familiar with the intricacies of diplomacy. He had covered all
the postwar political meetings in his capacity as European general manager for International News Service, and had already
visited Moscow, having gone there in 1947 to cover the abortive
Big Four foreign ministers' conference.

Frank was (and is) a prolific reader and student of history.
He was more conversant in this field than either Joe or myself,
with particular emphasis on modern European history and Russian political developments since the revolution. His memory
for dates and the names of peoples and places has always as-

tounded me. His intensive study of Communist history and the lives of Bolshevik leaders gave him a special perspective on the Moscow scene.

And finally, they were both true professionals, as was Bob Considine, who took Joe's place in 1957 when the latter's executive duties in the Hearst organization made it impossible for him to go with us on our second trip to Russia. With people of this caliber accompanying me, I felt confident in overriding the pleas of those who opposed my plans.

On December 23, 1954, Dave sent a special delivery letter to Konstantin G. Fedoseev, counselor of the Russian Embassy in Washington. It read:

"W. R. Hearst, Jr., chairman of the editorial board of the Hearst Newspapers, has requested me to take up an important matter with His Excellency, Soviet Ambassador Zaroubin. I would like to have a preliminary discussion of the matter at your convenience."

On Christmas eve, Dave received a cordial phone call from Fedoseev. He proposed they get together the next day. Dave suggested they meet at noon in the National Press Club bar. Only the bartender was present on this Christmas day when Sentner and Fedoseev gathered for this holiday drink. As Dave recalls it, there was a bit of conversational fencing, with Fedoseev insisting that things had changed greatly in Russia since the death of Stalin.

"But have they changed enough so that a man named William Randolph Hearst could get a visa?" Dave asked.

The Russian put down his glass and shrugged.

"I don't see why not," he said. "Permit me to say that I think it could be arranged."

Thus, casually, did the citadel fall. Dave recalls that Fedoseev balked when told of my proviso: that it was all—Hearst, Smith, and Conniff—or none. He asked for background information on

both of them, which Dave agreed to supply. They quickly agreed
to admit Joe, but held up on Frank. I simply repeated my initial
instruction: all or none.

While I was still gathering further material they requested
about Frank, we were suddenly informed that everything was
acceptable. All three visas would be granted, but would we stop
personally at the Russian Embassy in Washington to pick them
up? I thought it only proper to accept that condition. I had lived
in Washington previously for about five years and had never
accepted any of their invitations, but under the circumstances,
thought it correct to do so now.

As Frank and Dave and I walked up the marble stairs of the
Embassy on Sixteenth Street, we were confronted at the top
with a huge picture of Joseph Stalin beaming benignly down
on us. It struck me, and I mentioned it to Ambassador Zaroubin
after he broke out some first-class caviar and vodka from the
home country, that I would love to know what my father would
think about this chummy gathering at the Russian Embassy.
The Ambassador, a gruff, dour, but not unfriendly man,
grunted. He thought Pop might have approved it because the
project under discussion was a journalistic one.

We had one more tug of wills before final arrangements were
completed. Aerflotte Sovietskaya had recently concluded an
agreement with Air France permitting the transshipment of
Moscow-bound passengers at Prague. Ambassador Zarubin
suggested we use this route. I demurred and insisted that we depart for Moscow via Berlin. I wanted one final check with our
intelligence, diplomatic, and military people in that exposed
bastion before taking off into the unknown. An impasse developed, and again Dave Sentner despaired. Who were we to insist on conditions? But the Ambassador finally yielded.

Then, about a week later, as we were about to board a Pan
American Clipper for Paris, who should pop up at the counter

but the Ambassador. He had given no inkling over the caviar
of the possibility of his going to Moscow at the same time, and
on the same plane, for that matter. Once aboard, I stopped by his
seat, greeted him, and asked him if he had known he was going
to Moscow when we met the week before. "No," he said with
a smile. Then he jerked a big workingman's thumb over his
shoulder in the general direction of Moscow.

"They send," he said. "They send."

And so they had. In Paris we learned that Soviet ambassadors
from all the leading capitals had been summoned home suddenly. It became known only later, that the clan was being
gathered to be briefed on the new order. It turned out that a
fellow named Khrushchev was taking over, and he wanted them
to be the first to know.

When we arrived in Russia, a grave crisis gripped relations
between East and West: the dispute over Formosa, and more
specifically, over the two small islands of Quemoy and Matsu.
Congress had just voted almost unanimously to give President
Eisenhower a free hand in this matter, and administration policy
allowed for virtually no retreat. Admiral Robert B. Carney, then
Chief of Naval Operations, had predicted to a select group of
Washington correspondents that hostilities would flare up by
April 15. And Russia, as well as the United States, was committed to support its ally in a showdown. We seemed faced with
another Korea—or worse.

And events in Russia itself served to feed the war hysteria
which seized the world. The change in regime seemed especially
ominous. The harsh words spoken by the new leaders before the
Supreme Soviet, the threatening tone of their exhortations to
the party cadres, the largest appropriations for the defense since
the wartime budget of 1944, caused many a reflective and experienced student of Soviet affairs to predict a return to the
dark days of Stalinism. Others saw in the rise of Marshal Zhu-

kov to the Minister of Defense and membership on the Presidium a warning that the Red Army was at long last ready to make
its move for supremacy. The elimination of the intelligent Malenkov, highly respected for his ability and good sense by
Western diplomats, in favor of the boorish, little-known Khrushchev also appeared to bode no good.

But we three reporters, right on the scene in Moscow, found
a sign which directly contradicted these omens of imminent war.
Our first-hand observations and experiences led us to conclusions we could not ignore or explain away. There was the steady
chorus of "Peace and competitive coexistence" which we heard
from everyone in authority. There were such gestures as Bulganin's eloquent shrug when we questioned him about the
threatening talks in the Supreme Soviet, a shrug which plainly
asked, "Why don't you believe what we tell you, and ignore
what we say to keep up the party fervor?" Above all, there was
the treatment we received, the exhaustive series of interviews
we were granted, all of which strongly implied that the Soviets
had a new policy which they were extremely eager to get across
to us.

Even so, we might have dismissed all this as the familiar
mouthings of Communist propaganda, had it not been for our
interview with the man who was obviously responsible for making top-level decisions, the man who could be immediately recognized as boss in the reshuffled Soviet regime, the man who
would prove to be the key to Russian policy from that time on.
Our meeting with this heavy-set, bull-necked little man, whose
beady blue eyes, bald bullet head, and gap-toothed smile have
since become well known all over the world, soon crystallized
our suspicions into certainties. Here, very clearly, was the head
of the state; here was the man who would call the tune.

The details of this startling interview with Nikita Khrushchev
will be narrated fully later on. I will quote here only those words

which convinced us beyond all doubt that a new era had dawned in East-West relations.

"We are living on one and the same globe, and there is no place where we could step out of it.

"What is the conclusion to be drawn?

"You are against socialism. We are against capitalism. You want to build up your economy on a capitalist basis. We want to build ourselves up on a basis of socialism.

"There is no reason why you should not do so. The only thing necessary is that you should not try to prevent us from building up our economy on principles we think best.

"Some people might think it is the will of God. We believe it is due to the facts of historical development that these two systems have come into being. You believe capitalism is something that cannot be shaken. We believe the same about our own socialist system.

"Those, of course, are opposite solutions. But how can solutions be reached? For hotheads, war is a solution. That is a silly kind of solution.

"We believe, as Lenin said, that the solution lies in coexistence. In other words we can live together without fighting.

"Lenin spoke of long-term coexistence. How long no one can tell. It would depend on historical conditions. If the American people prefer to live under capitalism, there is no reason why they should be prevented from doing so.

"I sympathize with communism. You sympathize with capitalism."

At this point, the Soviet leader leaned over the table in his office and patted my arm. His blue eyes twinkled.

"You are a capitalist yourself, but we are having a peaceful talk here," he said. "If we can coexist around this table, I think we could coexist around the globe."

Sound familiar? It should. The same ideas, couched in practically the same words, poured out at you in September, 1959, from newspapers, radio, magazines, and television. The little man was saying them as the invited guest of the country, following Vice-President Nixon's journey to Moscow and the announcement of President Eisenhower's return visit to Russia.

We left Moscow only a few days after this climactic interview, and stopped over in London to think over and evaluate what we had seen and heard. We realized that we had a story of momentous importance, but our views were so contrary to those generally held in that troubled time that we knew we had to sum up our conclusions with extreme care. We were flailed by cables which seemed to arrive hourly from stateside editors demanding the immediate start of an "interpretive" series on Russia. And there was one other consideration which, I must confess, contributed to the general turmoil. We knew that readers of the Hearst papers probably expected not only a blast at the whole Communist system, but also red-hot warnings that the Red Army was about to launch a shooting war.

"We must be nuts," said Joe Smith. "We seem to be the only people in the world who don't think there's going to be a war."

We finally agreed on a general statement of our findings, which was released in late February of 1955. In part, it read:

"The Soviet Union can't stand a war with the West within the foreseeable future and therefore won't start one. . . . Russia's realistic rulers will exert a cooling influence to keep the Chinese teapot from boiling over.

"The only spark that might touch off an atomic showdown would be the failure of the West to keep up its guard and encourage the Kremlin to think we were weak and defenseless."

(We didn't hear a whisper about Soviet progress in rocketry during the 1955 visit. Reading the above paragraph over in the light of the U.S.S.R.'s brilliant achievements since 1955 makes me shiver a little.)

"The West is well equipped in any trial at arms. But are we prepared practically and philosophically to surpass communism in the thornier problems of peace?

"We are going to face a struggle that may prove more difficult for us to wage successfully than a military conflict: I am referring to the conflict of 'Competitive Co-existence.' This is intended to be an ideological and economical struggle aimed at achieving Communist domination by measures short of an all-out, East-West war.

"It will be far more subtle than the cold war was under Stalin. But its ultimate objective, as far as we are concerned, will be the same."

If these paragraphs have a familiar ring, it's because we are no longer in the minority in our opinions. But our conclusions were developed under the lash of a journalistic deadline and at a time when the world situation was being interpreted in exactly opposite fashion by many distinguished commentators. A newspaperman is happy when a story stands up for twenty-four hours; a week is a long time; but the basic judgments in our original report have stood up for five years. That's a lifetime by newspaper standards.

It is remarkable how little Khrushchev has changed his fundamental "line" since our first meeting in February, 1955. Some of his remarks were repeated almost verbatim on his 1959 American tour, and the same theme appears in every interview he has granted an American. Basically, it is a variation of the iron-fist-in-a-velvet-glove motif, with more emphasis on the velvet than on the iron: our two great nations should be friends and can be friends; we can engage in peaceful competition; let us coexist and compete and see which system is the best for coming generations; meanwhile, don't forget that we have an enormous military machine, are right up to date in the fields of science and technology, and don't intend to be pushed around.

Events either beyond Khrushchev's control, or set in motion by the dynamics of his new policy, have forced him to drop the sweetness-and-light theme from time to time. Witness Hungary. Khrushchev responded to this unexpected threat with a ferocity that would have drawn a grunt of admiration from Stalin himself. Witness his violent reaction to the Lebanon landings of our Marines. Witness his on-again-off-again family quarrel with Tito. But Khrushchev always seems to return to his fundamental program as soon as it is feasible.

Khrushchev and his colleagues in the Kremlin have shored up their world position by benefits derived from scientific innovations of World War II. It was during Stalin's reign that the decision was taken to go full-out on the rocket program, at a time when American strategic thought rested primarily on a manned bomber deterrent. But Khrushchev has used this power in ways Stalin would never have thought of. Stalin believed so deeply in fear as an instrument of policy that it is doubtful if he would have used the Russian rocket supremacy acquired in 1957 with the subtlety and finesse of Khrushchev. With Nikita, the threat is always there, but it is veiled.

In fact, Khrushchev has evidently decided that nuclear-headed war is an impossibility, because of the dreadful power of modern weapons. In a nuclear war, neither side can look forward to winning world leadership of anything save a wrecked and ravaged globe. Therefore, the continuing struggle for Communist world domination, which goes on unabated despite occasional switches in the party line, must be waged in new fields and with different methods. As in the familiar proverb, Khrushchev hopes the West will lose its cloak of armed protection not because the icy winds of Stalinism have whipped it off, but because the sunny warmth of Khrushchevian geniality has induced the West to remove it willingly.

This new policy does not rule out the use of tried-and-true

Communist techniques. Distortions and outright lies about American and Allied policy have figured just as strongly in Khrushchev's propaganda as they did in Stalinist days. The seeds of dissension and revolt are being spread in fallow territory as before. Opportunities for pushing Communist influence into new areas, most brilliantly illustrated by infiltration into the Middle East, are not neglected. The iron clutch on the satellites remains firm, despite the mild liberalization in Poland. All the ancient gimmicks of Communist penetration are still primed for use on targets such as Latin America, except that now they have been augmented by other, more insidious approaches not comprehensible to the inflexible Stalin.

But the general Communist shift from a "cold" to a "soft" war presents the United States with a marvelous opportunity, if we correctly perceive the battleground and prepare our tactics accordingly. That is why I have supported President Eisenhower's flexible approach toward these problems. There was a time when the picture of a big, powerful Uncle Sam, well armed and ready for a showdown, brought a certain reassurance to countries trying to get on their feet after the agony of World War II. Behind this battle-alert posture, they succeeded in reestablishing their economies with the help of American funds, and now no longer believe that the end of the world is coming the day after tomorrow.

But the image of Uncle Sam that served a useful purpose as recently as the mid-1950s no longer fits the realities of the present. Even though the basic differences separating the free and Communist worlds remain the same, they are now being fought out under different ground rules.

We have continued with this method of personalized journalism in covering the new tack of Communist strategy, and in following the career of the remarkable man who guides the destinies of the Soviet empire. In 1957, this time with Bob Consi-

dine along, we paid a second visit to Russia, on the theory that
the Russians would do something spectacular to commemorate
the fortieth anniversary of the revolution. We had no idea, however, that it would be Sputnik I which would provide the additional fireworks. Once more we obtained significant interviews
with the Russian leaders, including another revealing three-hour
session with Khrushchev. Then, in 1959, we covered both Vice-
President Nixon's visit to the Soviet Union and Khrushchev's
historic visit to this country.

Each time, first-hand observation and face-to-face confrontation have helped illuminate ever more clearly the personality, beliefs, and methods of this man who controls the destinies of so
many millions. And in describing our observations we hope to
transmit this sense of what the man is really like and what he
stands for. We cannot help but believe that this sort of on-the-
spot reporting can help our citizens to understand better the
world we live in and the challenges we face.

Besides, it beats hell out of sitting around the office.

CHAPTER 1

Operation improbable

Around 6:30 P.M. on February 8, 1955, there was a rap on the
door of the ornate apartment of William Randolph Hearst, Jr.,
on the third floor of the Hotel National in Moscow. Historians
may yet acknowledge that the knock was the cue for a new
phase in relations between the Western world and the Soviet
Union. At any rate, it signaled an end to the Stalinist years of
calculated hostility to all things Western, and the beginning of
a present accommodation which, with lamentable lack of im-
agination, we have come to call "peaceful coexistence."

At the time, the apartment throbbed with all the jangled
sound and fury of that Western phenomenon known as a cocktail party. For two weeks the itinerant Hearstmen had been
padding out the skimpy fare of the National's uninspired menu
with grateful dips into the more sumptuous larders available to
the chefs of the various embassies. No invitation to lunch or
dinner had been spurned by the three hungry journalists and as
a result, certain responsibilities had been incurred. The traditional American weapon for wiping the slate clean, the cocktail

party, had been organized around a basic supply of vodka, gin, and scotch scrounged from sympathetic friends, and canned grape juice liberated from the American Embassy commissary.

Elegant was hardly the word for it, but the assembled ambassadors, ministers, attachés, and junior secretaries seemed to be having a very agreeable time, judging by the high-decibel level of their conversation. But this group, set down by choice or destiny in Moscow at a crossing point in history, had plenty to talk about. Only five hours before, Premier Georgi Malenkov had astonished the diplomatic galleries at the Supreme Soviet by suddenly pleading inadequacy and asking the comrades to relieve him of his high office. And scarcely two hours before, at a second session of the Supreme Soviet, the First Secretary of the Communist Party, a man named Khrushchev, little known to any of the diplomats, had compounded their amazement by arising to propose that Nikolai Bulganin succeed Malenkov.

These gentlemen and their ladies had more than the usual shop talk to occupy them as they spaded caviar onto brown bread and sluiced it down with vodka and other accompaniment. Little wonder that the taciturn American Ambassador, Charles Bohlen, seemed more reserved than ever as he chatted with France's Leon Joxe. Or that Sir William Hayter, Great Britain's suave representative, listened gravely to the *doyen* of the diplomatic colony, Sweden's Rolf Sohlman, while the latter speculated on the significance of the sensational switch. The hosts meanwhile silently congratulated themselves: circumstances had made this a jimdandy affair, one they might later look back on with a glow of satisfaction, among other glows.

But in the midst of this animated scene came a knock at the door. The confrontation that followed will undoubtedly remain locked in the memory of everyone present. Framed in the doorway were the elite of communism's most envied caste, true celebrities whose names were not only household currency throughout the Soviet empire, but also known and admired in artistic circles the world over.

And when, after an uncertain pause, they strode regally over the threshold, the assembled diplomats knew for a certainty that something historic had indeed happened on this dour February day. Far more than the shifts in power witnessed that afternoon, this small group signified that a new chapter had begun in the troubled relations between East and West.

In the lead, as befitted her station, walked Galina Ulanova, prima ballerina of the Bolshoi ensemble, never seen anywhere before by those present except across the footlights. Next to her was Maya Plisetskaya, heiress apparent of the Bolshoi. A step or two behind, as if in tacit acknowledgment of royalty, was Yuri Zhdanov, male dancer of the Moscow ballet, and Nicolai Fadeyechen, another top-ranking performer. Chaperoning the delegation, evidently nervous and a bit self-conscious due to the importance of the occasion, was Georgi Orvid, *le directeur* of the Bolshoi.

For almost ten years there had been no socializing between Westerners and the people of Moscow except in the most formal sense. Balletomanes of the Western colony had for years worshipped Ulanova from a distance, well knowing they could never meet her because it was Stalin's psychotic decision that they should not. Ulanova had come down from the Leningrad ballet to conquer Moscow and had reached the years of a grandmother without any contact with Westerners. Now, suddenly and unexpectedly, she was here in the flesh, the living, breathing legend, in a whole roomful of Westerners.

Plisetskaya was almost too much. In her late twenties, already acclaimed all over the world, this tall, good-looking girl is endowed with the rare gift God lavishes on few women, an inner fire which is communicated to everyone who comes into her presence. One of the younger chaps from the British Em-

bassy made a bit of a fool of himself, hanging in ecstasy on her
every word, and one of the visiting American newspapermen
refused for several days to wash the hand she had gripped so
warmly.

How did these artists happen to be here? Well, Hearst, in
the course of a prearranged interview with Ulanova, had casually mentioned the cocktail party, and simply for the sake of
courtesy, had invited her and any of her friends she cared to
bring. He never dreamed she would come. One can only guess
at the phone calls made to higher authorities before Ulanova
received the clearance—nay, the order—to drop in on the Western festivities.

The appearance of the Bolshoi delegation provided a glamorous climax to this historic day. As the guests departed in the
snowy Moscow night, Russians and Americans exchanging
mumbled amenities, a rosier future for cultural exchanges, for
relaxed personal contacts between the two worlds, could easily
be predicted. For Ulanova, Plisetskaya, and their companions,
this was but the first triumph on a trail of glory that was to
take them to all the capitals of the West.

The cocktail party was also a fitting climax to the improbable
odyssey of three American reporters who had swooped down on
Moscow two weeks before with the vague hope of extracting
enough copy to justify the huge expenses of their visit. They
had hit the journalistic jackpot, and there was to be still another dividend in the Kremlin, although they did not yet know
it that night as they piled into a cramped compartment for four
on the night train for Leningrad.

Operation Improbable, they themselves called it. This journey, launched over a drink with a Soviet underling at the National Press Club bar in Washington always had an air of un-
reality about it, especially since the cold war was then at its

frostiest, the leader was named Hearst, and the expedition was to the dark side of the moon, or at least to its earthly equivalent in the year 1955: mysterious and hostile Russia.

The delights of Paris over a January weekend had muted the misgivings of the adventurers, and the Frankfurter Hof in Frankfurt and the Kempienski in West Berlin had given them a few more nights of familiar Western creature comforts. But in the chill dawn of January 25, the Kempienski porters had rapped urgently at the bedroom doors to send Messrs. Hearst, Conniff, and Kingsbury Smith on their way to Schoenfeld airport in East Berlin.

East Berlin? Right then and there the ulcer of doubt began to gnaw. The courage of the travelers waned sharply as their limousines tooled through the empty streets in the first light of a bitingly cold day. At the checkpoints separating freedom from the slave world, guards yawned sleepily and focused flashlights on their passports. All in order. Pass on. Schoenfeld Airport lies straight ahead.

A milky fog bathed the airport, reducing visibility to zero. Hope soared within the intrepid reporters. Obviously no one would fly in such weather. They would be reprieved for another night. But the station manager grumpily took their tickets, weighed their baggage, and declared it overweight. Two hundred dollars more, *bitte*. We had to pay through the nose for the privilege of an experience that already seemed a nightmare.

At 8 A.M. the plane was called. Heavy vapor still shrouded the runways. A motley band of passengers moved forward trancelike to meet its fate, which seemed to call for the plane crashing on take-off. There were three Indians swathed in greatcoats and fur caps, a couple of Red Army officers, several seedy-looking business men off on the odd commercial errands of this backward empire, and a few other nondescript types.

Our plane proved to be a battered old IL-12, the work horse

of Russian aviation until the advent of the Tupelov jets, a plane that looked like a cross between the DC-3 and Convair. There were no seat-belts. A dowdy young hostess assigned us seats, and the pilots, brawny fellows running fast toward forty, strolled nonchalantly into the front compartment.

They gunned one engine, then the other, and the plane rolled to the runway end. With no preliminary run-up of the motors, the plane swerved into the wind and rolled off into the cottony gloom. This was the moment of truth when, each of us confessed later, we all wondered what in hell we were doing there.

But the old ship got airborne somehow, and within a few minutes we had burst through the cloud cover. Everybody relaxed. The hostess distributed tea in steel-sheathed glasses, the Red Army colonel snored, the Indians chatted among themselves in exotic tongues, and the Americans began to have second thoughts. Maybe everything would turn out all right after all.

We stopped to refuel and admire the picture-postcard beauty of old Vilna, nestled among the snow-draped Lithuanian hills, where the Americans were forced to concede that the pilot had made a skillful landing on the narrow runway. In the airport restaurant they were introduced to the charms of Russian vodka, which tended to soothe any remaining traces of apprehension. By the time IL-12 swooped down from the overcast at Vnukovo airport in Moscow, we felt practically like old Russian hands, having already spent ten hours behind the Iron Curtain. The fine piloting and the good instrumentation assured us that men and machines *could* be operated skillfully and efficiently in Soviet Russia, contrary to some reports.

The Moscow airport is as crowded and confused as any in the West, and the arriving guests braced themselves for a long tangle with red tape. Here occurred the first miracle of the venture. Out of the mob milling in the dusk materialized a magician who for the next three weeks was to attack every logistical problem with single-minded intensity, who would slash protocol and get results almost unfailingly and instantaneously. The magician was Leonid Khortakov, official representative of Intourist Agency.

In the five years since our first meeting, Leonid Khortakov has ascended the ranks of Communist bureaucracy, and he now sits behind a desk in the Hotel National, bossing the entire Intourist operation. He is a young man marked for success, and his present post is by no means the limit of his career. Of medium height, quick and alert, tough-minded with Soviet officialdom when it hampered his movements, he possessed an assurance that suggested that he held high rank in the Party despite his comparative youth—he was scarcely thirty in 1955. Since then he has been to America twice on governmental missions. When we returned to America, we always recommended Leonid as a guide to prospective visitors, but few of them were able to secure this privilege.

"You can't get him any more," we were told. "He's become too important for that. They only use him for big stuff."

This was the man who quickly rushed the three newspapermen through customs and passport control with a minimum of inspection. For three weeks he was to be our constant companion, a competent chess opponent for Smith, a slyly humorous needler of Conniff, and a bright, agile-minded ideological opponent for all three in a running argument over the relative merits of communism and free enterprise.

Did the American visitors suddenly yearn to see the sold-out Bolshoi ballet a half-hour before curtain time? No trouble at all, evening after evening. Leonid magically produced the tickets, and twenty minutes later the Americans were seated in the best stalls in the house. The opera? Why not, although you've only given me fifteen minutes' notice. The Red Army Chorus? The circus? A concert by the Oistrakhs, *père et fils?* The puppet

show? And all the other entertainment delights of Moscow, even
though tickets are distributed weeks ahead and there is never an
empty seat when the curtain rises.

Only once did he intrude a personal suggestion into the entertainment plans of his charges. The ballet *Giselle* was to be
danced by Ulanova for the first time in a decade, and announcement of the performance instantly made it the gala of the winter.
Leonid had secured six tickets for the great event, and Hearst
said he intended to invite Ambassador and Mrs. Bohlen, balletomanes both, to go along.

"Please don't," said Leonid. "They are Muscovites—that is,
they live here all the time—and they'll get a chance to see it
again later. Please ask people for whom it will be the only opportunity."

The humorless Communist bureaucrat so often spoofed in
the West found no reflection in the amiable Mr. Khortakov. He
soon discovered in the portly Conniff a broad target for his wry
barbs. Once, while we were crossing Gorki Street in the twilight, a small Soviet car brushed against the ample form of Conniff, weighing in at a tidy 220 at the time, and Leonid pulled
him out of harm's way.

"Why, Leonid," said the grateful guest. "I didn't know you
cared. I'm touched that you didn't want me to get hurt."

"It wasn't that at all," said Leonid. "I happen to be a good
Soviet citizen. I was trying to save the car, which is Soviet
property. If it had bumped into you it would have been destroyed."

During a session of the Supreme Soviet, someone asked how
many passengers an elevator to the meeting floor could carry.
"Ordinarily it holds four," said Leonid. "But if Mr. Conniff is
one of the passengers, I think we had better keep it down to
three."

Once Hearst asked Leonid to estimate the traveling time between Moscow and Zagorsk, where we wished to visit a Russian Orthodox monastery.

"If we went straight through we could make it in three hours," he said. "But you know Mr. Conniff. He'll want to stop along the way to eat. You'd better allow four hours."

On ideological issues Leonid was as adamant as Andrei Gromyko on a particularly stubborn day. No amount of logic or of fact could shake his unyielding grip on the Party line. He wavered only once, after a vigorous defense of Communist intellectual freedom, illustrated by his freedom to read his way through the great Lenin library with its millions of volumes.

Minutes of painstaking argument finally forced Leonid to concede that this freedom was constricted so that the only volumes at his disposal were those approved by his Party superiors. Daunted only for a moment, Leonid pounced on an unassailable argument, one that beamed a shaft of light on the mental processes of the modern Communist.

"But I've got freedom to read *something,* don't you understand?" he said triumphantly. "My father and mother and grandparents didn't have it—they didn't know *how* to read. *But I've got it!"*

Leonid Khortakov figures prominently in this narrative because he was our first close contact with a representative of a certain type of Communist: a man whose beliefs were formed by an ideology we deplore, but a citizen of good character and high ethical standards. He refused all tips and gifts. He showed pictures of his wife and daughter with bourgeois pride, but forbade us to buy any presents for them. We were to meet other up-and-coming young Communists—the interpreters Oleg Troyanovsky and Victor Sukhodrev, Alex Rogov of Intourist, and other pleasant friends—but Leonid was the first and he particularly sticks in our memory.

The livin' was easy in our quarters at the National, a Czarist relic where a measure of bourgeois comfort still survived. Hearst had the main suite, curving from Manezhny Square around Gorki Street, and Smith and a smaller one down the corridor.

As for Conniff, he had just begun unpacking when Alex Rogow, then manager of the National Intourist bureau, solemnly informed him that he was in a room of some historical interest.

"Vladimir Ilyich lived here," Mr. Rogow announced portentously. "The great Lenin slept in this very room."

It was a ritual that has been repeated since on Walter Lippmann and other visiting Americans. Vladimir Ilyich Ulyanov—Nikolai Lenin—did live in suite 105–07 at the National for several months after the Bolshevik government moved down from St. Petersburg in the winter of 1918, while a Kremlin apartment was being prepared for him. Suite 105–07 connected with the apartment assigned Hearst, so comrade Lenin could proceed directly to the curved balcony overlooking the juncture of Gorki Street and Manezhny Square when the mood seized him to harangue the excited thousands milling below in the months of the revolution.

The work of the Hearst mission began immediately. Smith, our linguist, ordered up a Russian typewriter and a Russian stenographer and commenced dictating requests for interviews to Malenkov, Khrushchev, Zhukov, and a whole list of Russian notables. We always considered this a shrewd move, calculating that letters written in Russian would by-pass the need for translation and thus speed their passage through Communist red tape.

We also decided not to work through Leonid Ilychev, press director of the foreign ministry, but to deliver our requests directly, insofar as we could. This tactic seemed to pay off handsomely, although it earned us the bitter displeasure of Comrade Ilychev. Bureaucrats never like to be circumvented, and the animosity of bureaucrat Ilychev was to make itself felt on future visits. He, too, has since moved up the Communist ladder. As head of the important Agitprop (Agitation-Propaganda) Bureau of the Party, he fashioned the savage press attack on the American Exposition in Moscow in the summer of 1959, a campaign waged so crudely that it boomeranged on its sponsors.

We had been warned before leaving New York that we could expect all kinds of Communist duplicity, that our phones would be "bugged," microphones would be hidden in our apartment, that we would undoubtedly be shadowed by the secret police, and that beautiful Russian girls would attempt to extract vital American secrets from us. To cover these points in the order named, (a) we don't know whether our phones were tapped, (b) no microphones were ever found in our apartment (we looked), (c) if we were shadowed we were never aware of it, and (d) not a single Russian Mata Hari, alas, made a pass at us. We realize the last admission ruins the chance for a lurid cover in the paperback version of this book.

Microphones or no, Smith and Conniff soon designed an elaborate charade to put them to use. Hearst confessed later he was astonished to overhear their first diaolgue, spoken loudly in words well spaced out and carefully articulated, in the manner of amateur actors at their first reading of "As You Like it."

"Say—Mister—Smith—" (This from Conniff.) "What—did —you—say—about—that—letter—Mr. Hearst—has—for— Premier Malenkov?"

"I said—that Mr. Hearst—is to deliver it—personally—I said, *personally*—to Premier Malenkov.—Those were—the President's—instructions."

We naturally never had any letter or instructions from the President or anyone else for that matter, but we thought it only kind to give the poor fellow assigned to record our conversation something meaty to place on the desk of his chief in the morning.

Our one real security measure probably deserves mention. FBI director J. Edgar Hoover once told Hearst that the best and simplest way to counter a microphone is to turn on a water tap. Therefore most of our strategy conferences were held in Hearst's bathroom. The tap on the tub would be turned on, and while water gushed from the spout, the next moves would be freely debated. Hearst usually sat on the edge of the tub. When the water reached high enough to lap against his anatomy, he would leap to his feet and declare the conference over.

These summit meetings invariably waxed warm, and the participants often continued them in the living room, forgetting the "microphones" altogether. An argument about a proposed question to Khrushchev got so confused and prolonged at one session that we practically repeated every point for the benefit of anyone who might have been listening.

At our meeting with Ambassador Bohlen the morning after our arrival, the Ambassador drew the first of several astute deductions he was to make during our visit. Charles Klensch, then the International News Service correspondent in Moscow, who was a great help to us throughout our visit, shepherded us to the lemon-tinted Embassy on Sadovaya Ring, a forlorn and dilapidated building with plaster flaking off it, even though it had been constructed less than fifteen years before.

"I think your visit is going to have significance," the Ambassador said. "Your arrival was reported in *Pravda* this morning. They never put anything in *Pravda* unless it's supposed to mean something, and I think this means you'll have a successful trip."

Chip Bohlen and his charming wife, Avis, were both helpful and kind in the course of the Hearst visit. Bohlen's counsel was always available, and a copy of every news report and interview filed by the newspapermen was dispatched immediately to the Embassy or to Spaso House, the Ambassador's residence. On several occasions the visitors dined at Spaso House, where the Bohlen's entertained graciously.

As it must with every visitor, the novelty of Moscow began to wear thin after a few days, and the trio on the third floor at the National grew edgy. The tourist bit can be enjoyed only when you are not preoccupied with greater problems—such as the fate of some carefully typed and even more carefully delivered letters. Moscow was evidently master of the don't-call-us, we'll-call-you stall.

The first telephone call came on Friday, three days after our arrival. We were told only to expect another call at ten the next morning.

At ten the next morning the same heavy, mysterious voice said that Hearst and Smith were to be ready to leave the National at 10:45 P.M. A car would pick them up for an interview with comrade Molotov at the Foreign Ministry.

The eighty-minute interview that followed took place on the last Saturday of January, 1955. The date is important because the question of war or peace was then balanced on a knife's edge in the Formosan straits. The United States Congress just a few days previously had passed the resolution pledging support to Formosa (a resolution which, by the way, still governs our policy in that incendiary area). United States Navy units had begun the evacuation of Chiang's exposed garrisons on the Tachen Islands, and the world wondered whether the Red Chinese would launch shooting attacks on the convoys. On this delicate operation hinged the possibility of World War III.

Thus the two American newsmen felt tense and expectant as they faced Molotov in his Kremlin office.

And Molotov had news, big news, for his visitors. It was couched in the disarming parlance of diplomacy, but the paydirt was there all the same.

"If Chiang Kai-shek desired to withdraw his troops from any islands," he said, "hardly anyone would prevent him from trying to do so."

Carefully adding that he could not speak for the "Chinese People's Republic," the Foreign Minister nevertheless made it amply clear that Soviet Russia favored a reduction of tension in the Formosa area and indicated, in fact, that Russia might ask Communist China to agree to a temporary cease fire in the Straits.

Molotov's remarks on the Far Eastern crisis naturally provided the hottest item of the interview, but there was one other memorable answer which was to set in motion a whole chain of events. We had prepared questions in many fields of foreign policy, all of them hopefully designed to elicit newsworthy replies. It should be explained here that the preparation of suitable questions represents one of the most important and painstaking jobs of an interview with a high-ranking Communist leader. You don't just go to his office and start firing queries off the top of your head. Long hours were spent and much debate lavished on the wording of what we considered the most provocative questions. Then they were typed out in triplicate on small sheets of paper and distributed among the three reporters. This preinterview care was responsible for producing Molotov's answer to a question on Austria skillfully composed by Smith.

As INS General Manager for Europe, Smith had been present at all high-level postwar conferences and knew exactly the stated position of each country in regard to various issues. He knew that the United States and its Western Allies had proposed in 1954 that the four-power occupation of Austria be ended and a peace treaty signed. From his contacts among allied diplomats he knew the belief was growing that Russia was concerned about the presence of Western troops in Austria, hard by the satellite borders of Czechoslovakia and Hungary. At the

1954 meeting of the Big Four foreign ministers, Molotov had given indications right up to the last minute, when he finally said *nyet*, that he might be willing to negotiate an Austrian peace treaty.

Joe saw no reason for not giving another whirl to the oft-defeated proposal.

The exchange went like this:

Hearst: With a view toward getting the world started on the road to disarmament through the gradual reduction of military bases on both sides, and in order to create a favorable atmosphere for coexistence, would the government of the U.S.S.R. be prepared, pending the conclusion of a treaty of peace with Austria, to withdraw all of its military and air bases from its zone of occupation in Austria providing the Western powers would simultaneously withdraw the bases in their respective zones?

Molotov began his answer by repeating expected propaganda about American bases. But then he voiced words that were to galvanize the Austrian government into action and hasten the Austrian Ambassador in Moscow to the Hearst suite pleading for elaboration.

Molotov: The question arises in my mind, What is your view as to the possibility of extending that suggestion to other areas. I mean to say, if a start is made is Austria, how could it be done elsewhere?

Smith: It might prove contagious. As Hearst said, you have to start somewhere.

Molotov: Then you base yourself on that single hope. Is that sufficient?

The layman might study this exchange and look in vain for its significance. But observers trained in diplomatic language, particularly the Austrian experts who had been hoping for just such a gesture, recognized that Molotov had just opened the door for the evacuation of their country and an eventual peace treaty. We received calls of gratitude from Vienna, and the Austrian government asked us to return home by way of Vienna as guests of the state, an invitation we were unable to accept until two years later. In 1957 we came "out" via Vienna and spent several days there as guests of the country. From Chancellor Julius Raab on down, our hosts credited the 1955 interview with paving the way for Austrian independence. Following up the lead contained in our interview, the Austrian Ambassador was told, Yes, Molotov was ready to negotiate. Less than four months later, in May, 1955, the Austrian peace treaty was signed, and both the Russian troops and the Allied occupation forces left the country.

"Old Squarepants," as Molotov was sometimes called (though not to his face) was at the top of his game at this particular hour in Communist history. Cool, icily polite, and disdainful of small talk, he spoke authoritatively on foreign affairs, and it seemed that he had staked out the field as his own domain in the post-Stalin government. It later became apparent that he had not taken the full measure of a pudgy colleague in the Presidium, who was to dump him from power two years later.

When he said that "hardly anyone" would fire on Chiang Kai-shek's evacuating forces, there was no room for doubt that Russia had laid a restraining hand on its exuberant Asian ally. Ambassador Bohlen so interpreted it and fired off a signal to the State Department after studying the text of our interview. So certain was Smith that we had mined a golden nugget that he startled National residents and employees alike on our return. Usually sedate and reserved, Joe threw all restraint to the Moscow skies and pounded his cane vigorously against the floor of the lobby.

"We've made history!" he shouted as various delegations from all over the Marxist empire blinked in amazement. The maids and waiters took this more calmly, realizing that all

Americans were a little crazy and not generally downright dangerous.

"History!" he repeated. "We've made it today. We can go home now and be sure our trip was a success."

Chip Bohlen agreed with Smith's evaluation. As we sipped martinis later that evening at Spaso House and pored over the verbatim transcript of the interview, the Ambassador estimated that we had reached the high point of our visit. Evidently we had talked to the proper person in the Soviet regime, so far as information available to foreigners was concerned; we could hardly expect to top this day's triumph.

We had this verbatim transcript available for Chip Bohlen and other interested Western ambassadors because Smith, with his own crossbred system of speedwriting and shorthand, had taken down every word. The nuances of diplomacy are such that the real "message" may lie in an offbeat phrase tucked deep in the text. We have always taken complete question-and-answer transcripts on all our visits. Hearst and Conniff take complete notes, and Considine, on the second visit, proved remarkably fast and accurate at taking a transcript. James Reston and Bill Jorden followed the same procedure on their important Khrushchev interview in autumn, 1957, but the accounts of several other American newspapermen have been disappointing because they interpreted what they thought Khrushchev *meant* instead of first making public what he *said*. The interpretations can come later, and the Hearst taskers have inflicted their share on the public, but first of all should come the actual words of the interviewee, even though larded with propaganda, old party clichés, and just plain lies. End of journalism lesson.

Meanwhile, back at the National, the visitors returned from Cloud Nine in a more relaxed mood and hopefully awaited the next cue. We were in daily telephone contact with London. All our stories moved uncensored, via telephone to the outside world. Men in the INS office in London hung on every word, even though the line often faded, there were frequent cut-offs, and the signal became at times so scratchy that each word had to be spelled out.

At this point, we almost qualified as candidates for the booboo prize of the year, and only good luck and some remarkable circumstances saved us from committing it. We were asked—over the telephone, of course—if we were interested in seeing Defense Minister Bulganin. It was stipulated that the meeting would take place after the Supreme Soviet adjourned. Now, there is a strategy to journalism just as there is to war, and we had settled on Premier Malenkov and Party leader Khrushchev as the primary objectives. In dealing with the Russians, Smith and Conniff treated Hearst, against his wishes, as if he were a "chief of state," and one not to be fobbed off with lesser Communist powers than his own opposite number—Premier Malenkov. At least two of our triumvirate were convinced it was a sound tactic and one that impressed the Russians.

Therefore, with a touch of asperity, we informed the Russians that Hearst was not interested in minor cogs like Defense Minister Bulganin but was concerned only with meeting the bigs. Of course, we didn't know that less than a week later, Bulganin was to be named Premier. Lest the suspense get the best of you, we will admit that we finally *did* interview Premier Bulganin, thus setting up a smash finale to the visit.

Life in Moscow was pleasant enough. Leonid conducted us through the Kremlin—just being opened to the Russian public —St. Basil's, the Lenin and Stalin Mausoleum, Moscow University, and other noteworthy monuments. At night it was the ballet, the opera, the puppet show, or some such diversion. We were emerging into celebrity status ourselves, inasmuch as *Pravda* had taken the whole front page to print the Molotov interview, a sure sign to the faithful that the three visitors were something more than mere tourists. Some twelve thousand

Americans visited Moscow in 1959, but in 1955 there couldn't have been more than ten in town, excluding the diplomatic colony. Billy Prince, the remarkable Chicago merchant, was present negotiating an exchange of furs. Marshall MacDuffie, a lawyer who had met Khrushchev many years before while on a governmental mission, was also in Moscow at this time, and secured an informative interview with Mr. K. that eventually appeared in *Collier's*. But there were so few of us that we automatically attracted attention wherever we went, and we found the Russian people uniformly friendly and considerate to all of us.

Someone always stayed behind in the National with one ear cocked to the telephone. After our ultimatum about Bulganin, we hoped to know in a matter of days whether our high-handed strategy would work.

On Friday morning, February 4, the telephone in Hearst's apartment gave an asthmatic tinkle, and a heavy, mysterious voice intoned: "Be ready at 10:45 A.M. tomorrow for the car that will take you to Comrade Khrushchev's office at Communist headquarters." We were about to meet the question mark of the party, the man touted as Premier Malenkov's most formidable adversary in the Presidium of the Central Committee (formerly called the Politburo). Three days later, on Tuesday, Malenkov was to admit his defeat before this new power in the Kremlin.

The Soviet ambassadors in the chief diplomatic posts had been summoned home. *Pravda* and *Izvestia* had been carrying attacks by Khrushchev on those (among them Malenkov) who maintained that consumer goods could be produced without slowing the manufacture of heavy goods—what he called "production of the means of production." It was increasingly apparent that some inner turbulence was churning the Presidium, but when the storm broke in the Supreme Soviet on the Tuesday following our Khrushchev interview, its scope and intensity surpassed anything anticipated in the West.

Khrushchev received us in his long, narrow office in Commu-

nist party headquarters in downtown Moscow. He was a bit
more portly then than he is today. The doctors had not yet put
him on a rigid diet and limited his intake of alcohol. But the
same boundless energy, inner vitality, and agile intelligence that
were to astonish the Western world quickly impressed the three
American interviewers. Oleg Troyanovsky, the good-looking
young Communist who was to become familiar to the American
television audiences during Khrushchev's 1959 visit, did the in-
terpreting.

Within a matter of minutes, the First Secretary of the Communist Party issued an order that reflected the true state of the
power structure within the Presidium better than any grandiose
gesture or inflated statement possibly could. The telephone interrupted Khrushchev's answer to one of our first questions, and
he was patently annoyed. With one swift wave of his stubby
fingers, he made it clear that he was not to be disturbed. No
telephone calls were to be put through. When there is no one
higher in authority who can get through to you on the phone,
then you are indeed sure of your power. Such an edict would
have been unthinkable in Stalin's time—for anyone but Stalin.
In the Communist power pyramid, you are always available to
the man on top. There appeared to be no "top" over the confident Khrushchev.

One other pattern in this long interview—it was to last two
hours and forty-five minutes, to be exceeded only by the three
hour and thirty-five minute duration of our second meeting with
Khrushchev two years later—indicated that this blunt, blocky,
aggressive little man represented the strongest authority within
the Kremlin's "collective leadership." Molotov had confined himself to answers in the foreign field, and we took it for granted
that Khrushchev, likewise, had staked out a private sphere of
power—party affairs, say—for his own domain. Not at all. We
had prepared questions in all fields, just in case, and Khrushchev

had replies for all of them. At no time did he instruct us to take our inquiries in the military realm to Defense Minister (at that time) Bulganin or the Army marshals. Nor did he lob a question on foreign affairs into Molotov's court. He volleyed all shots back in swift, authoritative sentences, pausing seldom even to collect his thoughts. We were sitting in a room with a man who knew that as First Secretary of the Party he was occupying the only post of authority Stalin ever required—although, just like Stalin, he was later to take on the mantle of the premiership for reasons of prestige and protocol. It was clear that he was sure he knew how to employ all of the weapons in the arsenal of power, just like his old master.

The interview frequently took the form of an open debate, with the three of us stoutly defending American positions and denying that the United States alone was responsible for world tensions. Khrushchev accepted all such interventions in good grace. The theme of peaceful coexistence and of the need for closer contacts and improved trade balanced his more belligerent outbursts.

Despite his remarks on coexistence, many of which have been quoted earlier, Khrushchev maintained his belief in the eventual victory of communism.

"You believe capitalism will have the upper hand," he told us. "We believe communism will win in the long run. When that will happen it is impossible to tell. As far as the United States is concerned, it depends on the American people.

"No one else can decide the question for them. If you had asked Czar Nicholas ten years before the Revolution how long his system would last, he would answer, It will stand for ages. But ten years later it no longer existed.

"In the United States, the working class is very strong and some day will raise its voice."

"The working class *is* the American people right now,"

Hearst objected. "It raises its voice at every election. When you speak about leaving it up to the American people, I can assure you we leave it up to the American people at every election. If you would leave it up to the Russian people in the same manner, we think it would be a good thing."

The First Secretary accepted this sally in good humor. "There are a great many things in America which merit our copying," he said. "And I think Americans could find many good things in the U.S.S.R."

He thereupon reiterated his desire for peace and better relations.

"America is a good country," he said, "with good people, and we want nothing from them. On the other hand, is there anything America wants from Russia?"

"It is impossible to get anything from us by blackmail or through threats. If it is possible to get something from us, it can be done by trade and normal relations. We should seek to develop normal, businesslike trade relations so that in time they might be strengthened and transformed into friendly relations.

"A conflict of any kind is certainly not in the interest of our nations. I am certain that we shall find the strength and common sense to achieve an improvement in our relations."

We pointed out that one impediment to improved trade relations was the still unsettled question of payment for the eleven-billion-dollar American lend-lease contribution to the Russian war effort.

"It would be silly to deny that," he admitted, then added sternly, "but we paid with our blood for that assistance."

And then, as if to prove the sincerity of his declarations, Khrushchev made a startling statement concerning the crisis that was even then causing nightmares throughout the West.

"We are interested in peace," he said, "and we are prepared

to do what we can to find a solution to the Taiwan issue and prevent the conflict from developing into war. If America shows common sense—and I have no doubt about the common sense of the Chinese—I believe that with the participation of other countries in peace it may yet be possible to avert war. The possibility of Russian participation in such a conference is not excluded."

In other words, Khrushchev was declaring, in remarkably blunt and undiplomatic language, that the Soviet government was not in favor of the saber-rattling tactics of the Chinese Reds, and would lay a restraining hand upon their dangerously aggressive maneuvers. This momentous statement did much to relieve the war hysteria then threatening to sweep the world. As a matter of fact, no conference to work out a solution to the Formosa problem ever was held, but events made this unnecessary. And it is a fact that the explosive situation began to simmer down after Khrushchev's soothing words.

Rumors of a struggle for power between him and Premier Malenkov were ridiculed by Khrushchev. He called them "wishful thinking" on the part of the West. He related the story of a professor who gave his blindfolded pupils a glass of liquid and asked each one to describe the smell.

"Each gave a different answer," said Khrushchev. "The professor told them it was the same liquid—ink—and it smelled to each as each wanted it to smell."

So, Poof! to those stories of a struggle for power between the First Secretary of the Party and the Premier of the Soviet Union. Technically, of course, Khrushchev was correct. The struggle was over. Malenkov had been vanquished already, although we didn't know it yet.

The aspect of Khrushchev's character that impressed us perhaps most of all was his keen sense of humor. He used it at every opportunity, and seemed to delight in poking fun either at us or at himself. Once we asked him if he would like to visit the United States some day. Putting on a wry smile, he said:

"I think it would be difficult to find any influential person in America who would dare invite the First Secretary of the Communist Party to visit his country. Would it not be said that I was going there to subvert somebody or blow up something?"

Four years later an "influential person" named Eisenhower turned that joke upon him.

Our interview was charged with controversy, and at times became heated as we took exception to Khrushchev's sideswipes at American policy. At its conclusion, the Communist boss patted Hearst on the shoulder.

"Mr. Hearst," he said, "when you return to America and are called before the McCarthy committee investigating subversion —and you are sure to be, after sitting down for three hours with a Communist leader in Communist headquarters—I am prepared to testify for you that you defended your country's position well and ably"—this said with a big, broad smile, a hearty laugh.

A Communist with a sense of humor was certainly something new on the world scene. America's homegrown comrades have so abjectly aped every innovation from Moscow that we hoped this latest development would have some effect on them. Thus far, however, we have seen no sign that they have emulated their bouncy, fun-loving world leader.

After this extensive Khrushchev interview, our mission to Moscow exploded on the front pages of the world. There was hardly a country in which important newspapers failed to carry it. When the transcript was typed out, it ran to fourteen single-spaced typewritten pages. These were closely scanned that evening by Chip Bohlen, Great Britain's Bill Hayter, and other diplomats. Ambassador Bohlen sent a cable to the State Department following the interview, stating his belief that Malenkov was on his way out. "You were getting to see the big wheels of the country," he told us later. "And Malenkov was being passed over. I figured that he was going into eclipse." These are the small intimations which serve the diplomat seeking clues to the Russian riddle.

The day after our Khrushchev interview, as we read *Pravda* over our morning borscht at the National, we realized that Comrade Khrushchev was getting to be a mighty big boy in the Soviet Union. Our interview with the First Secretary ate up not only the entire front page, but the top half of the second page as well. Sort of uninspired editing, you might say, but a sure sign that the little man was here to stay.

With Molotov and Khrushchev in the bag, the hunting grew progressively easier. On Monday, the eve of the meeting of the Supreme Soviet, we were received by Marshal Georgi Zhukov at the Ministry of Defense, where he was serving as First Deputy. On the morrow he was to become Minister of Defense when Bulganin moved up to the premiership. His calm, easy manner indicated that he was at peace with events on this particular night.

The Marshal served tea on a small table in the corner of his office. His broad chest was bedecked with eight rows of medals, topped by three stars representing a triple award as Hero of the Soviet Union. He chatted easily and amiably with us. He said it was his dream to visit America one day, and he spoke several times of his affection and admiration for President Eisenhower. He recalled a conversation with Eisenhower in 1945, in which each said his own country would never attack the other.

The Marshal displayed a keen sense of humor, which, with Khrushchev's jolly jibes, suggested at least that the new "collective leadership" might be more entertaining than the old. Hearst told Zhukov that Conniff was the military expert in the group and had devoted considerable time to the memoirs and published records of World War II. He added that Conniff wanted to ask the Marshal a few questions about the German assault on Russia.

Zhukov spread his hands and smiled impishly.

"But how," he asked, "could I possibly answer the questions of such an expert?"

Conniff picked himself up off the floor and doggedly pursued the subject. The Marshal's answers to Conniff's two questions are herewith reported.

Conniff: What was Hitler's greatest strategical mistake in the invasion of Russia?

Zhukov: Hitler's greatest strategical mistake was the decision to invade Russia itself. By that I mean he launched an operation for which he never had the necessary means. The conquest of Russia was simply beyond the means at Hitler's disposal.

Conniff: What was Hitler's greatest tactical mistake?

Zhukov: Hitler's greatest tactical mistake was the dependence on aircraft at the expense of artillery. The Luftwaffe was a very formidable instrument, certainly, but there would be days at a time here in Russia, even weeks, especially during the winter months, when airplanes couldn't fly at all. Then he missed the artillery, which could function in any weather, and which we had in abundance.

Conniff also mentioned that a theory had developed in the West that the Battle of Moscow in the fall of 1941 was the turning point of the Russian-German war, and not the Battle of Stalingrad a year later, as was more popularly supposed. Marshal Zhukov opted for the popular view. He said that the Battle of Moscow proved that Germany could not win the war, but that the tide definitely turned against Hitler following the Stalingrad disaster.

Spare as these comments were, they are among the few that any top-echelon Russian commander has made on the war that

are free of Communist bias or propaganda. The spate of memoirs
from the Allied and Wehrmacht commanders has no counter-
part among their opposite numbers in the Red Army. Zhukov's
statement that Hitler lacked the means to conquer Russia jibes
with the views of many Western students who believe the vast
spaces and fighting power of the Russians were beyond the capabilities of the Wehrmacht, despite its undoubted skill and battle experience.

Zhukov insisted that the Red Army was an instrument for
peace, maintaining that it could have rolled on and conquered
all of Western Europe in the fall of 1945 if its aim had been
anything but peaceful. How could the Americans charge the
Russian government with warlike intentions, when it hadn't
taken advantage of that opportunity?

Hearst mentioned that the American monopoly of the atom
bomb might have been a deterrent to Russian aggression.

Zhukov shrugged. "You only had three bombs," he said.

"If you know we only had three bombs," Hearst said dryly,
"you have better information on the subject than the American
people."

A week later, when Prime Minister Churchill received the
Hearst group, he disagreed with Zhukov's estimate of the
number of atom bombs available in the fall of 1945. "You had
sixteen," he said.

Zhukov spoke with evident pride of his relationship with the
Communist Party, which he joined in 1919. His pride now
seems ironic, since he was removed from office for allegedly trying to weaken the Party's control over the Red Army.

Our interpreter for the Zhukov meeting was our guide Leonid
Khortakov. He took notes as he went along, stuffing them
casually in his pocket when the interview ended. Some hours
later he was summoned to the telephone and ordered to bring his
notes immediately to *Pravda*. For a few minutes Leonid was one

perturbed Communist as he searched his clothing for the required pages which, fortunately, he hadn't thrown away. A few
days later, after Marshal Zhukov had been named Minister of
Defense, the full interview appeared in *Pravda,* occupying the
whole front page.

Sandwiched between talks with high political brass were conversations with Communist notables in the arts, sciences, and
religion. Dmitri Shostakovich submitted to an hour's interrogation at the Moscow Conservatory of Music, under the baleful eye
of a Communist bureaucrat who did not hesitate to prod or guide
the distinguished musician whenever his answers faltered.
Shostakovich said that he welcomed the criticism of his party
superiors on both political and musical grounds. "When a comrade gets off the right path," he said, "it's only proper that his
comrades should help straighten him out." A fussy, nervous
little man who smoked incessantly, Russia's greatest composer
appeared so miserable that we soon terminated the conversation
out of sheer pity. We got an illuminating insight on high priority
given our requests when we learned that Shostakovich had been
summoned all the way from Leningrad to meet us. He had endured an uncomfortable, night-long train trip from the north,
and faced a similar journey back. When Big Brother beckons,
the Russian citizen, no matter how great his fame or reputation,
comes immediately.

Svetlana Stalin, the only daughter of the late dictator, was
also tapped for an interview. We were the first Americans to
enter her apartment, located in central Moscow in a block of flats
which resembled a New York tenement. It was a grimy, gray
building about ten stories high, with stone stairways, dim light-
ing, and an elevator that only took people up.

No sign of the Western conception of luxury marred the
workaday drabness of Svetlana's apartment, except perhaps for
the neatly clad maid who opened the door, and the upright piano

in the cramped little chamber which served as both sitting and dining room. Behind the maid at the door stood Svetlana, a red-haired, fair-complexioned woman with a rather pretty face and a pleasant smile.

She was slenderer than most Russian women and looked more Irish than Russian. Her fluffy hair was cut short. She wore a pink and beige pullover sweater, a brownish tweed skirt, and good-looking pumps. We judged her age at about thirty-five. Throughout the visit she was tense and apprehensive, especially when questioned about her father or the whereabouts of her controversial brother, Vassily. She told us she was teaching Soviet literature at the Moscow Academy of Social Science, and also volunteered that she was married and the mother of two children, one a ten-year-old boy, named Joseph after his grandfather, and a five-year-old girl.

When Hearst asked her about Vassily, tears openly welled in Svetlana's eyes. Moscow scuttlebutt at the time held that Vassily had been liquidated because of his drunkenness and high-living capers. He had once been a top-ranking officer in the Soviet Air Force.

"He is very, very ill and no longer on active duty," Svetlana said. "I hope he will be well again soon."

She also appeared deeply moved when questioned about her father. She was asked whether he had expressed to her in private his thoughts concerning the future of Russia and the world.

"His private views were the same," she said primly, "as those expressed in his public speeches."

Her dad, she replied to another question, had been too busy to write any memoirs, and his chief relaxations during the later years of his life were reading and puttering around the garden and orchard of his country home on the outskirts of Moscow. Unlike his great contemporaries, Roosevelt and Churchill, he never read detective stories.

"He preferred historical works, especially about ancient times," Svetlana said. "He liked to work nights, and also read late at night."

Despite her apprehension, Svetlana's manner was friendly and gracious. She proudly presented her two children, the boy Joseph, timid and shy, the girl, laughing and by no means displeased by the unexpected attention.

We haven't read or heard anything about Svetlana or Vassily Stalin in the five years since this interview. Presumably, Svetlana is alive and well, but nothing concerned with her activities appears in the Soviet press. It might be well to remember, however, that there is again a Joseph Stalin in the world, the grandson of the old buccaneer. He'd be about fifteen now, reaching the age when he could be expected to nourish a few political notions of his own. Could he be a chip off the old block?

"Religious feeling among Russian people is very strong. The strength of it is surprising. The people who believe in God are very firm in their belief. Their faith cannot be shaken."

These were the most impressive words in a very impressive interview we had with a representative of an institution which is publicly scorned and privately tolerated in the godless Communist state: the Russian Orthodox Church. This statement was made to us by a leading ecclesiastic, the acting chief monk at the famous monastery of St. Sergei, which we visited one cold and dreary day.

Named after the patron saint who founded the monastery in 1322, Father Sergei sat across a table from us in his tiny apartment in the seminary building of the walled, fortresslike headquarters of the Russian church at Zagorsk, about fifty miles northeast of Moscow. Through the frost-lined window behind him could be seen the beautiful bell tower of one of the ancient Byzantine churches that grace this holy shrine of Russia. With

his flowing beard, long hair covering his shoulders, and his black
robes of the priesthood, this man of God looked like a survivor
from Biblical times. And in the atheistic Soviet Union, he was
easily as anachronistic.

We had just finished a lunch that reflected the traditional
hospitality of the Russians. Caviar, toast, hot meat cakes,
borscht, baked chicken, rice, carrots, potatoes. Then a rich
pastry, followed by oranges and apples. All washed down with
vodka, red and white Georgian wine, Russian sweet champagne,
and brandy. This was certainly not the ordinary fare in Russia,
and we doubted that Father Sergei himself ate this well very
often. Apparently he had been informed in advance of our visit,
and was ordered to provide a banquet.

Present at the luncheon was the civilian "director" of the
monastery. He never left the side of Father Sergei during our
visit through the churches, the grounds, and the seminary itself,
and he answered most of the questions we put about religion in
Russia. A heavy-set, stern-faced man, he nonetheless seemed to
be on fairly friendly terms with Father Sergei; they were "coexisting" as pleasantly as they could under the circumstances.

We said we noted that most of the people in the churches were
elderly women. We inquired whether the younger generation
came regularly to religious services. The answer was that more
young people came when there were sermons. Nevertheless the
percentage was small.

We asked whether the church was allowed to teach religion to
the young, and whether there was anything like our Sunday
school classes. The answer was no. In response to our question
as to how the children learned about religion, since it was not
taught in the schools or in the churches, the "director" said,
"Children learn about religion from their families."

We said we understood that the government discouraged belief in religion, and that those who dared to send their children

to church or to have them baptized ran the risk of trouble with the authorities. If that was so, how could parents teach their children about religion? The director replied that it was only members of the Communist Party, not the populace in general, who were supposed to abjure religion.

We asked what were the relations between the government and the church.

"The church is completely separate from the state," the director replied. "Of course, it is necessary for it to have some relations with the government. Since 1944 there has existed a 'committee' on matters relating to the Russian Orthodox Church. All the church needs from the state are handled by this committee, which is composed of members of the church and the state."

We inquired how this committee affected the freedom of the church in religious matters. That seemed to touch a sensitive spot, and the voice of the director took on a slightly sharper tone.

"The church is more free than before the revolution," he said. "Under the czars, the state ran the church, today the state does not try to run the church."

Father Sergei sat silently through this outburst, looking wistful, even pathetic. He had nodded his head in agreement to some of the director's assertions, but in this case he remained quite still.

"As a principle," the director added, "we have freedom of religion." Noticing the skepticism in our faces, he quickly added, "Certainly it is possible that there have been some mistakes, but they have been rare—due to the fervor of some individuals. They are being corrected now. You may have heard of Comrade Khrushchev's decree."

Some years earlier Khrushchev had taken note of religious persecution by party officials and ordered that it be terminated, maintaining that "scientific" education—propaganda, not persecution—must be used to further atheism. Members of the Party were themselves being hounded by Communist vigilantes if they permitted their children to be baptized or had yielded to a bride's request for a church wedding. Most important, the antireligious campaign had led to a slowdown in production, and Khrushchev acted to ameliorate the situation, not through any moral compassion, but because he wanted to spur the assembly line.

We asked whether the state allowed new churches to be built or established. The director said that in order to "open" a church, twenty residents of the district in question had to sign a petition addressed to the Patriarch Alexei, head of the Russian Orthodox Church. The patriarch would, if he was disposed to support the petition, bring it to the attention of the committee.

"Would the committee automatically grant the request?" we inquired.

"It would be considered," was the reply.

We then directed our questions to Father Sergei and heard, in response to inquiries about the attitude of the people toward religion, the heartening statement quoted earlier.

"I often hear confessions," Father Sergei added, "and am surprised when, in the evenings, young girls come and ask forgiveness for small sins. The souls of these girls are good, and their belief in God is firm. I think this is a result of the profound religious feeling of the people."

Before lunch, Father Sergei and the director had escorted us around the grounds of the monastery and through the ancient churches. The foundations of the main church dated back to 1354. There were no pews or chairs inside the church, although a service was being held when we entered. It was a weekday. A score of women and a few men stood on the stone floor, all facing in the direction of the saint's tomb, where a bearded monk was chanting prayers. We were told these services were conducted by the monks from five o'clock in the morning until six in the evening. The walls and columns supporting the high-domed church were covered with priceless icons.

We felt awed by both the beauty and the spiritual atmosphere of this house of God, which had stood for so many centuries and through so many turbulent eras. And we emerged with a sense of great reverence and a strengthened conviction of the stability of Christianity.

In answer to our question, as we walked across the snow-covered courtyard, Father Sergei estimated that there are now in Russia between sixty and eighty convents and monasteries.

During our sumptuous luncheon we had told Father Sergei the highlights of our Moscow visit. The night before, we had attended a concert by the Red Army Chorus, and, as we told Father Sergei, the singing had been magnificent. As we rose to go, late in the afternoon, he held up his hand. One final treat had been prepared for us. He ushered us into an exquisitely decorated little music room which had been built for the seminary by Catherine the Great. There a chorus of some two hundred student monks had gathered. Somehow he had managed to summon them together after hearing our remarks about the Red Army Chorus. For forty-five minutes we listened enraptured while this marvelous group sang Russian Christmas songs. The fine musicianship and deep fervor of their singing moved us more deeply than any of our other experiences in Russia. Father Sergei smiled. He had shown that men of God could sing as well as soldiers.

Before leaving Moscow, Hearst was able to visit the Patriarch Alexei himself in his home in Moscow. It was not unlike a cardinal's residence, with religious paintings and icons on the walls. They sat around a large, bare, highly polished table. The Patriarch wore the familiar somber vestments, and a bejeweled cross hung on a silver chain around his neck. They talked for a while about Hearst's impressions of Russia.

"You know," Hearst said, "it has occurred to me that one of the reasons our two countries have such difficulties in believing one another is that we believe in God, as you do, while the governing body of Russia, the Communist Party, insists on godlessness—atheism—in its ruling hierarchy."

The Patriarch evaded a direct response, asserting that there was religious freedom, and that there were many religions in Russia. He mentioned that in the eastern regions of the Soviet Union there was Mohammedanism, and even Buddhism.

He said, tapping his heart with his hand, "Who knows. I think perhaps there are times when they do think of God."

With that, he rose and asked if Hearst would like to see his chapel. He led him through a door into a candlelit room filled with icons. As the Patriarch stood by, Hearst silently asked God for a blessing in behalf of his wife, his children, and his mother. They then returned to his reception room, and as Hearst bade him farewell, the Patriarch gave him a little mother-of-pearl crucifix on a gold chain. It is still a treasured memento.

Two years later, when the Hearst team again visited Moscow, in his momentous interview, Khrushchev was to deliver his own frank, blunt views on religion, views which would make the hopes expressed by the Patriarch seem optimistic indeed. And later, we were to see that persecution for religious beliefs and associations was far from being relegated to the Stalinist past, when we saw the first evil stirrings of a wave of anti-Semitism that is even now gaining in virulence. But at this time we could not help but be impressed by the signs of religious feeling in the people, nourished in near-secrecy in a hostile dictatorship.

The home stretch now lay before the three reporters. The cocktail party had been set for late afternoon, February 8. Leonid had procured a compartment on the night train for Leningrad at 9 P.M.; now only a day of sightseeing in that stately city, and the day's session of the Supreme Soviet was between them and the breakout to Helsinki and home.

It was this meeting of the Supreme Soviet that was to topple Malenkov from power and set Nikita Khrushchev on his march to unquestioned authority. But there was little at the meeting itself—at least insofar as the non-Russian speaker was concerned —to indicate events of such magnitude had taken place.

The first session started at 1 P.M. and adjourned about fifteen minutes later. Premier Georgi Malenkov was the principal speaker. We were sitting in the press gallery, high above the floor filled with 1,300 delegates. Our translator had been translating for us in a routine low-pitched monotone, and showed no particular emotion when Malenkov began his fateful speech. Suddenly his eyes went glassy, and he slurred to a stop. No words came from his shaking lips.

"It's sensational!" he said finally. "Sensational!"

We hadn't the slightest clue as to what was so sensational. Malenkov continued to speak in a calm, factual manner. Smith seized the translator by the collar and shook him unmercifully.

"Speak up, man," he said. "What's going on down there?"

"It's sensational," mumbled our translator. "Premier Malenkov has just quit."

Malenkov sat down amid mild applause, and the meeting was adjourned until 4 P.M., at which time the new Premier was to be announced. This gave the diplomats and journalists several hours in which to speculate about Malenkov's successor. The consensus was that Khrushchev himself, having displayed his power, would now move into the top spot. We were pleased to hear this, because, after all, hadn't we exhaustively interviewed him only three days before?

The four o'clock meeting was as cut-and-dried as the earlier one—except that consternation gripped us when Secretary Khrushchev arose and suggested to the delegates that Comrade

Bulganin would make an excellent Premier. Now—too late!—
we understood why Bulganin had been suggested for an interview a week previously. We also grasped the full significance of
the stipulation that he could only talk to us *after* the meeting of
the Supreme Soviet. Our Communist hosts had tried to present
us with a world scoop of staggering dimensions, and we had
coolly turned it down. Now we were scheduled to leave without
seeing either the outgoing or the incoming Premier. For, as you
can well imagine, the 1,300 delegates, without a dissenting noise,
raised their hands and voted aye to Khrushchev's "suggestion"
that Bulganin was the man for the job.

Our morale hit a low ebb at the hotel when we returned to find
a cable from Barry Faris, editor-in-chief of INS, urging us by all
means to try and interview the new Premier. A request was duti-
fully dispatched to the Kremlin asking for an appointment, but
our hopes of success were virtually nil. Besides, we were leaving
for Leningrad in a few hours, and for Helsinki, two days hence.
Our schedule was too tight to permit any serious hopes. We
needed the cheer and warmth of the farewell cocktail party that
soon erupted in Hearst's apartment; the glamor of Ulanova and
Plisetskaya and the Bolshoi group also helped to dispel our
gloom. We *had* at any rate seen Khrushchev, Molotov, and
Zhukov, we told ourselves. You can't win them all.

But when luck is running for you, sometimes it comes up all
sevens. We had our one-day tourist's view of Leningrad, although for Conniff the visit was flawed by an attack of his recurrent gout. One can easily be afflicted with this allegedly aristo-
cratic ailment in the workers' paradise; vodka-cum-caviar twice
a day for nigh onto three weeks will bring it on anywhere.

The trio rose early on Thursday and prepared to depart for
the airport to catch the ten o'clock Helsinki plane, but it was
delayed by a low ceiling at the Leningrad airport. So we stayed
on at the hotel to kill a few hours. Hearst began writing his

regular Sunday "Editor's Report." We were then notified that
the plane had arrived, and we left for the airport. Our baggage
was checked through the tedious Soviet customs and loaded
aboard the aircraft. All that was needed was the signal to board
the plane.

Joe Smith and Leonid Khortakov spent the last few minutes
in a grim chess game, with the honor of free enterprise versus
communism practically dangling on the outcome. Hearst fiddled
with a dilapidated old radio, while an Intourist interpreter
sought to translate for us the Russian version of our Khrushchev
interview, at that moment being broadcast by Radio Leningrad.
Conniff sat in a corner, stroking his aching foot.

The loudspeaker announced our flight. We were halfway out
the door before an airport attendant came rushing up.

"Engine trouble," he said. "Another half-hour."

And it was in those twenty minutes of grace that a phone call
arrived from Moscow. Charles Klensch, INS bureau chief, had
news for us. "Premier Bulganin," he panted, "will see you
tomorrow or Saturday."

Off with the baggage. Cancel the plane tickets to Helsinki.
Frantic efforts to get reservations on the night train back to
Moscow, all accomplished through some magic by the invaluable
Leonid. Just as we left the airport, we saw the Helsinki plane
take off into the mist.

We just managed to catch the Moscow train, and there was
no time to eat dinner beforehand. An hour out of Leningrad,
Leonid hopped off the train at a five-minute station stop and
returned bearing sandwiches. "Fat sandwiches," he said. "Just
what we need to keep us warm on this cold night." Smith took
one look at the slices of blubber placed between two slabs of
moldy bread and became slightly green around the mandibles.
He turned over in his berth with his face to the wall and looked

no more that night on his companions. Hearst nibbled just once and followed suit.

Once again, American manliness was being put to the test. Conniff steeled himself to the sacrifice, hummed a few bars of "The Star-Spangled Banner," and began gnawing away on the blubber sandwiches. "Just great," he mumbled to Leonid. "We ought to have sandwiches like this in America. Beats pizza all to hell." Conniff realized that he just had to eat the greasy concoctions: Leonid would never have believed *he* wasn't hungry.

The interview with Premier Bulganin turned out to be something of an anticlimax. The goateed, gentlemanly career Bolshevik added nothing really new to the outline sketched by Khrushchev the Saturday before. The stress upon "peaceful co-existence" strengthened the growing conviction in the Hearst Task Force that Russian policy was really veering off on a new tack. We mentioned to Bulganin that in a telephone conversation with New York an hour before, Randolph Hearst had told us that the American people were alarmed by the bellicose tone adopted by the top Communists during the Supreme Soviet meeting. Bulganin shrugged his shoulders as if to suggest that he hoped we didn't believe what was said for home consumption. What Khrushchev had told us and what he was now telling us was the real message. The Soviet government hoped for a lessening of world tension and for a *rapprochement* with the United States.

We took a liking to Nikolai Bulganin, although his party record indicated he was a ruthless schemer of the first degree. His appearance was almost professorial. He wore conservative Western clothes, spoke in soft, cultured tones, and seemed an ideal front-man for the regime, a man whose polished urbanity neatly counterbalanced the rugged free-wheeling style of the

First Secretary. He appeared to blend perfectly into the atmosphere of sweet reasonableness in which Khrushchev intended to bathe the party line. On our second visit, two years later, he knew his number was up. To every request for an interview, he smiled sadly and said, "See Comrade Khrushchev. He's the one you should talk to." By spring of 1958, Khrushchev had replaced him.

There was one final festive evening before our delayed departure for home. On our last free evening in Moscow, we went once more to the ballet. This time the Maly—the "small" ballet theater, in contrast to the Bolshoi or "big"—held the main attraction in town, a production of the Tartar ballet *Shuralae* featuring the incomparable Plisetskaya. In the middle of the orchestra stalls sat the great Ulanova. When she entered the theater a few minutes before curtain time, the whole audience rose in a roar of welcome. Ulanova was for the Russians a combination of Joe Di Maggio, Jack Dempsey, Marilyn Monroe, and any other celebrity you care to mention. When she spotted the three Americans who had been her hosts seated in a side box, she graciously turned and bowed in their direction. The audience, still applauding, swiveled toward them, too. Any Americans who rated such a public acknowledgment from their greatest heroine must be people of importance. Plisteskaya compounded our embarrassment by dedicating the performance to us, and again the balletgoers scanned us long and carefully.

Naturally a furious storm, typical of the Russian winter, was blowing up when we left Moscow the next morning. Snow streaked across the Vnukovo runways in bitter gusts, coating the aircraft and bringing visibility to almost zero. But the ground crew went about preparations for departure as if such weather was an everyday event, which, of course, it was. Their equipment was rather primitive, if effective. To unfreeze solid sheets of ice

from the wings of our IL-12, they simply sprayed hot water on
the machine. We crawled into the glacially cold cabin and the
pilots went up to the cockpit.

The trip out was uneventful. We had breakfast in Moscow
before leaving, lunch in Vilna, dinner at the Tempelhof airport
in Berlin, where we transferred to a Pan American plane, and
supper that midnight at Claridge's in London. It was at
Claridge's, surrounded by the smooth service and luxury that
this greatest of hostelries provides, that the full significance of
our whole adventure, Operation Improbable, began to sink in.

CHAPTER 2

The blacksmith's boy
makes good

In the years following our first visit to Russia, "getting to know
Khrushchev" became of major importance in the work and
travels of the Hearst reporters. We were convinced after our
first contact that it was vital to learn as much about the personality and career of this man as we could. To dismiss him as
a bibulous braggart could be suicidal for the Western world,
yet to descend into a jellylike fear of the man would be equally
unwise. Somehow, we felt, we had to search out the truth about
this elusive character.

He is not easy to know. As Communist leaders go, Khrushchev has been comparatively shy about revealing his origins
and background. There are great gaps in the available story of
his life, gaps which have not been filled in either by fact or fiction,
by sycophant or critic.

He appears to be in no mood to shed more than flickering light
on his shadowy past. The exposure of his family on his trip to
the United States from the secrecy in which his private life had
been veiled was an astonishing change. On trips to Russia in

1955 and 1957, our questions about Madam Khrushchev and the Khrushchev children had been met with either blank stares or banal generalities. It was noted by the team during the 1957 visit that Madam Khrushchev's picture had never appeared in a Russian (or any other) periodical. Two years later, for at least a brief period, she was possibly the most photographed woman in the world.

A week before the arrival of the Khrushchev family, inquiries at the State Department and the Soviet Embassy had failed to elicit any information whatsoever on Madam Khrushchev. The Embassy was not able to give us even the first and maiden names of the Soviet Union's First Lady. During most of the thirteen days the Khrushchevs were in the United States, it was written and rewritten that they had married in 1938, after the death of the Premier's first wife, and that Madam Khrushchev had raised Khrushchev's children by the first wife.

These stories went completely unchallenged almost until the end of the visit when Madam Khrushchev received the women reporters covering the tour and gave them an interview. She then mentioned quite casually that she and Khrushchev had been married in 1924, not 1938; that the first wife had died "in a famine"; and that she was the mother of Sergei, Rada, a married daughter, and Yelena, a student at the University of Moscow. Khrushchev had two children by his first wife, a son, Leonid, killed with the Red Air Force during World War II, and a daughter, Yulia.

This is but one example of the formidable difficulties in assembling a Khrushchev biography. The biographical details presented here represent a winnowing job in which vital facts that are seriously in question have been sacrificed with the chaff.

Nikita Sergeyevitch Khrushchev was born April 17, 1894, in the hamlet of Kalinovka, of which Kursk was the administrative center, on the edge of the Ukraine. "I used to live in a mud hut," he likes to say when barnstorming through an underprivileged area. This is his man-of-the-people approach, not unlike that of American politicians who found it expedient to dwell on their log-cabin origins.

Actually, the Khrushchevs were better off than many families in the village of Kalinovka. His father was the local blacksmith, a sturdy, hard-drinking, big-eating man who claimed to be a descendant of a Zaporog Cossack banished to the region by a forgotten czar. He appears also to have been the local locksmith, and probably worked as a coal miner at some period during his life—for Khrushchev has frequently alluded to the fact that he, like his father, was at one time a miner.

Nikita Sergeyevitch was one of ten children. If any of the others are alive today, it must be regarded as one of the best-kept secrets of the times.

Little Nikita's first known work was that of shepherd for the family's cow, goats, and pigs, which grazed on a comparatively sizable plot (the equivalent of 16 acres) which his father had inherited. This phase of his life was recalled several times during his United States visit, with mingled pride and a trace of self-pity. He may have been seven or eight years old when assigned this task.

His early schooling was unquestionably sketchy. It came from a Russian Orthodox priest named Amvrossi, who doubled as the village school teacher. There is evidence that it was confined to four years, between the ages of seven and eleven. At the latter age, his father took him out of school and began his apprenticeship as blacksmith-locksmith. He was eventually to resume his schoolwork with voracious zeal and in time acquire a remarkable store of knowledge in fields as unrelated as agriculture, heavy industry, and political history. But his uncultured manner of speech still reflects the gaping wound in his early schooling.

What Nikita Khrushchev lacked in formal education he made

up in sheer energy and gall. The elders of Kalinovka remember him as a bouncy extrovert who liked to play the flute and could dance the *gopak* with almost excessive fire and gestures. He excelled, too, at *lapta,* a handball game, and delighted in dueling with his contemporaries with sticks.

He was also reputed to have a sharp eye for the sturdy babushka-wearing girls of Kalinovka. His appreciation for feminine beauty has apparently remained undiminished since. (During his hard-drinking visit to Belgrade in 1955, where he reached a short-lived accord with Tito and signed a trade and barter treaty, Khrushchev remarked jovially to the Yugoslav dictator, "The treaty becomes null and void if you fail to barter your wife for the wife of Nikita Sergeyevich Khrushchev, member of the Presidium of the Supreme Soviet.")

Khrushchev's alcoholic consumption has been severely cut in recent years on the orders of his doctors and the insistence of his wife. His tippling was probably overestimated, although he was publicly drunk in Belgrade on at least one occasion during his visit in 1955. His reputation as a tosspot springs mainly from the many photographs showing him with a glass in his hand. Actually, almost all public pictures of Khrushchev as he emerged from anonymity were made at diplomatic receptions. At such functions, which are all but nightly affairs in Moscow, it is customary for all guests to toy with a drink for toasting purposes. Khrushchev has gotten through many an evening at a foreign embassy in Moscow with hardly a sip, but almost invariably has been pictured to the world the next day as a man holding his tenth.

The fact is that he couldn't have been a heavy drinker during his rise to eminence. He had need of his full and unclouded wits through virtually every waking hour of that ascent. He lived— and still lives—in a jungle of intrigue and treachery in which one slip, either of the foot or tongue, could mean disaster, if not death. During his early career his extracurricular distinction was not as a heavy drinker, but as an entertainer—a teller of earthy jokes, a man who could make hilarious fun of people his superiors did not like, and a man who could always get up and dance.

Khrushchev's Russian biographer Victor Alexandrov relates this possibly apocryphal but nonetheless significant incident in Khrushchev's youth to explain the origin of his revolutionary fervor:

A stomach ulcer prevented his father from working, and Nikita had to take his place. His thick-set figure could often be seen at the anvil, wielding a hammer with might and main. He now worked steadily and did not often make his appearance on the village green to share in the amusements of the other young people as in the past. Nikita was beginning to take life seriously. The only relaxation in which he now indulged was fishing. He had bought a small boat, a kind of canoe, and armed with a paddle and some fishing lines he used to make his way downstream towards the marshlands owned by Prince Kozlovsky, which were connected with the river by a large pond. Nikita's boat, which drew very little water, could reach the marshlands by way of the pond. Thereupon he would open a bag which he had hidden in a box, and take out a kind of dragnet which he lowered into the marsh. His catch always consisted of several dozen plump tench which agreeably supplemented the family's ordinary diet. Moreover, fish-food had become a necessity to Sergei Khrushchev, whose illness was getting worse, and Nikita redoubled his efforts to maintain an ample supply of fish for his father's benefit.

One day he was caught red-handed by the Prince's gamekeeper, who, after knocking him about, tied him hand and foot and delivered him up to the local police sergeant. This dignitary decided to take the law into his own hands. He confiscated the canoe, the fishing lines and dragnet for his own personal benefit, and, after giving Nikita a taste of his "nagaika," a whip whose lash was weighted with a piece of lead at the end of it, he let him go.

In this way, young Khrushchev, a descendant of the proud Zaporog Cossacks, gained his first experience of social injustice and fell afoul of one of the authorities of Imperial Russia. This incident fundamentally affected the subsequent course of his life.

... Nikita (thereafter) showed himself rarely in the village. Everybody there had heard what had happened to him, and he had a feeling that he was being laughed at. He therefore took to roaming about in the woods by himself, and on these occasions he carried a small book with him, the work of a terrorist named Kravchinsky who was condemned to death during the reign of Alexander II. He had escaped from Russia and later settled in England, where he became known as an author under the name of Stepniak.

"Let us proceed to conquer our country by force of arms. Let us sweep away social injustice. Death to the Tsar's police!" These words formed the keynote of the book.

Young Khrushchev was carried away by the discovery of a world hitherto new to him. In his eyes the police sergeant's "nagaika" typified the horrors of Tsarist Russia which Stepniak-Kravchinsky urged his readers to destroy. The bruises which he still bore on his body were precisely those "stigmas of shame" which, Stepniak-Kravchinsky insisted, must be wiped out by bloodshed.

After this, Nikita decided that he could no longer live in peasant surroundings, the most ignominious aspect of Imperial Russia. He told his mother that he intended to leave home and find employment at Kharkov. The workshop would have to be sold. And in the Spring of 1911 he went to Kharkov, the capital of the Ukraine.

Even in this stiff and probably biased account, there is a good deal of plausible detail. Khrushchev was seventeen at the time, and probably as impressionable as any other embittered youth. The distant relatives with whom he went to live in Kharkov found work for him as a turner's mate in a farm-machinery plant and introduced him to a little group of revolution-minded fellow workers. They were in ferment over the recent hanging of the radical Dimitri Dogrov, who had assassinated a hated czarist official in a Kiev theater. Nikita joined with 3,000 other workers in a protest meeting—his first.

He also made his first speech on this occasion, to be followed by countless others. A book by Makar Ptitza, published in Kiev in 1940, gives this eyewitness account:

Comrade Khrushchev was the last speaker. He was still very young, scarcely 20 [actually 17]. He was introduced as "The young comrade from the Helferich-Sade Factory," and with considerable feeling he uttered a few sentences. He ended his remarks by saying, "Other strugglers will take Bogrov's place."

The publicity young Khrushchev gained from this maiden effort was not healthy. The police came looking for him the next day at the plant, and Khrushchev, forewarned, made the first of many strategic retreats which were to mark his dizzy rise to the top. He found work in Karan in the Donets Basin. (He sometimes begins a talk today, "As a former metalworker in the Donets Basin. . . .")

He stayed there a year, then moved on to Mariupol where he boarded with a Jewish family named Yankyelyevich. This was again a gesture of protest. Subsequent events have proved him to be no great friend of the Jew in Russia. But at that time the Czar was embarked on an anti-Semitic campaign. That was enough for Nikita. During his stay, he was credited with helping to break up a pogrom-minded gang of toughs about to descend on the neighborhood. He moved on after a year, an itinerant mechanic, working where he could, studying, now and then breaking loose for an evening on the town, associating with every radical group he could locate, but staying out of trouble.

Millions of American televiewers who watched him arrive in the United States looking comparatively trim and dapper in a black silk suit made by his Italian tailor, will be surprised at the portrait of him in 1914 by Vladimir S. Andriyevsky in *The Memoirs of an Agrarian.*

I met him in a large beerhall near the station at Kharkov. He was with two young ladies whom he introduced to me as his cousins.

... He was dressed in a manner which, by the standards of the Kharkov working classes, was considered smart. He wore a grey woolen cap, a dark blue coat of diagonal cloth; light blue bell-bottomed trousers, all the rage among the Odessa toughs, who had copied them from the sailors, and now an essential item in the uniform of the Russian proletarian dandies.

... He was drinking beer. Now and then he cautiously took a bottle of vodka out of his trouser pocket, and after sipping it, put it back with equal caution.

"Beer's all right for Germans," he said, "but vodka's the stuff for Russians."

Khrushchev, who was to hold the rank of lieutenant general in World War II, was deferred in World War I as a skilled mechanic. He gave over his spare hours to making up for the lost years of formal education. An article about him in the *Voroshilovgrad News* in 1938 speaks of his joining the Popular Library at Lugansk at this time, and of hungrily devouring great chunks of Gogol, Pushkin, Lermontov, Goncharov, Spielhagen, Zola, Balzac, Goethe, de Maupassant, Dickens, Nekrassov, and Schiller. He was pictured as an avid reader in science. In night classes at The Popular University, he studied mathematics, science, spelling, history, and geography.

The Lvov-Kerensky revolution of February, 1917, which ended the long reign of the czars and momentarily established Russia as a constitutional democracy, had a deep effect on Khrushchev. He quit job and classroom in Lugansk and joined in an excited march to Kharkov where a great burst of celebrations was taking place. Aside from this gesture, however, we do not know to what extent he favored this short-lived regime.

He did briefly hold office in the new order; he was "Chairman of the Distribution Committee" in his home town of Kalinovka.

This was part of an agrarian-reform program aimed at breaking up large estates and sharing out the land among the peasants. How he came by the job is not known, but it may have been by pure chance. He was visiting his mother in Kalinovka at the time of his appointment, and perhaps his status as a hometown boy who had made good as a mechanic, plus his book-learned knowledge of agricultural problems, were the deciding factors.

But orthodox-minded Kremlin historians are careful to point out that Khrushchev was not taken in by the "imperialistic" aspects of the Kerensky government. A biographical sketch of Khrushchev printed in *Trud* in 1937, by which time he had become one of Stalin's chief political hatchet men, describes a speech Khrushchev made during World War I, denouncing the popular theory that Russia should demand the Dardenelles as her price for continuing to fight for the Allies. His grounds were that this proposal was being made solely to prolong the war for the enrichment of imperialists. Thus, *Trud* concluded, Khrushchev was even then in ideological harmony with Lenin, who was soon to overthrow the provisional government and take Russia out of the war.

So it is not surprising that Khrushchev made a nimble switch from petty officialdom in the provisional regime to a place in the apparatus the Bolsheviks set up after "The Great October" in 1917.

Again, chance, this time in the guise of a pretty girl, seems to have played an important role. An attractive cousin, in whose company he spent much time when in Kharkov, had joined the Communist Party there and been assigned to work in Lugansk. Khrushchev followed her there and was working at the prosaic task of metal-fitting when the Bolsheviks carried out their coup against the moderates.

Perhaps through his cousin, and perhaps through his keen salesmanship, Khrushchev was elected a member of the Lugansk soviet a month after the revolution. He was promptly given the first of countless assignments which became for him the rungs of a ladder to the top. His earthy muscularity and vigorous manner of speech prompted his superiors to appoint him a recruiting officer. Russia was filled with jobless stragglers from the demolished and demoralized army and navy. They had come home to find the country in the grip of civil conflict. Some signed up with Cossacks, others with the White Guards—which in time had the support of United States, British, French, and Italian troops. Khrushchev's task was to find men to fight with the Red Guards. Perhaps as a gesture, but probably because there was nothing else to do, he himself became one of the first to enlist on the side of the Reds in the bloody war that followed.

Khrushchev apparently saw action during a month of skirmishes against the Cossacks and the Whites at such places as Rutchenkovo, Yuzovo, Gorlovka, Pavolgrad, Melitopol, and Taganrog. There, a sizable force of Reds was put to embarrassing rout by several hundred cadets of a military school. Khrushchev was wounded and spent the first three months of 1918 in a Lugansk hospital.

In April he was back with the Red Guards, this time as commander of the First Proletarian Regiment of the Donbass, part of a 30,000-man force commanded by Klimenti Voroshilov. The enemy, in this instance, was a large German force advancing on Kharkov under Gen. von Eichborn.

The Red Guards went out of the city in a desperate effort to stop the Germans, and were beaten. They fell back to Kharkov and—such being the chaos of the day—found themselves forced to fight several Russian counter-revolutionary groups which had seized pockets of the city. The German steamroller crunched onward, and the battle plan was to sweep right through the city.

Khrushchev knew Kharkov like the palm of his hand. He maneuvered his men into positions in a part of the city which

would afford them the best natural cover, and is credited with
holding up the German advance for a full day—during which
time most of Voroshilov's beaten troops were able to escape with
much of their gear and material. Khrushchev personally issued
the orders to evacuate Kharkov and was presumably one of the
last to leave. He reached Byelgorod in late April, 1918, and there
made formal application to become a member of the Bolshevik
party.

The remarkable thing about Khrushchev's boast that his
record in the Communist Party was stainless is that he was
close to speaking truth. Through the years he was not only one
of the most loyal party men, but surely among the most astute.
He appeared to sense in advance every major shift in policy, un-
erringly picking the right coattails to hang from.

He was accepted into the Party immediately after his application. His first assignments, curiously enough, were minor
bureaucratic posts. One of these concerned agrarian reform in
the Kursk area. His report was lucid enough to attract the eye
of a Moscow official who, in turn, mentioned him favorably to
Lenin. The revered leader gave the bustling, peasantlike Khrushchev a short audience not long after that. Nevertheless, at the
time, one might have supposed that Khrushchev's chances of
becoming Lenin's eventual successor were slim indeed.

When the war with Germany ended, Red forces quickly filled
the vacuum left in the Ukraine by the Kaiser's departing forces.
Lawlessness and Ukrainian nationalism were rife. It was
Khrushchev's job to define both and crush them. He had hardly
commenced his duties, however, when the White Russian Army
struck. He was back in action in a civil war whose first casualty
appears to have been the Geneva Convention. It was war by night,
in the forests; a war in which no man dared risk capture. For a
time, Khrushchev served as a prosecutor attached to military
courts, which gave quasirespectability to invariable verdicts of
death for prisoners.

In the wake of the eventual Red victory, Trotsky came to Kharkov—it was January, 1920—to make the principal speech at a tense celebration, and to distribute medals among the faithful. The edgy atmosphere was due to Trotsky's excoriation of the people of the city, the hungry and haggard hosts of successive military oppressions.

"Kharkov is like a radish, red outside and white inside," he scolded them. "When our Red armies left your city in 1919 the inhabitants fired on us. Even the proletarians of Kharkov did not give full support to the Soviet government. There was only one small group which defended the city to the last against the hordes of German imperialists. The First proletarian regiment of the Donets was the one which saved the proletarian honor of your city, which has become once again an honest Soviet city. Glory to that regiment! Glory to its First battalion which held out at Kharkov to the last."

Khrushchev, among others, was called to the victory stand, and from Trotsky received the first of many decorations. He was grateful but hardly overwhelmed. When it came time to cast his lot either with Trotsky or Stalin—the latter a man he didn't know—he chose Stalin.

Another impeccable decision Khrushchev made in 1920 was to turn down a commission in the Red Army. Instead, he asked to be sent to school. His superiors sent him to a school to formalize his already considerable knowledge of agriculture. Most of his classmates were in their late teens or early twenties; Khrushchev was twenty-six, case-hardened by war and bursting with the will to succeed.

Biographer Alexandrov states that this school, located in a hostel in Kharkov, differed from other coeducational institutions of the time in its lack of promiscuity. This was the Soviet Union's brief period of "free love," of rebellion against marriage, which the early Communist planners approved as a means of breaking down family and religious resistance to the new regime.

At this agricultural school, however, lovers were wont to get married.

Nikita, too, had a love affair at the hostel, and one day in the spring of 1922 he married a Miss Surkova, who was also studying agriculture. There were three children of this marriage, a daughter and two sons, one of whom, an airman, was killed in the last war. Nikita and his wife soon left the hostel, and by means of wire-pulling he obtained a small flat. His marriage made no change in his educational plans. He had already attracted the attention of his teachers by a number of essays on his special subject, and one of these essays, which dealt with the rotation of crops in the Kursk area, brought him a prize of ten rubles. Nikita made up his mind, with the help of his wife, to write a book on the rotation of crops throughout the Ukraine. He spent much time in the library of the agricultural college, [and] ... his wife ... helped him by her research work.

This gives the student of Khrushchev cause to be somewhat puzzled. The present Madam Khrushchev firmly gave her own account of the family history before she left America in September, 1959. Khrushchev's first wife died in a "famine" in 1922, she said. There were two children, not three. She and Alexandrov agree only that the eldest was killed while serving in the Red Air Force. There is no reason to doubt Mrs. Khrushchev's word about the children: Yulia, the eldest of the girls, is small, dark, wiry, and sharp faced, while the features of the younger children all strongly resemble the broad-boned, flattened faces of Mr. and Mrs. Khrushchev. But there is no way of completely reconciling these two accounts.

Madam Khrushchev also revealed to Western journalists that she met her future husband in the city of Yuzovka (now Stalino), in the Donets Basin of the Ukraine. "I came there as a teacher of political science," she recalled, "and he was already a student at the workers' faculty, studying to be a mining engineer. We met in the same city, but I did not teach him anything and he did not teach me."

Beyond this, astonishingly little is known of the present First Lady of the U.S.S.R. She has since further broken with tradition by appearing in print under her own by-line. In the December, 1959, issue of *Soviet Woman* Mrs. Khrushchev commented on how kindly and courteously she had been treated by American women during her visit, and in her folksy way praised Mrs. Eisenhower and Mrs. Eleanor Roosevelt, who, she said, "extended us sincere hospitality and cordiality and acquainted us with their children and grandchildren."

What prompted her to write the article? In answering this question she gave one more tantalizing fact about her background. "I write this report in response to requests from old friends at the Moscow Electric Light Bulb Factory where I worked thirty years ago."

The most important event in Khrushchev's career in the twenties was a dutiful but unpopular campaign against Trotsky in the Ukraine. By 1924, when Stalin sent Lazar Kaganovich to Kharkov to root out Trotskyism, especially among students, Khrushchev was virtually a minority of one among the younger and more aggressive Communists of the region. Kaganovich, hampered not only by the unpopularity of his task, but also because as a Jew he suffered from a wave of anti-Semitism in the Ukraine, found young Khrushchev an admirable ally. He called Khrushchev to his office, questioned him at great length, was satisfied with what he heard, and then ordered him to leave school. Khrushchev became a propagandist for the party in the Ukraine, his job to demolish the reputation of the man who had decorated him during the civil war.

Kaganovich was delighted with Khrushchev's work. The young Stalinist looked and dressed and spoke like a true proletarian, but he had a mind that cut through reactionary resistance like a buzz saw. He seemed to have committed Marx, Engels, and Lenin to memory, and with equal ease confounded intellectual opponents in debate and established close communion with his "fellow workers of the Donets."

He was mentioned favorably in Kaganovich's reports to Stalin, and his star appeared to be in ascendancy. But then, with no warning, Kaganovich was recalled to Moscow, and his place was taken by a crusty old Bolshevik, Skrypnik. Skrypnik did not cotton to Khrushchev, whom he considered an uncouth ruffian. Khrushchev became one of the chief targets of Skrypnik's ultimatum that all party officials in the Ukraine must be able to speak fluent Ukrainian.

Now, although the people of the Kursk area, in which Khrushchev was born, were under the Ukrainian administration, linguistically they were neither fish nor fowl. Khrushchev spoke a curious patois made of Russian and Ukrainian, but if he had mastered either of the two languages, it was Russian. An early defector from communism, and an associate of Skrypnik, Gregor Bessedovsky, wrote in his *Memoirs of a Diplomat:*

I came into contact with quite a number of functionaries of the central committee of the party at Kharkov. Nearly all of them were dismayed at the thought of having to learn Ukrainian. Many of these functionaries, though of Ukrainian origin, did not know our language and had no desire to learn it.

Among those members of the central committee who were of Ukrainian origin, but who had not succeeded in learning their native language, I came across a certain Khrushchev, from Kursk. ... One day he made a speech before a group of commissars for foreign affairs, whose permanent secretary, Nikolas Lyubtchenko, was a well-known Ukrainian author. Khrushchev had, of course, spoken in Russian, and after his speech Lyubtchenko rose and said:

"Before discussing the question dealt with by Comrade Khrushchev, I will give you a Ukrainian translation of his speech."

Skrypnik apparently "rode" Khrushchev without mercy. His star dimmed, and probably his income, too. It could have been about this time that his better-educated wife went to work in the light-bulb plant. Khrushchev searched about for friendlier contacts within the Party. He found sympathetic friends at the Kiev Industrial Academy, and cannily applied to be sent there to study industrial organization.

This was arranged, but Khrushchev never forgave Skrypnik. In 1934, Khrushchev testified against the old Bolshevik, who was up before the central committee in Moscow on loose charges of being a deviationist. "You are a traitor," Khrushchev shouted at the old man. "Were you not one of those who urged that the Cyrillic alphabet be replaced by the Latin alphabet in the Ukraine? That is rank treason! Pilsudski is in favor of the same scheme. That means that you are nothing but a Polish agent!" The staunch old Communist was stripped of his remaining authority. He went straight off to his room in the National Hotel and committed suicide.

At Kiev Industrial Academy Khrushchev began to move forward once more. He reestablished contact with Kaganovich by mail, and after two years of broad hints and entreaties was able to persuade his patron to have him transferred to the Joseph Stalin Industrial Academy in Moscow.

As in Kharkov earlier, Kaganovich needed a tough-minded trouble-shooter. Stalin had triumphed over Trotsky and had liquidated his supporters, but so-called "rightists" were now giving him trouble—Rykov, Bukharin, Tomsky, Piatakov, and Sokolnikov. They were especially strong in Moscow, core of a growing Communist bureaucracy. Khrushchev's job was to "restore order," another way of saying "purge."

Krushchev's first purge is credited with being a direct cause of the suicide in November, 1932, of Nadyezhda Aliluyeva, Stalin's wife. She took her life in protest against what her husband, through Khrushchev, was doing to old associates. Her death helped Khrushchev's career. It permitted Stalin to legalize his long relationship with Rosa Kaganovich, sister of Khrushchev's patron. As Kaganovich rose, Khrushchev was pulled along. He began to be invited to the parties of the hierarchy, even to the informal fetes which the new Mrs. Stalin gave at their *dacha* outside Moscow. A French governess of the Stalin children wrote later:

Among other regular guests was a Ukrainian, secretary of a committee at Moscow. He danced well, sometimes alone, sometimes with his hostess. He was a good singer and also liked telling anecdotes which made even Stalin laugh. On one occasion, too, he brought with him his little boy who played with Basil, the son of Stalin.

Pleased by the way he had eradicated "unreliables," Stalin promoted Khrushchev to second secretary of the party committee of the city of Moscow in 1932, and to first secretary the following year, where he was Kaganovich's assistant. Khrushchev became political overseer during the costly construction of the Moscow Subway. Out of Stalin's pleasure over this grandiose subterranean monument to Bolshevik power came Nikita's first villa.

Stalin then began making direct use of Khrushchev. In 1937 he sent him to Rostov-on-Don with an unusual assignment: to bring about the arrest and "confession" of a Stalin relative named Sheboldayev, who had made more than the customary botch of the tasks assigned him. The methods Khrushchev employed are not known, but the official in time signed a document accusing himself as a "Saboteur ... Fascist ... Spy in the pay of Turkey."

The two men returned to Moscow on the same train. Stalin's kinsman was put to death in Lubyanka Prison. Khrushchev received the first of his major decorations.

The Ukraine was to see much of and learn to quake at the name of Khrushchev. As Eugene Lyons described it to the Congress, just before Khrushchev's trip to the United States:

"He was sent in 1937 as Stalin's trusted killer [to the Ukraine]. . . . His first move was to summon a conference of the entire Ukrainian government, staged as a social occasion. The gathering was surrounded by the secret police, arrested en masse, and most of his 'guests' died in the cellars of the Kiev and Moscow secret police. When his two-year Ukrainian purge was over, an estimated 400,000 had been killed and terror gripped the whole population."

When the Nazis struck Russia, Khrushchev, like other important civilians high up in Kremlin circles—he had become a full member of the Politburo in 1939—assumed a uniform and an imposing rank. He became a lieutenant general and "President of the Defense Committee for the Kiev Area," under Marshal Budenny.

Budenny was soon removed, and Khrushchev was named commander-in-chief of a partisan force in the Ukraine, working out of Bryanskiy Forest. He was in on the Kharkov offensive of May, 1942, and at Stalingrad later in the year. He became embroiled in the feud between Marshals Rokossovsky and Zhukov and flew to Moscow to take the latter's side before the Politburo. Once again, his skilled intuition was at work: Zhukov one day was to save his neck.

When the Red Army rolled the Nazis out of the Ukraine in 1943, Khrushchev was sent in its wake to punish the Ukrainians who had welcomed the Germans as liberators. There are no reliable figures of the number killed, imprisoned, and exiled, but scattered accounts by a few lucky escapees indicate that the campaign was a true blood bath.

After the war, Khrushchev helped change the face of Russia, moving thousands of farming families out of their hovels into barrackslike buildings and even apartment houses. He was, in effect, commissar of the communal system, turning the farmer into a faceless employee of the state. It was work which was close to the soil, and Khrushchev enjoyed it. But Stalin gave him little rest.

The old dictator had plunged suddenly into senility. He wanted no advice from his Politburo, but demanded simple and abject loyalty. Two men gave it to him without question— Georgi Malenkov and Khrushchev. Stalin was darkly suspicious of all others. Though these two henchmen must have privately recognized the paranoid absurdity of the accusations, they were key figures in the group that, late in 1952, carried out Stalin's prosecution of the Jewish doctors, ". . . murderers in white overalls."

Malenkov was the best-known party figure at the time of Stalin's death on March 5, 1953, and it was confidently expected in the West that he would succeed the old dictator. This expectation appeared realized when Malenkov took over, not only as Premier, but as head of the reformed Party secretariat. Khrushchev was listed right behind him and Mikhail Suslov ranked third.

During the first weeks of Malenkov's tenure, the pages of *Pravda* reflected what must have been an intense internal drama. During the first week, three separate pictures of the new Premier adorned its columns, presented in a manner strikingly similar to that in which Stalin had been built up years before. The third picture showed Malenkov in a close huddle with Mao Tse-tung —a sure sign of his eminence, especially when it was discovered that other high leaders had been tidily cropped out of the photograph.

But the build-up then came to a sudden end. After the first week there were no more individual pictures of Premier Malenkov. The theme of "collective leadership" became the leitmotiv of the new regime. And then on March 21—two weeks after Stalin's death—a short official announcement gave the outside world a peek at Kremlin intrigue. Malenkov voluntarily relinquished his duties in the Party secretariat to concentrate on his administrative chores as Premier while Nikita S. Khrushchev was named First Secretary of the Communist Party of the U.S.S.R.

Malenkov either lacked the strength to wrest party leadership from Khrushchev, or elected to take the Premiership alone in the hope of eventually solidifying the base of his power. Did he have any reasonable grounds for hope?

Malenkov apparently hoped to challenge the position of the Party from within the Russian government itself: that is, the administrators, bureaucrats, and functionaries who actually run the machinery of rule. There is reason to believe that Malenkov gambled that as Premier he could so organize the administration and the administrators that he could govern Russia without recourse to party clearance or fear of party veto. As a party leader himself, he must have recognized the desperate odds against his gamble. Some Westerners believe he made his lunge for control within the first five days of Stalin's death, that he failed, and that in so doing he prepared for his own exit.

The Communist Party, it must be remembered, is the ruling apparatus of Russia. Party members permeate every branch of government, the army, the secret police, the schools, the scientific and technological systems. A Russian's real power derives from his position in the Party, not from his nominal rank in a government agency. A party counselor in an embassy can conceivably exert more real influence in a political sense than an ambassador; a junior officer with the right placement in party circles is more potent than a commander who lacks such links.

Meanwhile, Khrushchev began picking off his other foes, one by one. On his return to Moscow from a speaking tour with Malenkov he found Bulganin and Beria, chief executioner during Stalin's last years, at odds. Khrushchev supported Bulganin, realizing that NKVD and its sadistic leader represented a dangerous threat to the power of the party. In the closing years of Stalin's life, when the aging dictator saw threats to his safety from his closest associates, Beria had awesome power. He reported directly to the old chief and ruled with imperial sway in a large domain of his own.

Marshal Tito during one of his first periods of disillusionment with his Russian ally in the late 1940s thus described Beria's sinister power:

"During the past 15 years an important position has been acquired by the intelligence service—the NKVD. Instead of being a weapon to fight counter-revolution, it has grown into a power in itself. . . . The entire activity of the country, the party, foreign policy, all rests upon the intelligence service. Its reports are given priority; it really rules the country.

"Stalin himself has become the slave of the intelligence service he created and developed—its willing slave. Consequently in the Soviet Union today, no one trusts anyone else; everything is a cause for suspicion."

There is evidence that even Beria came under Stalin's suspicion in the last months of his life. The dictator's death, at any rate, served to crystallize opposition to his former headsman.

No official report of the events surrounding Beria's liquidation has ever been released, but Khrushchev himself is reputed to have given a pungent description of it to Pierre Commins, member of a French Socialist delegation which visited Moscow in May, 1956. This account appeared two months afterward in a Socialist publication:

"Very soon after the death of Stalin we in the Presidium began to get reports of some double game Beria was playing. We began to have him followed and in a few weeks we established the fact that our suspicions were justified. He was clearly preparing a conspiracy against the Presidium. After waiting for a favorable moment, we designated a special session of the

Presidium to which, of course, Beria was invited, too. He appeared, apparently not suspecting that we knew anything. And right there we began to question him, to adduce facts, data, to put questions to him, in other words, we put him through a cross-examination that lasted four hours.

"For all of us it was clear he was really guilty, and that this man could be dangerous to the party and the country.

"We left him alone in the room, in this very room where we are now conversing, with him sitting in the very chair in which you are sitting now. And we went into another room and there had a discussion of what should be done with him.

"Our inner conviction of his guilt was unshakable. But at that time we did not have at our disposal a sufficient amount of judicial evidence of his guilt. And we found ourselves in a difficult position. Evidence for his consignment to a court we did not have, yet to leave him at liberty was impossible.

"We came to the conclusion that the only correct measure for the defense of the Revolution was to shoot him immediately. This decision was adopted by us and carried out on the spot.

"But we felt much easier when, some time after the condemnation, we received sufficient and irrefutable evidence of his guilt."

These details may sound melodramatic, but it is certain that the elimination of Beria was carried out with ruthless dispatch.

The secret police have since been made to perform the tasks for which they were originally intended, as an arm of the Party designed to keep errant comrades under tight discipline. If the organization is no longer a formidable political instrument, its members are nicely placed to keep an eye on Russia's administration. They man the border, monitor the telephones, and control communications, and their chain of command goes up to the Central Committee of the Party for direction and guidance.

Khrushchev then moved into action against Malenkov. The

means of undermining the Premier were extremely subtle, and were bound up with Malenkov's budget appropriations for heavy and light industry. By sounding alarms in military circles, to the effect that Malenkov was favoring butter over bullets, Khrushchev won support from that important group. Through Dmitri Shepilov, editor of *Pravda,* he was able to get a great amount of publicity as the champion of heavy industry and, therefore, of national defense. Whenever he had the opportunity, he put in a plug for Nicolai Bulganin, but not for Malenkov.

At the climax of this duel, Malenkov's 1955 budget was rejected by the Central Committee. The Premier resigned, accusing himself of "incompetence," and declaring, "I am responsible for the failure of Soviet agriculture. . . ."

It was at this time—when Khrushchev was still an obscure figure outside his own land—that the Hearst team received its first interview with him, and received intimations of his radical new policy.

CHAPTER 3

... And still champion

The year 1955 was a period of salesmanship for Khrushchev, as he unveiled his new "line" to a wary world. Rollicking bibulously through Yugoslavia, giving India a full dose of his bumptious charm, assisted by the suave Bulganin, with a subdued interlude in Geneva thrown in for a change of pace, the bouncy First Secretary tried to sell the nations on the peacefulness and good will of communism.

This was a period which created many false notions about Khrushchev which still persist in some quarters. It was easy to take lightly a fat little fellow who needed guidance from Mikoyan in negotiating the steps after a Belgrade party. He flaunted crazy hats in India and Burma and cut up for the photographers upon demand. At Geneva he was seen in the back of open convertibles waving gaily to passers-by but played down his role in the deliberative councils. One could not help wondering whether his clever colleagues from the Stalin era—Molotov, Kaganovich, Zhukov, and the downgraded Malenkov—were not taking advantage of his frequent absences to prepare his overthrow. It hardly seemed possible that he could have been keeping an eye on the store while cavorting in distant places.

The years 1956–57 were indeed to constitute a grim, testing grapple for Khrushchev's survival. It became apparent that he had not neglected his business while flitting abroad and that his assets were strong enough to withstand the intrigues of his partners in the "collective leadership."

For apparently Molotov, Kaganovich, and the rest of the Stalinist Old Guard shared the Western delusion that their brash comrade could be driven into political bankruptcy whenever they chose to turn against him. When they did finally strike, they must have been confident of success, for they all understood the penalty of failure. But somehow they failed to grasp what the proposed victim had been doing for several years to escape their toils.

The old pros appeared to place little value on the way the party organization was being stacked against them by the executive in charge of assignments, promotions, titles, and salaries. It nevertheless seems hardly conceivable that they failed to notice how many comrades from the Ukrainian and Moscow *apparats* were slowly taking over in key positions. How could the opposition of the revitalized Central Committee have been a mystery to them? Khrushchev had risen to First Secretary of the Party from a position in the Moscow machine, just as Stalin had, and before that Nikita had been powerful in the Ukraine. One by one comrades from these areas departed for choice positions in the provinces, or settled into important posts in the capital itself. The Central Committee had been heavily salted with Khrushchev supporters beginning in spring, 1953, and the process gathered momentum after the upheaval of February, 1955. And had Molotov and his clique failed to observe the friendship between Khrushchev and Marshal Zhukov, who largely controlled the powerful Red Army?

The true tale of the undercover machinations in these eventful years remains cloaked in conjecture. The army of Soviet specialists attempting to analyze them disagree on details, vary concerning the motives of the principals, and differ over the voting alignment in showdown ballots. Nevertheless, a dim pattern emerges from these events, suggesting how Khrushchev consolidated both his own power within the Party and the power of his new policy. And the first step took place at the famous Twentieth Congress.

On the night of February 24, 1956, First Secretary Khrushchev rose to speak before the Twentieth Congress of the All-Union Communist Party in the Kremlin. He suddenly launched into a seven-hour, 30,000-word peroration which slashed at the father-figure who had led them for a generation. Nothing anti-Communist writers had ever said about Josef Stalin equaled the charges leveled at him that night by his successor.

A week before, Anastas Mikoyan had given them an inkling of what was to come with a savage swipe at his old mentor. But it was a passing shot, a glancing blow, and perhaps only intended to drop a hint of what might be expected when Khrushchev took the floor. But nothing in the way of a cue from Mikoyan or a hint from insiders could have prepared the majority of delegates for the vitriolic attack they were to hear.

The Communists have a tradition of punctuating their written accounts of party meetings with stock phrases indicating the emotional state of the auditors— "Commotion in the hall . . . Indignation in the hall . . . Laughter in the hall . . . Applause . . . Prolonged applause . . . Tumultuous, prolonged applause . . . Stormy, tumultuous, prolonged applause," are some of them. Interjected into the text of the usual dull Communist speech, such reactions seemed forced and a little phony, and evidently more dutiful than spontaneous. Studying the text of Khrushchev's remarks, peppered throughout with commotion, indig-

nation, laughter, and the rest, one feels that no special prompting
was necessary on this occasion. These reactions were for sure
and for real.

Khrushchev's assault upon Stalin still shocks Westerners who
were long aware of the dictator's transgressions. The delegates,
too, knew that there had been terror and persecution and injustice in that grim generation. Still, they must have gripped
their chairs in stunned disbelief as Khrushchev tolled the long
list of Stalin's crimes: the violations of "Socialist legality," the
respected and proven party workers who had been liquidated at
Stalin's whim, his coarse military mistakes which almost
brought disaster to Mother Russia, the threat that hung over his
closest associates in his last years.

"It is not excluded," said Khrushchev, "that had Stalin remained at the helm for another several months, Comrades
Mikoyan and Molotov would probably not have delivered any
speeches at this Congress."

There was grim humor in some of Khrushchev's revelations.
While describing how the "cult of personality" had extolled
Stalin's alleged accomplishments to the heavens, Khrushchev
told the delegates that most of the laudatory material had been
prepared under the direct supervision of the dictator. This was
especially true of the edition of his *Short Biography*, published
in 1948.

"This book is an expression of the most dissolute flattery,"
Khrushchev said. "It is an example of making a man into a
Godhead, of transforming him into an infallible sage, the
greatest leader, sublime strategist of all times and nations. . . .
We need not give here examples of the loathsome adulation
filling the book. All we need to add is that they all were approved
and edited by Stalin personally and some of them were added
in his own handwriting to the draft text of the book."

Then, after showing how Stalin had personally composed the

most flowery tributes to his own genius, Khrushchev told the delegates that the Great Man had insisted upon the inclusion of the following paragraph:

"Although he performed his task of leader of the party and the people with consummate skill, and enjoyed the unreserved support of the entire Soviet people, Stalin never allowed his work to be marred by the slightest hint of vanity, conceit, or self-adulation."

Laughter in the hall!

There was pathos, too, in some of Khrushchev's disclosures, as when he read the letter written by the old Bolshevik, Kedrov, to the Central Committee, appealing the unjust verdict against him during one of the big purges:

"I am calling to you for help from a gloomy cell of the Lefortorsky prison. Let my cry of horror reach your ears. Do not remain deaf. Take me under your protection. Please, help remove the nightmare of interrogations and show this is all a mistake.

"I suffer innocently. Please believe me. Time will testify to the truth. . . . I am an old Bolshevik free of any stain. I have honestly fought for almost 40 years in the ranks of the party for the good and prosperity of the nation.

"Today I, a 62-year-old man, am being threatened by the investigative judges with more severe, cruel, and degrading methods of physical pressure. They are no longer capable of becoming aware of their error and of recognizing that their handling of my case is illegal and impermissible. . . . Let the party know I am innocent and that there is nothing that can turn a loyal son of the party into an enemy, even right up to his last dying breath.

"But I have no way out. I cannot divert from myself the hastily approaching new and powerful blows.

"Everything, however, has its limits. My torture has reached the extreme. My health is broken, my strength and my energy are waning, the end is drawing near. To die in a Soviet prison branded as a vile traitor to the Fatherland—what can be more monstrous to an honest man? And how monstrous all this is! Unsurpassed bitterness and pain grips my heart. No! No! This will not happen; this cannot be, I cry. Neither the party, nor the Soviet government, nor the people's commissar, L. P. Beria, will permit this cruel, irreparable injustice. I am firmly certain that given a quiet, objective examination, without any foul rantings, without any anger and without the fearful tortures, it would be easy to prove the baselessness of the charges. I believe deeply that truth and justice will prevail. I believe, I believe!"

"The old Bolshevik, Comrade Kedrov, was found innocent by the Military Collegium," Khrushchev added, with a fine sense of dramatic contrast. "But despite this, he was shot by Beria's orders."

Indignation in the hall!

It was at the Twentieth Congress that the party officially learned of Lenin's famous testament characterizing Stalin as "excessively rude," and of the codicil recommending his removal as General Secretary. Two other documents were read to the Congress—one from Krupskaya, Lenin's wife, to Kamenev, in which she fiercely upbraided Stalin for his rudeness to her during Lenin's lingering illness, and a second, from Lenin to Stalin, when the former heard of the incident:

"Dear Comrade Stalin:

"You permitted yourself a rude summons to my wife to the telephone and a rude reprimand to her. Despite the fact that she told you that she agreed to forget what was said, nevertheless Zinoviev and Kamenev heard about it from her. I have no intention to forget so easily that which is being done against me and I need not stress here that I consider as directed against me that which is being done against my wife. I ask you, therefore,

that you weigh carefully whether you are agreeable to retracting
your words and apologizing or whether you prefer the severence
of relations between us.

Sincerely: Lenin."

Indignation in the hall!

The delegates must have been stunned when Khrushchev
quoted to them the fate of their predecessors at the Seventeenth
Congress in 1934:

"It was determined that of the 139 members and candidates
of the party's Central Committee who were elected at the 17th
Congress, 98 persons, that is, 70 per cent, were arrested and
shot, mostly in 1937–38. ... The same fate met not only the
Central Committee members but also the majority of the delegates to the 17th party congress. Of 1,966 delegates with either
voting or advisory rights, 1,108 were arrested on charges of
revolutionary crimes, that is, decidedly more than a majority."

Amazement in the hall!

This remarkable document is a source of never-ending fascina-
tion for anyone interested in Stalin—or in Khrushchev himself,
for that matter. The essential question it raises about Khrushchev is, Why did he make this speech?

When Khrushchev gained control of the party machinery in
1955, he intended from the outset to turn Russia to a new path,
one tentatively plotted by Malenkov during his short regime. He
was willing to run spectacular risks to change Soviet policy;
many of them must have shocked the party members. The chains
of Stalinism still shackled the minds of many of them. Khrushchev's most daring gambits—his reconciliation with Tito, his
overtures to the United States, his willingness to abandon
Stalin's belligerent stance—failed to sway the cadres to the
new order, or to convince them that a switch away from Stalinism was necessary or desirable.

The destruction of the Stalin myth was intended, we believe, to accomplish these purposes. Only a hardnosed Stalinist of the old school could deny that a change was indicated after Khrushchev's attack upon Stalin's excesses in his chapter-and-verse attack. While hammering home that the new team was serious in its pursuit of the new course, Khrushchev was also convincing the Party that the change was long overdue.

There may have been one other powerful consideration motivating Khrushchev: a long-range one. The stress upon "socialist legality," the accent upon the annihilation of delegates to the Seventeenth Party Congress was intended, we believe, to convey a frightening picture of what happens when individuals are permitted to operate without any reference to the rules of the Party. Never let this happen again! So vivid were his examples of irresponsibility that they undoubtedly left their impress on the delegates. In not too long a time, he was to use this point to demolish his remaining enemies.

Of all the risks Khrushchev has run, this speech ranks as unquestionably the most daring. For there were those in the audience who never had it so good as in the bad old days; who were directly connected with the worst crimes attacked in Khrushchev's indictment; who must have realized that a showdown was inevitable with this bumptious creature. Such were Molotov, Malenkov, Kaganovich, and Voroshilov. All of them were caught in the line of fire at one point or another. Voroshilov was scornfully informed that he might now want to correct some of the military myths about Stalin, myths which he had helped create. Molotov and Kaganovich had been linked by name to one of Stalin's most brutal orders, dictating a speed-up in the trials and executions during the 1936–37 purge. Malenkov's link, through the Kremlin secretariat, to Stalin's bloodiest plans was also alluded to. These revelations brought simmering quarrels into the open. This attack upon them must have solidified the intentions of Khrushchev's enemies to liquidate him.

And the effects of Khrushchev's speech, when it leaked to the outside world provided fuel for anyone hoping to undermine Nikita S. Khrushchev. Communist prestige took a terrible jolt; defections from the Party outside Russia became severe. Old members and fellow travelers who had sympathized with Stalin through the decades, those who had even managed to stomach the temporary partnership with Hitler, found themselves without an illusion to stand on. Anti-Communists were jubilant, seeing in Khrushchev's admissions an acknowledgment of their own exposures. But in terms of his relationship to the Party inside Russia, Khrushchev evidently figured the risk was worth while. Events seem to have proved him right.

One of Khrushchev's most ambitious experiments in personal salesmanship, possibly designed to shore up shaken Communist prestige, followed close upon the Twentieth Congress. This was the famous tour of "B. and K." to England in the spring of 1956. Malenkov was pulled from obscurity and sent ahead on a trial run. His trip was a huge success. Britons liked the little fellow and gave him a warm welcome. Malenkov kissed babies and mingled freely with the people. Americans tingled with alarm, fearful that the British had lost their ancient antipathy to dictatorship and would give Bulganin and Khrushchev an enthusiastic reception.

"Don't you worry," David Niven told his friend Hearst. "They know Malenkov is only an extra. When the real wheels get there the reception will be entirely different. Fly over and see."

Hearst and Conniff were posted in the cleared lobby of Claridge's when B. and K. first stalked into that most fashionable of hotels on April 18, 1956. The only other person in the lobby, aside from Scotland Yard and MVD security agents and members of Claridge's staff, was Merle Oberon, the stylish motion picture star, who had stopped by the office to pick up her jewels from the safe for the evening. Reginald Van Tyne, the elegant and efficient manager of Claridge's, escorted Bulganin and Khrushchev into the lift as if they were ordinary guests. They had apartments on the third floor, directly above the quarters occupied by Conniff and Hearst. Instead of staying at their own Embassy, their usual procedure, they had insisted on having a go at the most exclusive hotel in the world.

We trusted that the Russian bigwigs were suitably humble; the staff at Claridge's are expert at putting upstarts in their places. Many years before, Hearst and Conniff had taken over a Claridge's suite and reveled in its dignified luxury. Their spacious apartment seemed to stretch away into infinity, and Hearst remarked favorably on its size. An old Claridge's retainer decided to give young Mr. Hearst some sense of perspective.

"Your father," he said icily, "always took the whole floor."

A crowd of several hundred had gathered outside Claridge's before Khrushchev's arrival. They greeted the Russian leaders in frosty silence. This reception set the mood for the entire visit. The British were at all times correct and cordial, but at no point did they lose their traditional calm. Day after day, and night after night the visitors met a glacial response from the English. Little wonder that Khrushchev's temper finally ignited. At a meeting with Labor members of Parliament, he was closely questioned about the fate of several well-known union workers whose whereabouts—somewhere behind the Iron Curtain—were unknown. George Brown, a respected old-line Socialist, led the interrogation. Khrushchev finally blew his top. He roundly denounced the gathering and stalked off into the night, leaving behind him an antagonistic group and unfavorable headlines.

Bulganin and Khrushchev scheduled an appearance at an industrial fair in Birmingham, and we chartered a plane to follow them. A luncheon had been prepared in their honor. To reach the dining room, the team had to walk down the aisle of the exhibit hall. Workmen, exhibitors, and spectators lined both sides. It looked at least a quarter-mile long, and to the visitors it must have seemed much longer. As they padded down the corridor, they ran a gauntlet of utter, complete silence. No applause. No cheers. The wall of reserve would have wilted the stoutest heart. Khrushchev couldn't take it. When he was called upon to speak after lunch, he lashed out with threats, prating of the atomic weapons at Russia's disposal. His hosts were appalled. It was decidedly a bad show. Damned bad show.

The social highlight of the London visit was a reception given by the Russian Ambassador at Claridge's. It was a mess. The ballroom overflowed with the invited, plus assorted gate-crashers, and the guests of honor had to take refuge in a small anteroom. Charlie Chaplin was among the guests, and the two visiting Russians conducted him into the side room with them. Apart from several security guards, the only other persons present were Mrs. Chaplin, Oleg Troyanovsky, the Russian interpreter—and Conniff. He had sneaked into the inner sanctum alongside B. and K. and no one questioned his right to be there. The Russian MVD agents thought he was an operative from Scotland Yard, while the latter made the same mistake in reverse.

Conniff was thus in a position to chronicle for posterity the words of the Mutual Admiration Society formed by Bulganin and Khrushchev and the millionaire comedian.

"Your noble words will live in history," said Chaplin to the smiling Communist boss.

"You are a genius," Khrushchev replied. "They repudiate you, but we recognize you."

"Your words here have been inspiring," said Chaplin again. "We have been thrilled by your speeches."

"We still have to do a lot to break through," said Khrushchev, as interpreted by Troyanovsky. "You have been a big help. We love your pictures even though they repudiate you."

Chaplin seemed a bit flustered by the high praise of the Russian leader. He had already introduced his wife outside, but now repeated the ritual. The former Oona O'Neill was much less extravagant than her husband.

"I am very happy to meet you," she said simply.

"If they will only listen to your words, everything will be well," Chaplin said. "They have been an inspiration to us all."

Bulganin's contribution to the repartee was an occasional affirmative shake of the head. Finally a security officer asked Conniff to identify himself.

"Why, I'm a newspaper reporter," said Conniff. "Just trying to pick up a story."

He was asked to leave. The incident caused a bit of a flap in London. It was considered very sticky when a reporter could break Scoltand Yard's famed security so easily. The newspapers ran stories about it; questions were asked in Parliament. Max Aitken, son of Lord Beaverbrook and publisher of the *London Evening Standard,* had said only a few days previously that such a violation of Scotland Yard security could never occur, and he was properly aghast.

Somehow or other, the team limped to the end of its British trip and were, in fact, extricated from a public-relations fiasco through another security lapse on the part of their hosts. A former Royal Navy frogman named Lionel Crabb had descended alongside the Russian ships, possibly for purposes of espionage or sabotage. The frogman's motive was never made clear, partly because the man himself disappeared. The resultant furor took the heat off Bulganin and Khrushchev. They beat a hasty retreat to Russia, and that summer recovered their aplomb at seaside *dachas* near Sochi in the Crimea.

They had need of a good pelt of tan as well as a thick skin to fend off the troubles that were to confront the Bulganin-Khrushchev government in the autumn of 1956.

The explosions in Poland and Hungary, coming ten months after the anti-Stalin speech, brightly spotlighted the dangers to the Red empire of Khrushchev's more lenient policies. But when the Hungarian revolt burst upon the Communist world, Khrushchev reacted with Stalinist savagery. He defied world opinion by ordering Russian tanks to suppress the revolution, and by liquidating or driving into exile the Hungarian rebels.

Again Khrushchev gambled and won; the West fulminated against the outrage, the United Nations passed a belated resolution, but the brave talk of "rollbacks" and of "massive retaliation" proved to be no more than that. Moreover, Khrushchev showed that he could differentiate between "revolutions" by taking a soft approach to the Polish uprising. Wladyslaw Gomulka was, after all, a lifelong Communist and an essentially dependable one. Time could be expected to draw Gomulka's Poland closer to Moscow. Khrushchev therefore consented to the removal of Marshal Konstantin Rokossovsky as Polish Minister of Defense, and the granting of concessions to the Roman Catholic Church. Poland's geographic position renders the country an unhappy prisoner of the Communist net and gives it important strategic meaning in the defense of Soviet Russia. Khrushchev showed a cynical virtuosity in his differing attitudes toward the Hungarian and the Polish revolts. He even admitted later that "some of the comrades" opposed the use of force to quell the Hungarian disturbance. Khrushchev elected to run the risk, and it must be grudgingly conceded that he carried it off.

Some of the heat was taken off the crisis in Hungary when the Russians were able to capitalize on dissension among the Western allies over the Suez crisis. A statement was whipped off under Bulganin's name calling attention to Russia's nuclear

potential and its ability to bomb England itself, if necessary. Although, in actuality, it was the refusal of the United States support which forced the withdrawal of the British and French
from Suez, the Russians scored a propaganda victory with their
bluster, especially in the Middle East. When Considine and Conniff visited Cairo in 1958, they found many Moslems still cher-
ishing the belief that the Russian manifesto had scared off the
imperialists.

The early months of 1957, coming on top of the previous
year's excitement, were devoid of such fireworks on the international scene. There was plenty of heat inside the Kremlin,
however, as the party members struggled over the complex problem of economic reorganization. In addition, everyone in the
hierarchy was aware that before the year was out, Russia was to
attain prestige never before dreamed of. The jockeying for position must have reached feverish proportions. The first successful
Sputnik was almost ready, with Sputnik II scheduled to soar
from its launching pad shortly after. Party leaders knew that
whoever was in charge at this time would reap enormous lever-
age in power. It is possible this spurred the "anti-party group"
—to use Khrushchev's own designation of the Molotov-Malen-
kov-Kaganovich-Shepilov dissidents—to bring on a showdown.
When Bulganin and Khrushchev opened the summer season by
departing for Finland on another personal-appearance tour, the
Old Guard saw their opportunity.

The climax of the drama that began with Stalin's death now
approached. The men around him had been waiting for this moment. Molotov, cool and inscrutable, whose memory could en-
compass the whole revolution, who was the first editor of *Pravda*
in 1917, whose name has appeared on party resolutions ever
since, who was himself Premier from 1931 to 1941 until Stalin
took over the title, and high up in party councils ever since—
Molotov was ready. Malenkov, the mysterious *eminence gris* of

the Kremlin in Stalin purge years, who vaulted into the top spot when the old man died and was then unceremoniously ousted from power, who has since smoldered in the exile to which Khrushchev consigned him—Malenkov was ready. Kaganovich, the tough, tired old man who discovered Khrushchev in the Ukraine, who first saw in the ruthless, untidy upstart the elements of Communist greatness, brought him to Moscow and Stalin's attention, who sat by and nodded approval as the stripling proved his savagery—Kaganovich was ready. Shepilov, poor, bumbling Dmitri Shepilov, who bumbled his great chance to make career-capital of the Russian breakthrough in the Middle East—Shepilov was as ready as he would ever be. These were the principals in the plot to lead their leader to the slaughter.

The intended victim was not prepared for the sacrifice.

The conspirators had simply underestimated the ingenuity of their adversary. Molotov, was, as Lenin had called him, "a file clerk"—the best in the Soviet Union, granted, but still a file clerk. With no power base of its own, neither the Party, nor the Army, nor the secret police, the Molotov group was foredoomed to failure when it tried to shelve Nikita Khrushchev. And in any event, it was the tough party secretary who pulled the rule book on the file clerks and consummated their destruction.

As in all such moments of decision within Communist aristocracy, details are vague. The result alone is known. But here is the best accepted version of how Khrushchev prevailed over his enemies at the plenary session of the Communist Party's Central Committee, June 22 to 29, 1957.

Khrushchev was tricked into a Presidium meeting on June 17, ostensibly called for the members to go over their speeches for the 250th Leningrad anniversary celebrations coming up on June 23. When Khrushchev arrived at the meeting, only seven of the eleven members of the Presidium were present.

Maxim Saburov was in Prague at an economic conference; Suslov was unaccounted for and somewhere out of Moscow, Anastas Mikoyan was away, and Kirichenko was keeping a speaking date at a Ukrainian Party meeting in Kiev. That left Voroshilov, Khrushchev, Bulganin, Kaganovich, Malenkov, Molotov, and Pervukhin present for the meeting.

At that time, Khrushchev probably didn't have a majority in the Presidium on a showdown vote anyway, but with this grouping, his only safe votes would be his own, Bulganin's, and Voroshilov's, leaving him on the wrong way of a three-to-four vote.

When the meeting opened the Leningrad speeches were never mentioned. Instead, Khrushchev's leadership was put on the griddle. The opposition had his removal all planned and a slate of candidates ready to take over. Shepilov was supposed to replace Khrushchev, and things were so arranged that Khrushchev would be dropped out of the Presidium, but probably retained as a Central Committee member, for a while at any rate.

After Stalin's death, the Presidium members had set up a sort of mutual protective society within the Presidium. Each man agreed to go along with the majority vote. That way they planned to split the power between themselves, and not be forced to take issues before the larger and less trustworthy Central Committee.

When the vote was taken, Malenkov, Molotov, Pervukhin, and Kaganovich were the obvious winners; Bulganin and Voroshilov decided to stick with the majority. The final vote was six to one, with Khrushchev the only voter for Khrushchev.

It was here that Khrushchev pulled out the rule book. In the past, the Central Committee always routinely approved whatever decisions were made by the Presidium, although technically the Committee could vote independently. Khrushchev demanded the exercise of this formality. He refused to acknowledge the vote of the Presidium alone, and said that since he had been originally elected by the Committee, only the Committee could vote him out.

The file clerks sat there, mouths agape.

Khrushchev then opened a Russian filibuster and sent out word for help. While he talked on and on, carrying the meeting through the night, his army of supporters within the party organization rallied. By next morning they were able to present a petition to the Presidium demanding a special session of the Central Committee. By June 18, Mikoyan was back in Moscow. Marshal Zhukov, who had the tremendous power of the army behind him, had also arrived.

By the Central Committee meeting on June 22, Khrushchev had the votes for the majority he had lacked in the Presidium. There was considerable debate on points of party policy and ideology, but it was obvious Khrushchev had the Party behind him. The debate virtually ended when Zhukov announced that the Army was sticking with Khrushchev as the elected party authority, and would not stand for any defiance of party rule.

A vote was taken and the file clerks, not Khrushchev, were thrown out.

The plenary session of the Central Committee unanimously (with Molotov abstaining) voted to expel Georgi Malenkov, Vyacheslav Molotov, and Lazar Kaganovich as members of the Presidium, and Dmitri Shepilov as an alternate to the Presidium, on grounds they were members of an anti-party faction. It was charged that they had attempted to "change the party policy and return to that incorrect method of leadership condemned by the 20th Party Congress." Maxim Saburov was also thrown out of the Presidium and Mikhail Pervukhin was demoted to the position of an alternate (nonvoting) member because they had shown a wavering and ineffectual stand against the anti-party leaders. It was not announced at the time, but Nikolai Bulganin was also given a severe reprimand for voting against Khrushchev. He pledged to reform and was kept on—for a while.

Molotov was made ambassador to Outer Mongolia. Malenkov is a director of an electrical plant in Siberia. Kaganovich is an executive in a cement factory in the Urals. Shepilov is "teaching" somewhere near Moscow. Saburov is a deputy in the U.S.S.R.'s foreign aid program at a low executive level.

The paths of Communist glory lead many places. For two men to a massive mausoleum in Red Square. For hundreds of others, a cellar in Lubyanka prison and a bullet in the neck. For others, exile and oblivion.

An old man was standing in a corridor of the Supreme Soviet, scarcely noticed by the other delegates hustling past into the Moscow dusk. He was tired and stooped and his black overcoat looked shabby. He was adjusting his fur-fringed hat when the Russian-speaking American reporter Serge Fliegers approached him. What did he think of the party leader's speech?

The rheumy eyes focused on the newspaperman. The voice was cracked and faraway. "Comrade Khrushchev gave a good description of how things stand."

The reporter pressed him. What particular points in the party leader's speech were outstanding?

The old man peered at the reporter. Why couldn't they let him depart for his factory in peace? "Comrade Khrushchev touched on all the points that were essential," he said. "You must excuse me." There was tired finality in his voice. "Just say that Comrade Khrushchev's speech was very good. Now I must go."

The old man shuffled into the night. His protégé was a big man now. Lazar Kaganovich pulled the overcoat tight around him. Things could be worse. He was at least alive.

At the time of the party shake-up, Western speculation about its meaning ran high. For many Americans it was a pleasant surprise. Some were simply gladdened at the periodic sight of the Russian political machine erupting into sudden and violent action against its own leading members. To them, it indicated that the Russian government could not last, since internal power struggles like this would surely one day rupture the party framework. Others were not so optimistic about the prospects of the Party devouring itself. But they took heart from the fact that Zhukov was a friend of Ike's from the war, and that he knew Americans and got along with them. Many hoped for an easing in East-West relations.

Several observers believed that Zhukov and the army now held the balance of political power. They felt Khrushchev owed Zhukov too much, and someday would have to make good on his debt. Zhukov might even try to usurp Khrushchev's place.

In fact, the illusion has persisted in the West that the Red Army would some day gain the whip hand, especially after Stalin's death. The notion seems to have infected certain elements of the Red Army itself, who thought the end of the Stalin era presaged a whole new structure of power within the Soviet Union. They reckoned without the indefatigable and perspicacious Khrushchev, an even more ruthless party leader in his manner than Stalin.

Following the dramatic climax of Khrushchev's victory over the Molotov faction, the downgrading of Marshal Zhukov was only a mean and shabby aftermath. By the curious logic of Communist dynamics, Zhukov sealed his own doom when he assumed his pivotal role in the party crisis. By saving Khrushchev's neck, he extended his own for the ax. Since Khrushchev could not repay him, he betrayed him.

Khrushchev was too skilled to move in immediately on Zhukov, who appears to have been genuinely popular with the army's rank and file. A bit of tunneling was indicated. His chief henchman, Mikoyan, started by tapping his fellow Armenian, Marshal Bagramian, for a little intrigue against Zhukov within the Red

Army's upper crust. Strangely enough, this did not prove a difficult task. Zhukov was a proud, touchy individual, whose arrogance had rubbed more than one high officer in a raw place.

Furthermore, as in every human endeavor, enmities, jealousies, and clashing ambitions festered within the Red Army leadership, frictions which Bagramian craftily cultivated. The conspiracy proceeded smoothly through the summer, and the victim seems not to have suspected.

An opportunity for action presented itself in early October. Sputnik I whirled into space to dazzle the world and send a glow of pride through every Russian. And at this propitious moment when the attention of the world was diverted, Zhukov, a first-class strategist, committed a basic tactical error: he moved away from his base, and allowed his lines of communication to clog up behind him.

One can almost savor the relish with which the Khrushchev technicians heard the announcement that Marshal Zhukov was off on a fortnight's tour to Yugoslavia and Albania. Behind his back they prepared to take charge in the Ministry of Defense.

Zhukov finally tumbled when his old pal and confidant, Marshal Rokossovsky, was summarily ordered to assume command in the Caucasus. This was a major transfer, one that ordinarily called for the concurrence of the Minister of Defense. But he hadn't been consulted.

Zhukov had the wind up, but primitive Albania had barely heard of newfangled gadgets like the telephone. The outflanked general finally got a signal through demanding that a TU-104A jet be dispatched forthwith to fetch him home. Back from Moscow came the melancholy answer: Sorry, Marshal, bad weather up here. Big jet planes can't get through.

By the time Zhukov's plane, a simple old Illyushin-14, touched down at Vnukovo Airport early in the evening of October 25, a white-faced junior aide was the sole representative of his vast department to greet him. Zhukov's hours were numbered, but he rushed to the Kremlin. There the party elders awaited their victim. Zhukov fought hard, but Premier Bulganin, whose own position was shaky, reportedly ended the discussion by moving that the case be referred to the Central Committee. "Besides," he said to the chagrined Zhukov, "we're due at the Iranian Embassy for a reception. Mustn't be late, you know."

The same army apparatus which Zhukov had placed at the disposal of Khrushchev in June was thrown into gear to consummate his doom. Red Army planes again flew the Central Committee in for a showdown. And the army's elaborate signal system, a key device in controlling the country, was utterly beyond the Marshal's reach. Zhukov couldn't even make a telephone call out of Moscow.

There were no repercussions. The Red Army brass who might have been expected to support their stricken leader were too busy writing the denunciatory speeches they would deliver against him in the Central Committee.

The chorus of abuse was led by his friend Marshal Rokossovsky, and by Marshal Ivan Konev, whose jealousy of the better-known commander was hardly a secret. Konev had commanded the army group which enveloped Berlin from the rear, and was known to believe that Zhukov had received inordinate credit for the city's capture because he bossed the army group which assaulted Berlin frontally.

It was assumed that Konev, fanatical party man and one of vigorous military views, would be named to succeed Zhukov. There was some surprise when the choice fell on Marshal Rodion Malinovsky, a competent professional but a man used to taking orders and abuse from his party superiors. For instance, Marshal Tito, visiting the Kremlin during the war, once overheard Stalin berating the hapless general over the telephone:

"Malinovsky," Stalin roared, "an old woman could operate tanks better than you."

Konev is still important in Moscow as head of the Warsaw

Pact armed forces, but the docile, phlegmatic Rodion Malinovsky more neatly fits the blueprint for a Red Army chief. He
recognizes the preeminence of the Party over the armed forces
and that is exactly what Khrushchev demands.

Zhukov's relief as Minister of Defense was announced by
Pravda on October 26 in a twenty-four-word announcement.
Apparently this sparse bulletin was to test party and public reaction. When everyone proved more interested in ascending
rockets than in descending marshals, the party chiefs felt free
to make public the deliberations of the Presidium and denunciations of his fellow officers.

One other little-noticed gambit was undertaken at the same
time. General Kiril Moskalenko, commander of the Moscow
garrison, was suddenly promoted to Army Marshal. If the army
high command had tried to seize supreme power, the most ad-
vantageous moment would probably have been November 7,
1957, the fortieth anniversary of the October revolution. A Defense Minister aiming at a *coup d'état,* by carefully selecting the
troops and commanders in the Moscow area, and confident of
their utter loyalty, might move these units into position under
cover of their appearance in the Anniversary Day parade and
celebration. Harrison Salisbury, in his book, *An American Reporter in Russia,* narrates how Beria moved MVD units into
complete control of Moscow in the hours immediately following
the death of Stalin. For one day (but for one day only) he was
master of the city.

The lesson of the Beria coup must have impressed Khrushchev with the approach of Anniversary Day, and may have
had much to do with the timing of Zhukov's downfall, less than
a fortnight before the celebration. For his reward, Moskalenko
was allowed to stand with the party leaders reviewing the parade, the height of Communist glory.

The celebration of the fortieth anniversary of the October

revolution in November, 1957, serves as a fitting terminal point for this whole flamboyant period. And as First Secretary Khrushchev beamed on Communist princelings assembled from near and far, he had good cause for self-congratulation. The Stalin myth lay in ashes, the "anti-party" group had been sent into the wilderness, the Sputniks danced in the heavens, and Marshal Zhukov, like other good old soldiers before him, was fading away.

It was at this time that the Hearst team once more penetrated the Iron Curtain, and once more secured a revealing interview with this man of destiny.

CHAPTER 4

They also serve

It was early evening of November 7, 1957, fortieth anniversary of "The Great October," when the Hearst team reached our now-familiar quarters at the National Hotel. The air was cool, crisp, and clear. The great parade, complete with a token display of missile strength, was over and darkness had fallen, but the crowds were reluctant to leave the complex of squares and cleared places in the Kremlin area.

Overhead, brilliantly etched against the black dome of night, swayed a huge painting of Lenin, suspended from an almost invisible anchored balloon and cleverly spotlighted from the ground.

Pravda said next day that a million Muscovites and visitors had remained in the area after the parade, and for once *Pravda* didn't appear to overestimate. The great Manezhnaya Square, which our balcony faced, was clear of automobile traffic, which was just as well, for there would have been no room for cars. Beyond, Red Square was even more jammed. Loud-speakers on towering streetlights blared emphatic martial music. Groups of four, six, sometimes as many as a dozen persons marched through the squares, singing, laughing, and generally making the noise that accompanies a good time anywhere.

The carnival air had pervaded the somewhat stately old National, relic of the czarist past. The chambermaids on our floor let out yips of joy at the sight of Hearst (who had sent them Christmas cards and other little gifts in the past). *"Gospodin Gearst!"* a mammoth, jolly maid shouted, and enveloped him in a prodigious bear hug. *Gospodin* means "citizen," or "comrade," and the English letter *H* becomes *G* in Russian, as in "Gerbert Goover."

The carnival air infected the visitors, too. The phone in the ornate living room was ringing urgently as we lumbered in. Hearst picked it up, and we could hear a great cackle of Russian out of the receiver. He listened for a time, then snapped, "Speak American. We've taken over!" and hung up on what must have been a very startled Russian.

Somebody opened the big window-doors which led to the broad balcony jutting out perhaps fifty feet over the crowded pavement, the famous balcony from which the immortal Lenin had spoken. The sound of celebration swept over us like the crescendo of a strange symphony. In the distance we could see an edge of the mausoleum of Lenin and Stalin.

"These don't look like slave people," a puzzled Considine said to Serge Fliegers. "I didn't expect them to look . . . happy."

"They *are* happy," Fliegers explained. "They've never been happier in their lives."

"Because it's the fortieth anniversary of the revolution?"

Fliegers looked at him patiently. "Of course not," he said. "They're happy because this is the first time in their lives that they've ever been permitted to walk *across* Red Square."

The mood was in stark contrast to that of Prague, which we

had left earlier that day. Prague was the distressed and nervous servant; Moscow the fat, jolly, celebrating master.

We had been the reluctant guests of the People's Democracy of Czechoslovakia for three restless days, during which time we were ostentatiously followed by two inept members of the secret police—clichés right down to their greasy raincoats and slouch hats.

About the only department of Prague's Alcron Hotel the Communists had not been able to terrorize was the kitchen. The food was magnificent, a reminder of the standard of living which democracy—dead in Czechoslovakia for a decade—had nurtured in this land. The rest of the hotel had taken on the bleak, gray chill that is found principally in prisons and the office buildings of minor Communist officials. The rooms were garish cells, and the offerings at the newsstand were shrill with self-glorification and abuse of the West.

It was Considine's birthday, and we spent part of it at the Alcron bar, where a Czech in a white coat presided over his slim supplies and did what he could to sustain the pretense that all was well in this land of plenty. George was his name. He spoke with pride of his bar and of his travels. Once he had been as far off as Paris. How were things there now? Well, that was nice, but things were fine in Prague, too.

As the night wore on, there were no more Czechs at the bar, and the tense little lounge emptied, too. George poured himself a drink, carefully put it on our check, and then relaxed.

"Myself, I am a Catholic," he confided in the low voice he might have used to confess he was a spy.

Next morning Katherine Clark of INS and her husband took us to the airport. We started early enough to see some of the smoky city, including three impressive radio towers rising from Petrin Hill, overlooking Prague.

"The one on the left is for the Czechs," Katherine said. "The other two are for jamming the Voice of America and the BBC."

We pulled into the airport, followed by the two elaborately
indifferent men in their greasy raincoats and slouch hats. The
TU-104 was waiting.

This mainstay of the Soviet Airlines is a handsome, rakish,
swept-wing jet which much more closely resembled its parent,
the Red Air Force's medium range bomber, Bison, than our
Boeing 707 resembles its forebear the B-47. The Russian aeronautical engineers have not even bothered to redesign the cockpit and crew section, except perhaps to replace with navigation
equipment the bombsight which was once in the plexiglass nose.

Seventy passengers, most of us Moscow-bound, assembled
and waited. The hour of departure came and passed. There was
no public announcement nor, for that matter, a public address
system. The Czechs behind the counter could offer no information. Hearst found a Scandinavian Airways man who surmised
that either the weather might be bad in Moscow—and the Russians didn't want to admit it—or that the plane was being held
for the arrival of a big wheel en route to the festivities. (As it
turned out, it was a combination of both. The weather was foul,
and France's Duclos and Italy's Togliatti were both being
awaited.)

The passengers were kept at the airport all day and not dismissed until late afternoon.

"Tomorrow," a helpless Czech said.

The morning of the sixth of November was foul and smoggy.
Before leaving the hotel, Katherine Clark went to the travel desk
at the Alcron.

"Certainly the plane is going this morning," the man said in
answer to her query. "It is scheduled to go, it will go." If his
booth was "bugged" he could at least prove to the authorities
that he was a man of unlimited faith in Soviet aviation.

We spent the entire day at the airport. The monotony was

broken, to a degree, by several tests of the plane's two jet engines. The crew revved the turbines up to what must have been
full throttle. The Russians are not concerned with the costly
niceties of the Jet Age: the engines were not equipped with
noise-suppressing ducts. They just bellowed for all they were
worth, and there is reason to believe that they are worth, individually, 20,000 pounds of thrust. We who ventured out on
the foggy ramp to watch fled for the protection of a stone wall
and crouched behind it, hands clapped to our battered ears.

When, late in the day, the lot of us were again dismissed for
the night, we went back to the counter.

Hearst asked the distressed looking Czech, "Why didn't you
tell us this hours ago?"

The man looked around uneasily, and said with inexpressible
resignation, "The Russians won't tell us anything."

We came to know George at the Alcron even better that night.
The next morning, the seventh, produced a deluge. Surely, no
plane could take off in a downpour like this. We would be stuck
another day in this newsless realm, while the Russians flexed
their muscles in the parade past the mausoleum, while Laika
orbited the earth issuing bulletins on how she felt. It was most
discouraging.

But at the airport, where we had been duly followed by our
faithful shadows, there was the kind of bustle that needed no
interpretation. The TU-104 was definitely going to Moscow.
Apparently it had been waiting for nothing except the driving
rain which now pounded over its streamlined skin.

"You will be required to pay for an exit permit," someone
announced.

We queued into a grubby little office, where a shabby official
filled out the forms with a leaky pen, adding to the amassed
paper work of Europe (which, if piled, would dwarf the Alps).
He looked up at us and said something in Czech. A tired-looking

assistant acting as interpreter announced, "That will be ten dollars."

We counted our Czech money; it came to a little over the equivalent of ten dollars. The man in charge shook his head and again spoke. His assistant sighed and interpreted. "We are not permitted to accept Czechoslovakian money from persons leaving Czechoslovakia," he said. "It must be in dollars."

Hearst made some reflection on the lack of confidence the puppet government had in its currency.

"That is our law," spoke up the man in charge, in perfect English. We paid in dollars and hurried to the barren departure room. The names of passengers entitled to board the waiting TU-104 were being read out by a uniformed Czech girl—but not as individuals. This was plainly a VIP flight we had stumbled upon, with a passenger list made up of delegations to the ceremonies already under way.

"Deligazie Sudanese!" the girl shouted. Seven or eight towering Negro Communists from the Sudan marched through the rest of us and out into the cold, drenching rain. Most of them had wrapped coarse khaki woolen scarfs around their heads from chin to scalp for warmth. On top they had placed cheap fedora hats which looked ludicrously small perched on top of their wrapped heads.

In time, *"Deligazie* Hearst" was called, and we walked out through the rain to the steps that led into the rear of the TU-104. The line was long.

"Come this way." It was the SAS man.

He led us up to empty steps leading into the forward section of the jet. We ran along partly under the plane to stay out of the rain and for the first time noticed the almost incredible size of the nacelles which enclose the engines.

We took off our wet coats and settled down into a luxurious compartment of wide, roomy, and downy seats. This was living

—at least for five minutes. Then, along came a pleasant-looking but muscular stewardess and examined our tickets. She made a "Get up" gesture and led us back to the crowded "two and three" seats in the rear of the cabin. The airline of the classless society had evidently discovered tourist class.

The TU-104 takes an uncomfortably long run on the ground —usually around fifty-five seconds—before it gets up enough speed to take off. The plane was now further handicapped by puddles, if not quagmires, on the strip. After thirty seconds of run at full power, Hearst started making the little gesture that all pilots flying as passengers do: he touched fingers and made persuasive little movements back toward his belly as if handling the stick of a small plane. But this was a very big plane, and obviously it was rushing us all to our finish.

As it turned out, we had just enough runway. The big jet hammered up through the rain and mist, yawing like a fighter. In time it broke through the overcast into the world of blue sky and golden sunshine which lay above Prague.

On high, at what the stewardess described as "nearly 600 miles an hour and more than 30,000 feet" luncheon was served. It was pretty tired: a few slivers of veal, sodden vegetables, and a little glass of red wine.

The passengers were not displeased with the fare in any way. They were plainly excited about the prospect of joining their ideological superiors in Moscow. One jumped up in the middle of the aisle in our compartment, picked up his little glass of wine from his tray, and above the roar of the not-very-well-insulated 40,000 horsepower shouted a toast to the Soviet Union and Nikita Khrushchev.

That seemed fair enough. When the comrades had toasted, Considine proposed one to the President of the United States. The three Americans alone clicked glasses. Then Conniff, in a louder voice, proposed another toast: "To the president of the

National Association of Manufacturers!" There were puzzled faces. Several delegates, apparently fearful of offending, joined in the toast.

The TU-104 flew beautifully to Moscow. As it came in on its long approach we saw, on the port side, amid scorched birches and pines, the burned remnants of a smaller, propeller-driven plane, plainly the aircraft of the Rumanian Communist leader we heard had crashed on the way to the party.

Our landing was expertly executed. We didn't know it at the time, and were not to find out about it until we accompanied Vice-President Richard M. Nixon to the U.S.S.R. in 1959, but the TU-104 needs the aid of one or more parachutes in order to come to a proper stop after putting down. The chute or chutes serve as supplementary brakes. The Russians have not as yet discovered "spoiler" flaps or "clamshell" reverse blocks on their engines.

Anyway, we did stop, taxied back to the terminal—which is a kind of small-time LaGuardia with the Cyrillic lettering of M O C B A across its proscenium—and up nudged the first self-propelled airliner steps we had ever seen. More importantly, once we got to the terminal, there was Fliegers.

Serge Fliegers is an unusual young man. He was born too late to have been the model of Van Gogh's "Young Man in a Pork Pie" and too soon to have been a beatnik. He became one of the most gifted and sophisticated journalists of our time, fluent in four or five languages, and with a good reporter's infinite curiosity.

He got us through customs in perhaps an hour less time than it would have taken us on our own, thanks to his complete command of the language and knowledge of the harrowing paper work.

While we waited, two strapping young men in civilian clothes approached us and rather guardedly confided that they were U.S.

Air Force attachés from the American Embassy. They had come out to the airport, not to welcome us, but on a tip that the TU-114, Tupolev's gigantic four-engined turbo-prop, might be there. It wasn't, but flew in later to become one of the top exhibits the Russians showed their cousins from the Communist hinterlands.

The Air Force men, one of whom was later declared *persona non grata* and made to leave the Soviet Union, did have another look at the TU-104. It wasn't difficult. There were eight of the new planes on the ground—nearly a year before the first Boeing 707 was delivered to a United States airline.

"At least 20,000 pounds thrust, I'd say," one of the airmen in mufti said of the engines.

"I'd make it closer to 30,000," the other said.

Plainly, the Russians were not sharing such information with our side.

We drove into the city along a broad highway through a preserve of deep, green pine and frosty, white-trunked birch, and the University of Moscow soon loomed ahead. Its 700-odd foot tower makes it the highest building in Europe. The great red star above the tower looks down on enormous additional structures, mainly schools of science, and on a campus that the Russians say covers fourteen times as much ground as Columbia University in New York.

For Hearst and Conniff, the grandiose scale of the university was old stuff, but not the apartment housing development going up nearby. There were not simply blocks of these apartment houses; there were literally miles, stretching not only along the main road into the city, but also for several parallel streets on either side. All were eight stories tall, made generally of carrot-colored brick and, we were told, would in time house 2,000,000 Muscovites.

As our car swung away from the University into Lenin Hills, there was another surprise. Below us, across a tributary of the

Moscow River, glistened a magnificent assembly of sports arenas, dominated by Lenin Stadium, a perfectly proportioned bowl seating 100,000.

"Two years ago that whole place was a dump," Hearst recalled.

We reached the festive city as early darkness fell. Once settled, we went down into the crowded square. Moscow was jumping. Lenin's countenance was George Orwell's Big Brother come true. His face was everywhere, suspended from the fronts of buildings and garishly lighted. On our previous trip, the face of Stalin was the face on the land.

There were other faces displayed on building fronts as well. One, near the hotel, featured huge lithographed portraits of the members of the Presidium, beginning with the figurehead, Bulganin. That Khrushchev was next in line was not as impressive as the fact that Marshal Zhukov was pointedly not there at all.

Hearst and Conniff went off to the Kremlin, invited to the reception in honor of the visiting Communist leaders. Considine, whose invitation had not come through, remained with Fliegers at the hotel, getting background on the parade, the types of missiles displayed, the reception given Marshal Malinovsky at his first appearance since replacing Zhukov.

Hearst and Conniff finally returned from the Kremlin. It had been a splendid affair in a splendid setting, enlivened principally by the informal conduct of Khrushchev. The party boss had dominated the toasting in the roped-off and well-guarded section of the great George Hall reserved for Presidium members, other ranking members of the Soviet hierarchy, and such luminaries as China's Mao Tse-tung and Poland's Wladyslaw Gomulka.

Khrushchev had brushed Premier Bulganin and the rest aside as he led the guests of honor out of the enclosure and through the crowded hall, en route to rooms where there would be dancing and a concert by the Red Army chorus.

"He shook hands here and there like a Tammany politician," Conniff reported.

"I got Bulganin's eye and he remembered me," Hearst recounted. "When I said something to him he held up his hand a moment, then called an interpreter to his side. We chatted through the interpreter for a bit and then I said, 'We want to see you. We want an interview with you.' He smiled cordially enough, shook his head and said, 'You should see Khrushchev, not me.' He sounded a little defeated. I told him we were eager to see him, Bulganin. But he shook his head again, as if such an interview would be a waste of his time and ours, and repeated, 'No, it is Khrushchev you should see.' "

During this exchange, Khrushchev was displaying more than usual confidence and ebullience. He "broke" a couple in the midst of a dance, bussed the lady on the cheek and whirled her around the floor at a lively clip. A bit later, he strode into the midst of the Red Army chorus, and took over the direction of a number—joining in with the singers as he did so.

We were soon ready to file our first story to the West. Flieger's Russian negotiated the language barriers at the telephone company and he got through to INS London. The connection was fine. Considine took the phone and started dictating the story. Halfway down the first typewritten page there was the sound of clicking on the wire, and London was gone. The voice on the wire was now speaking Russian, and rather sharply.

Fliegers took the phone, and there followed a brisk exchange in Russian. Serge hung up the phone with a clatter. "We're not permitted to file out of here by phone," he said. "Everything has to go through the censor's office at the Telegraph Building."

There was now silence and emptiness in the streets below. The loud-speakers had been turned off for the night, and only the spookily suspended image of Lenin remained. The illuminated red stars atop the Kremlin gates looked suddenly ominous. We were in Khrushchev's Soviet Union.

Obtaining interviews with top Soviet officials calls for a certain amount of endurance and optimism. Our chances in this bleak November of 1957 hung by somewhat slim threads: a short talk between Fliegers and Premier Bulganin at a diplomatic reception the previous month, in which the Premier denoted that he would not be opposed to such an interview, and his brief though discouraging exchange with Hearst at the Kremlin reception. There was also circumstantial evidence. Why else would the Soviet Embassy in Washington have approved the team's visas?

On the first morning of what turned out to be a stay of nearly three weeks (involving a considerable investment, which began with a charge of $90 a day for our suite of rooms) we were in touch with Leonid Ilychev, whose enmity Hearst, Conniff, and Smith had gained on the first trip. Interviews? He repeated the word as if it smelled bad. But Premier Bulganin had said only last night . . . ? Ilychev would look into it. Write a letter.

Fliegers arranged for a Cyrillic-keyboard typewriter, and a girl from Intourist who could play it. Hearst dictated a formal request for interviews with Bulganin and Khrushchev, recalling and dwelling on the Task Force's previous cordial meeting with same.

The letter was sealed in an envelope and dropped into a mailbox on a Kremlin wall as per instructions.

It seemed so odd, so involved, so slipshod. But those were the rules of the game, and if we didn't want to play we could go home.

A hard-working, tweedy, muscular little Intourist guide, Zoya Novikovo, assigned to us during our stay, did what she could to find us entertainment while we awaited the summons to appear for interviews. It was not an unusually difficult task, for the Russians had made a carnival time of Moscow.

We saw the great Soviet puppet show, the unforgettable little one-ring circus that featured Popov, the magnificent clown, and a hippopotamus which mingled with the front-row customers. We attended *Swan Lake* at the Bolshoi the night Khrushchev had Mao Tse-tung as his guest. They sat in orchestra seats, ignoring the great state box on the mezzanine, occupied that night only by Anastas Mikoyan.

The American colony took us in, too, to lessen the tension and then the embarrassment of not receiving any answer to our requests. Irving R. Levine of the National Broadcasting Company and his delightful wife, Nancy, lived two floors above us in the National. Ambassador Llewellyn Thompson and the charming Mrs. Thompson had us for dinner at Spaso House. Another night, we were guests of the U.S. Marine Guard for the Embassy, also at Spaso House. This is an annual affair and couldn't be more heartwarming to the American visitors. The Marines of the guard contribute for a full year to a party fund to be spent on celebrating the anniversary of the founding of the Corps. They send to Denmark, France, England, and the United States for the food which graces their buffet, decorate Spaso House beautifully, and conduct a party which has more than style and tradition. It is a party that recreates, thousands of miles behind the Iron Curtain, a bit of America.

One night, by accident, we provided our own amusement. Conniff was taking a bath. Considine was hammering away at his typewriter, oblivious of the sounds of milling thousands outside and the trumpeting music of the street loud-speakers. Suddenly Hearst yelled, "Hey, we're on fire!"

He flung open the doors leading out to the balcony. The big hammer-and-sickle flag decorating the balcony had become drenched with the rain that had fallen through most of the day. One of the flags had become entangled with the neon sign which hung just below the balcony railing, spelling out *PECTOPAH,* or, "Restaurant." A short-circuit had resulted, and the flag, despite its sogginess, was smoking like fury.

It is not an especially comforting thought in Moscow to have a Soviet banner burning on the balcony. Sharp suspicions of sabotage and desecration must instinctively come to the minds of those on the street below—especially those who knew that Western imperialists resided there.

Hearst picked up a pitcher of drinking water and flung it toward the burning flag. It missed. Considine ran out on the balcony with another pitcher, heaved its contents, and most of that water missed, too. He looked down to the street below and, to his dismay, saw a lot of angry-looking Muscovites brushing water off their clothes.

Hearst was back now with a bucket of water and that, too, went partly on the flag, but mostly on the bystanders. Here was a dilemma that made the team temporarily forget the growing mortification of not having heard a word from Ilychev. Should we continue trying to put out the fire and insult the Russians, or let it burn and insult the Russians?

Smoke crept into the living room of the suite. We called for chambermaids, then the management. The flag still burned, and *PECTOPAH* occasionally gave off an electric snort and showers of sparks. Hearst and Considine thought idly of electrocution as they took aim and threw water.

Conniff arrived in the living room, towel wrapped around his middle. Hearst and Considine quickly told him what was happening.

He fanned away a bit of smoke.

"What fire?" he asked loudly. "I don't know anything about a fire. When the secret police arrive I will say the same thing."

The secret police didn't show up, but a small army of janitors, maids, and presumably electricians marched into the suite, put out the fire, and then removed all flags from our balcony. Some of them did not seem especially friendly. It is not likely that they would have believed our story even if we had been able to tell it to them.

Conniff's loud disclaimer sprang from our suspicion that our suite at the National was "bugged." Two years before, the Hearst team had caucused in the bathroom with the water running. The second wave of the Task Force took no such precautions. But there was sporadic banter about the possibility of being overheard.

"Why doesn't that s.o.b. Khrushchev give us a call?" Considine might mourn at the end of a restless day of waiting.

"Mr. Khrushchev?" Conniff would ask, speaking directly toward an ornate chandelier that extended down from the ceiling featuring a fresco of a well-padded Russian beauty being pulled along in her troika by peacocks. "Glad you mentioned Mr. Khrushchev. I'd just like to say that Mr. Khrushchev will be remembered among the greatest statesmen of our times."

And the wait went on.

Then a tantalizing nibble. "Submit questions to Mr. Khrushchev," Ilychev announced over the phone.

These we had been mulling over for some time. Hearst had contacted INS offices in London, Paris, Rome, Berlin, and Tokyo, asking bureau chiefs to forward pertinent questions. We recognized that phrasing would mean a lot. We would keep the questions general, hoping to develop specific points if and when the ice was broken at the interview itself. Hence, we discarded whatever might get Khrushchev's back up, such as, Why did you fire Marshal Zhukov? or, Will you permit East Germans to vote on whether they would prefer to live under communism or the democracy of West Germany?

Instead, the questions we submitted, in letter form and in

Russian, took the tone of, "What can be done to alleviate present tensions?" and "What are your disarmament proposals?"

Now we were in business. We had been writing warm-up pieces: Hearst's Sunday column, Considine's daily column, features about Russian Sputnik experts, and Conniff's pieces about sleeping in Lenin's old bed and his interview with the violinist David Oistrakh. But now came the first interview Andrei Gromyko had given as Foreign Minister.

He received us gravely outside his office in the towering rococo foreign ministry. Would we step inside? The four of us —including Fliegers, with his gift of tongues—started in. An aide politely but firmly blocked Serge's path.

"Not you," he said.

The doors closed on a room whose *décor* was to become familiar: a badly-lighted, boxlike chamber (it was late afternoon and already dark outside) with a thoughtful study of Lenin looking down from the wall, and a long conference table lined with chairs. Gromyko, heavier and apparently more sure of himself than he had been at the UN in New York, took his place at the end of the table and beckoned us into chairs. Young Oleg Troyanovsky, brought up in Washington and educated at Syracuse University (his father was a Soviet Ambassador to the United States), was interpreter.

Hearst brought along a little tape recorder and began to take it out of his case as the small talk plodded on.

"What's that?" Gromyko asked, a shadow of suspicion on his granite face. "A bomb?"

Hearst laughed. "If it were a bomb do you think we'd be saps enough to be in here with it?"

"Let me examine it to see if it is ticking," Gromyko said. For a moment we were not sure whether he was joking. He held the little machine cautiously to his ear, then with the trace of a smile—a hard thing for Gromyko to achieve—he said:

"Ah, it doesn't tick. It keeps saying 'bleep ... bleep ...

bleep.' " Then he laughed heartily. For this was at that time the great joke in the Soviet Union. They had satellites in orbit; ours were still falling over on their launching pads at Cape Canaveral.

"I brought it along so we could double check your answers to our questions," Hearst explained. "We wouldn't want to misquote you."

Grudgingly Gromyko consented, but it turned out to be wasted effort. The Foreign Minister, who speaks perfect English and had been chatting so easily in the first few informal exchanges, answered the first formal question in Russian. We could only conclude that Gromyko may have felt his office was "bugged." If hauled up later and asked to explain certain quotes, he might ask that his Russian answers be studied, not his answers as interpreted by Western journalists.

In the light of events that followed, it is interesting to examine some points made in the Gromyko interview.

Conniff asked him, "After American troops are completely evacuated from Japan, and tension is relaxed, is Russia prepared to return the southern Kurile Islands to Japan?"

Gromyko held a dead cigarette in his mouth as he replied, "These are two different questions. There is no reason to intermix them. Our position regarding the Kuriles is . . . a definite one. The question does not arise either separately or in connection with the withdrawal of American troops. The Kurile Islands are part of the territory of the U.S.S.R."

"Is there a U.S.S.R. solution to the Israeli-Arab friction besides selling arms to only one side?" Hearst asked.

"One point must be underlined," Gromyko asserted. "The policy of Israel is such at present that it is making its position even more difficult and complicated and dangerous. It is provocative and dangerous.

"I have in mind last year's [1956] Israeli attack on Egypt. Israel states that it wants to improve its relations with the Arab nations, but its policy leads to a further deterioration of the situation. Israel is reaping the fruits of its own policy."

At this point Hearst and Considine had a whispered conference to discuss the wording of the next question. The frown Gromyko had worn when he blazed at Israel was replaced by a knowing smile.

"Ah, an internal matter," he said waggishly. "We won't interfere."

"What is the Soviet attitude toward Western Germany as of now?"

"The Soviet Union favors good relations with Western Germany," Gromyko answered, "but the attitude of the Adenauer government is such, it in no way contributes to such relations. Western Germany is pursuing a dangerous policy. For example, the rearming program. Plans are afoot to arm Western Germany with atomic weapons. Then there is the locating of foreign atomic bombs on Western German territory. Besides, Western Germany does not notice the existence of the German Democratic Republic [East Germany]."

"Will the East Germans ever have a chance," Hearst asked, "to vote on whether they want to be part of Western Germany again?"

Gromyko shook his head. "The question of German unity should be a matter of agreement at government level between East and West Germany."

"No plebiscite?" Hearst persisted.

Gromyko ended this discussion immediately. "There can be no other way than the one which I have stated. A new approach to disarmament is demanded," the Foreign Minister went on, changing the subject. "Methods till now have failed, have yielded no positive results. The talks at London were confined to five powers, four of them NATO powers. These talks must be enlarged so that all can participate. The talks should be public and not behind closed doors and the commission should be permanent.

"The United States is too busy hunting for votes in the United Nations, instead of consultations among all nations. The pressure of the United States on all little states in the United Nations is an indisputable fact. Representatives of the small states have assured me personally that they couldn't express an opinion because of the pressure put on them by the United States. Spend only one day in the United Nations and that is enough to prove the existence of this pressure. The United States has not even tried to deny it."

Hearst spoke up. "Are you implying that the United States controls the vote of every other free country in the United Nations?"

Gromyko replied sonorously in Russian, and when the translation came through he had amended his use of the word "all" to "many."

"Why do you persist in stating that Western powers do not want disarmament?" Conniff asked him.

"There are economic and political reasons for the West's continuing the arms race," Gromyko replied. "There is a proverb. It goes 'It is difficult to hide a sin.' In certain quarters there are clearly many advantages gained by continuing the arms race. There are economic advantages and political. I refer particularly to balancing on the brink of war."

This ended our informative but rather disheartening interview with the flinty Foreign Minister. Now the road seemed clear for the tensely awaited meeting with Khrushchev. But it wasn't that easy. Either Khrushchev was too busy serving as one of the architects of a new Communist Manifesto of Solidarity which was about to be released, or Ilychev decided our probation period must continue.

Whatever the reason, we next found ourselves seated in an

office almost exactly like Gromyko's, but this time the man at the end of the conference table was the beefy former editor of *Pravda*, Yuri Zhukov, whom we had interviewed on our first visit, and who by now had risen to become Chairman of the Soviet Union's Committee on Cultural Relations with Foreign Countries.

Fliegers was permitted to sit in on the talk with Zhukov, but, for reasons which will soon be apparent, it was to be his last such appearance in behalf of the Hearst team.

The fluent English Zhukov had spoken on the previous occasion he met Hearst and Conniff now vanished. Zhukov had two interpreters in for this occasion and spoke only Russian. He called loudly for American-Soviet exchanges of students, atomic scientists, doctors, teachers, and technicians in other fields, including film-making. The exchange plan was presented in the nature of a challenge. Zhukov insinuated that he would be surprised if the United States accepted.

"Last time we were here you charged us with having an iron curtain of our own," Hearst recalled. "It had something to do with twenty-nine students, Russians, who were trying to get into our country. When we got back to Washington we talked to President Eisenhower, as we promised you we would, and the matter was attended to. So are you now prepared to do something for us in return? For example, when will Russia stop jamming radio broadcasts. Jamming has stopped everywhere else. What are you afraid of?"

Zhukov waited for a translation, tapping a finger impatiently on the green cloth top of the long conference table.

"The United States has lifted its iron curtain a little by eliminating fingerprinting," Zhukov said with a nod. "This will facilitate contacts. Your press seems calm. There have been no noticeable provocations during the negotiations. The behavior of your press is a good sign. Now, if only the Voice of America would stop poisoning the ether. It speaks of American industry and culture all the time. We would be very glad to hear it referring sometime to an American earth satellite."

Zhukov and his interpreters laughed heartily.

"Suppose the Voice of America just sent American news?" Hearst asked.

"That would be fine," Zhukov answered, "but you don't do that. You interfere with our affairs, so we defend ourselves. Let me put it this way: When a man is trying to throw a stone into your window you try to protect your window. You close your blind . . . I give you one little example: Last year when Premier Bulganin and Khrushchev visited Britain, the BBC stopped throwing stones into our windows. This lasted six months. During that time everybody was free here to listen to events in Britain as broadcast by BBC.

"But then, after certain events that took place in Hungary, the Conservative Eden thought BBC's tone should be changed."

This is the way one of Zhukov's interpreters relayed his Russian response to us. Fliegers immediately stopped him.

"Mr. Zhukov did not call Mr. Eden a 'Conservative,' " Serge said with some heat. "He called him a 'Fascist!' "

Zhukov looked somewhat bleakly at Serge and conceded in English that he had.

Zhukov snapped a command at one of the interpreters, and the man hurried off and soon returned with the text of a recent statement Khrushchev had made about jamming. Zhukov cleared his throat and read:

"In our country, people like music and you know many good singers come from Russia. Therefore, if we hear a good voice we don't jam it. We try to make it clearer on our radios and we send it through the country. But if it is not a good voice and harms our ears, we shut off the radio. If a person for some reason can't shut off his radio we are obliged to jam. If the Voice of America was really America's voice we would cease jamming. We like Americans.

"But when the Voice of America is some other voice we must prevent our people from hearing what they may think is indeed the true Voice of America."

"Do we really have anything in common, at this stage, beyond our mutual interest in President Eisenhower's atoms-for-peace program?" Considine asked.

Zhukov conceded that the atoms plan was a bond, and added that the people of the United States wanted peace personally just as much as the Russian people and that both countries were interested in scientific research.

"Where the countries separate is on the education level," he said pointedly. "The Soviet people are more interested in literature, American people more interested in television. But there are no unsolvable differences between us."

That same night, at a Belgian Embassy reception, the topic of exchanges on a higher level—seemingly out of the question at that time—were discussed. Fliegers spotted the Red Army marshal, Ivan Bagramian, who had been instrumental in dumping Marshal Zhukov, drinking with members of his staff in a quiet corner of the crowded Embassy, and took Considine over to meet him.

The big egg-bald soldier said the Russian people would enjoy a visit from President Eisenhower, "if he took the rock out from under his armpit."

Considine replied, "I saw the President not long ago and I could have sworn he didn't have a rock under his armpit."

Bagramian, the Red Army's inspector general, was equal to the challenge. He lifted his tunic, bedecked with sheriff-sized stars and four rows of campaign ribbons. "As you see, I have no rock either," he said.

Considine asked, "Do the Russian people think it would be right for President Eisenhower to visit here?"

"Your President was here just after the war, and he visited the Tomb of Lenin," Marshal Bagramian answered with a shrug. "We gave him our highest decoration. He would be made most welcome. He would be honored if he came back again. All honors would be paid to him."

It was the first opportunity to talk to a Russian who had been close to the ousted Marshal Zhukov. We knew also that Bagramian was supposed to have had something to do with this ousting. Considine remarked that there had been much concern felt in America about Zhukov, from the President down.

"Marshal Zhukov is on a leave of absence," Bagramian said firmly. "He has been ill. When he is recovered a suitable place will be found for him."

Nothing more about the faded general was forthcoming.

We told Bagramian that Russian sputnik scientists, when asked if they would tell other countries more about the missiles used to get the Soviet earth satellites in orbit, had said, "This is a question which the military men will answer."

"Well, what is it you want to know?" Bagramian asked expansively.

"I suppose we would want to receive, as part of the International Geophysical Year program, details on fuel, the thrust of the rocket engines, the number of stages involved, the guidance system, and things like that."

Bagramian was pleased.

"Ah, wouldn't you like to know!" he cried. And that was that.

But we were still getting no closer to Khrushchev. We could look from our hotel windows across Meneszh Square to the Kremlin walls, hardly a brassie shot, yet we began to feel that we were on another continent. Such is the utter isolation of the

Kremlin and such is the insularity which the system can impose upon the visitor. In the latter case, it is a form of brainwashing. Again we were called upon to "submit questions." But we *had* submitted questions. "Submit questions." New questions? "Submit questions."

Then another call from Ilychev. "You can expect to see Mr. Khrushchev the day after tomorrow. I will call."

In the meantime, we were faced with writing daily, and it got to be an exhilarating game to see what could pass the censor. For example:

As everyone here knows, the so-called American game of basket-ball was invented by Prof. Naismithski of the Institute of Physical Culture.

And this also passed without question:

Moscow: The new 1958 cars are coming out here, just as in the streets of America. In some respects the changes are more striking than anything emerging from Detroit this year.

For example, the Russian car stylists discovered two-tone decoration this year. A real snazzy idea. One part of the body is painted, let's say, blue, and the other part cream. Makes quite a contrast to the all black or all dun-colored cars built here since production began in 1930. Hope the idea will catch on in America.

The Russians at that time claimed, and perhaps correctly, that ten million Russians were studying English. If so, an overwhelming majority stayed away from the Hearst team. So Hearst invented a sort of muscular Berlitz course in Russian.

Ice is a simple word you would think would be on the tip of every Russian's tongue. But they persist in indicating they never heard of it. A nice waitress called Victoria, of all names, nodded happily after we had said the word in American, English, French, and German. She soon brought us a large bowl of sheep eyes.

Hearst then stepped into the breech. Putting on several coats, he hugged himself and said, "Brrrrrr!" Victoria skipped off and returned with a bowl of ice. Hearst's easy Russian is as simple as that.

There's a brand of Russian cigarettes called *Belmorsky Kanal,* meaning "White Sea Canal." Few Americans can order them, but Hearst found a simple way. He said to the girl at the cigarette counter, while making the motions of smoking, "Rufff!" The girl was momentarily puzzled. "Brfffufff!" Hearst repeated, practically spelling it out for her. Slowly it dawned on her, and her face lit up. She handed him a package of *Belmorsky Kanals.* The package has the picture of a dog on it.

Such were the diversions which helped fill the hours that led to "the day after tomorrow." When this day of days finally dawned, we got up early, dressed in our best, and waited for the call to Khrushchev's office. We waited all day and into the night, while a wet snow fell on the sad street outside. The revelers of the "Great October" celebration had departed. The Rumanian Communist leader who had been killed in a crash while approaching the Moscow airport had been swept past our balcony on a caisson, with enough of a cortege to denote the passing of a field marshal. Moscow was at its dreariest, as cold and gray and sloshy as a long-dead fish. We matched.

It was senseless to stay on any longer. Hearst got in touch with the Scandinavian Airlines office in the hotel and arranged for tickets to Helsinki, Stockholm, and home for the following Saturday. We chartered the Russian-speaking typewriter again, dropped a note to Ilychev saying it was nice being in Moscow and regretting he had not arranged the Khrushchev interview, and prepared to leave. Serge Fliegers dropped the note in the Kremlin mailbox. More than ever it seemed like tossing it into a bottomless pit.

But then came the call. "Friday morning at eleven, without fail," Ilychev phoned. "Central headquarters."

CHAPTER 5

Person to person

A uniformed flunky met us at the door of the undistinguished building which houses the Central Party headquarters. He led us to a little elevator, then up four floors, and down a corridor which might have been that of a cloistered private school. We stopped at a stained oak door on which was tacked a small framed nameplate, which read:

Comrade Khrushchev, NS

No other title was attached, nor did it differ in size from the nameplates on other doors along the corridor.

It led into a conventional outer office hardly distinguishable from the outer offices of any American executive, except that the several secretaries were older, stockier, and dressed more for warmth than effect. An assistant ordered Hearst to surrender his little tape recorder.

Khrushchev came out to greet us, accompanied by Ilychev and an interpreter, Victor Sukhodrev. It was plain the First

131

Secretary was in good, testy spirits. When the introductions reached Considine, Hearst explained that Considine was replacing Kingsbury Smith on this particular trip. Khrushchev looked the substitute up and down, not unlike a man measuring another before a fight. Then he grinned. "He's bigger than Smith," he said, "but is he as good?" This sally apparently broke up Ilychev.

Khrushchev led us into his office. It differed from others we had seen not so much in size, shape, and lack of elegance (Lenin was still the featured wall art), but in the happy disorder of the First Secretary's desk. It was cluttered with airplane models, souvenirs, and a bewildering variety of other gewgaws, together with a mountain of paper work.

Khrushchev took a seat at the end of the long conference table. Ilychev sat on his left, and four or five chairs up, a matronly stenographer took her place and opened her pad. The interpreter sat at the head of the table. Hearst was beckoned into the seat immediately opposite Khrushchev, and to his right sat Conniff and Considine.

Now began the longest interview Khrushchev had ever given up until that time.

It started gruffly. Hearst, wishing not to begin with the questions the team had carefully divided among themselves and now had spread out in front of them at the table, chatted about their previous meeting in the same office.

"It *is* the same office, isn't it?" he asked, when Khrushchev didn't reply.

"Yes," Khrushchev said. "We don't change in this country, as you do in yours."

Hearst tried another approach.

"Frank Conniff and I have noticed a lot of changes in Moscow since our visit of two years ago," he said. "Changes for the better. For instance, there are many more cars on the streets. . . ."

"We're not interested in automobile production," Khrushchev interrupted. "It has no important role in our economy."

We seemed to be foundering. Our long wait seemed to have been for naught. We had not only a reluctant witness but a truculent one.

There was an unhappy period of silence. Then Khrushchev said, "Now, about these questions. . . ." He stopped there and started thumbing through our submitted inquiries as if for the first time, which may well have been the case.

"We were instructed to submit questions to you," Hearst said. "You'll recall that the last time we talked, you didn't ask for written questions in advance. . . ."

Khrushchev took another brief look at the sheaf, tossed them aside, and said, "Ask me whatever you wish."

Our days and nights of working and reworking our questions had been largely a waste of time. But it didn't matter. Clearly, we were being given one of the rarest opportunities ever known to correspondents—an on-the-record, no-holds-barred interview with a man who now, assuredly, was not only the number one of the Soviet Union but, in terms of unbridled personal power, perhaps the number one man in the world.

Khrushchev covered a vast range of topics and referred to notes only once during the incredible performance, which ran so long that he said, with his customary heavy humor, after three hours had passed:

"Remember, Mr. Hearst, we have trade unions here in the Soviet Union too. They would say I am being overworked, that I am being exploited by and am under the enslavement of a capitalist."

Khrushchev jumped up from his chair more or less indig-

nantly during one exchange and started for a door that leads out
of the rear of the office. But it developed that his only purpose
in heading so resolutely for the door was to pick up a bottle of
Russian seltzer from a small table near the door, and bring it
back to the conference table. We momentarily thought he was
bolting the long-awaited interview.

But Khrushchev proved to be generally cooperative, and he
spoke mainly of peace in often blunt and sometimes humorously
barbed exchanges with the reporters.

"We do not want to continue the arms race," he said expansively. "We have already won over you. We have the absolute weapon. We have the most modern rockets. I say this not
to intimidate the United States or any other nation. But it is
just a fact that we have the ICBM and various other rockets of
all sorts and systems. We have all the bombs, A-bombs and
H-bombs. In this respect we have proved our superiority.

"If war should break out—and it could be started only by the
United States, because no other nation would dare—this could
lead to a great great war," Khrushchev said dispassionately.
"Your cities and bases could be stricken from the earth. This,
I repeat, is not a threat. It is simply that we are obliged by
circumstances to take the defensive.

"And remember, your overseas bases are yours but they are
surrounded by the peoples of those countries. You will see, one
day they will awaken from their slumber and recognize the folly
of depending upon NATO and such alliances for their protection.

"The people in the United States now living never fought
on their own territory. They do not understand war. They must
understand that the next war, if there is one, will not be fought
in Africa, or Europe, or Asia or someplace like that. But from
the very outset, and immediately, it will be fought on United
States soil.

"The ICBM permits this. We might strike Norway or Denmark or places like that, but they are not the main adversary, though of course in case of war we would have to eliminate bases there. The United States is the country of the main adversary. The American people would suffer huge losses in any ICBM war. Then, too, our submarines could launch lesser rockets from closer positions off-shore.

"But to repeat, we do not want to compete in this field of arms. We want a renunciation of war, with the necessary controls to follow."

Hearst leaned across the long conference table and asked, "Do you really believe the United States wants war?"

Khrushchev regarded Hearst for a time and replied:

"What is the United States you speak of? The people? Certainly they do not want war. They are afraid of war. So is the American bourgeoisie, some of its capitalists, its intellectuals and so forth. But the monopolists do! They profit by war. They forget that a Cold War can become a Hot War, however."

Hearst turned to Victor Sukhodrev, the young interpreter, and said to him, "Tell Mr. Khrushchev nobody wants war. We realize it would mean catastrophe. President Eisenhower and Secretary Dulles don't want war," Hearst went on heatedly. "Not a single soul in the United States wants war."

Khrushchev tapped a long letter opener on the table in front of him, put on his rimmed glasses, and glared across the table as if Hearst understood the Russian being spouted at him.

"If that is so, what prevents the United States from eliminating the Cold War?" he asked. "That would be alleviation that would lead to better understanding."

Hearst responded resignedly, "That's where we came in."

Khrushchev pounded the desk during the course of a ten-minute statement that followed. He listed a number of incidents in which he said the Russians made specific concessions during disarmament talks, only to find the United States, Britain, and France had retreated to a new position with which the Soviet Union could not agree. He concluded by suggesting the Warsaw Pact nations and NATO nations "agree on a nonaggression pact. That," he said, "would be a contribution to the alleviation of tension."

Conniff asked Khrushchev if the stress of the word "immediate" retaliation against American cities and bases meant that ICBMs and other missiles were at that time aimed at those targets, awaiting the touch of a button.

Khrushchev shrugged. "You should ask that of the general staff," he said. "They are the specialists in that department. That is what the general staff exists for—to pursue a line to destroy enemy targets as quickly as possible, in order to avenge an attack on their own country."

His face clouded as he continued, "I would like to voice my opinion and worry over such statements as those of American military men who state that about one half of your planes— bombers—are always in the air ready for action against us.

"A war psychosis has possessed your minds. How many planes in the air? How many people? Think of the psychotic state involved. If a signal is given—or if the pilot even thinks a signal has been given—he will fly toward his objective in the Soviet Union.

"The loss of a man's mind can lead to war under such psychotic conditions and bring about a terrible retaliatory blow immediately! We must preclude this, or it can break out in war even if both sides do not want war."

Hearst said that he thought the figure was one third of the American bombing force in the air at the same time, not one half.

Khrushchev snorted:

"One third alone is a lot. War may rest, after all, on only one pilot's decision."

Hearst asked him what was meant in the lengthy Communist Declaration which followed talks between Red leaders by the reference to "strengthening" the Warsaw Pact countries. Did it mean that Russia would supply these forces with missiles and nuclear weapons?

"That relates to the military," Khrushchev said. "The military did not participate in this Declaration. However, arming the Warsaw Pact countries depends on the circumstances, and the line taken by the so-called NATO bloc. Moreover, we have designed rockets to be used from our own territory and therefore we have no real cause to locate launching sites on the territory of these friendly countries. After all, we have our army in the German Democratic Republic [East Germany] and it has all the types of weapons it needs."

We deducted from this that the Red Army in East Germany has nuclear arms.

Considine asked, "In line with your promise to share all International Geophysical Year information, will you tell the United States how to launch its own Sputnik, give the United States plans for your ICBM which launched it, and the new fuel, if any, that propelled the Sputnik into orbit?"

"Certainly!" Khrushchev responded buoyantly. "Certainly we are ready to do so, but first let us agree on disarmament. Our satellites of course were launched by the ICBM. If we give you this information we will be giving you the ICBM. It is possible that you may not be able to develop this Intercontinental Ballistics Missile. But we would give it to you instantly, when and if the Cold War ends.

"The fact that we were able to launch the first Sputnik and then a month later launch the second shows that we can launch ten, even twenty satellites tomorrow. The satellite is the ICBM with a different warhead. We change that warhead from a bomb to a scientific instrument, and we launch a satellite.

"We will share anything. But first let us have trust. Let us sink all ICBMs in the sea and then we will truly have peace."

Hearst asked him about his feelings in regard to inspection, a major bone of contention at the bogged-down disarmament talks.

"What sort of inspection do you mean?" he asked. "When both sides bristle with arms, that is an unhealthy condition. The United States, Britain, and France have refused inspection plans submitted by the Soviet Union. You seem to say, first inspection, then confidence will follow.

"We stand for confidence or a combination of confidence and partial inspection, then absolute inspection based on absolute confidence. If we have inspection without confidence this would be military intelligence. Both sides would be choosing the happy moment for aggression.

"Suppose we had an inspection arrangement with India, let's say. India is a peace-loving state. We have no designs against India nor has India any designs against the Soviet Union. There would be no trouble with inspection. But when American generals and politicians say they can rub off the surface of the earth anything or anybody with whom they disagree, when they boast of their strength, how can we speak of inspection in such an atmosphere wherein passions are being constantly inflamed?

"We continue to regard and still stand on our position that to preclude surprise attack should be our aim. So we propose inspection posts at railroad stations, airdromes, important crossroads, and ports. Not everywhere—but points of departure or embarkation. Also we agreed on aerial inspection, for example over an 800-kilometer area on both sides of the dividing line in West Germany. But the United States, Britain, and France rejected this."

We moved on to other subjects. The Communist Boss was in a placid mood on the matter of the downgrading of Marshal Zhukov. Asked to define what "adventurism in foreign affairs" meant in the charges against the Marshal, Khrushchev answered:

"It means just that, an unreal attitude toward external affairs and affairs at home."

Zhukov's downgrading, Khrushchev said, had nothing to do with Russian policy in Syria or Turkey, "or Hungary."

"Lenin was known to bring back certain deviationists on the ground that they were still good Communists," Conniff commented. "Can Marshal Zhukov be brought back?"

Khrushchev replied, "Nothing is precluded or excluded in politics. Marshal Zhukov is still in the Communist Party. He is a great military specialist. When his services are required again, he will give all his strength to the Party and the people. He was punished only to the necessary degree. He is not a hopeless case."

We discussed the First Secretary's favorite subject, trade.

"Instead of the arms race let us trade," Khrushchev announced. "If you don't want to trade with us in strategic materials, well and good. Don't trade. But let's not eliminate all trade—let's end the discriminations in trade. So many opportunities to establish friendships come through trade.

"You have the most powerful state, the greatest capabilities, the most highly developed. We should compete in strengthening the peace through trade. Such is our effort. We arm only to repel any attack against us.

"We do have the ICBM, but I tell you in the name of myself and the Communist Party, we will never use it against the

United States unless the United States starts things first, or if a United States satellite nation attacks us.

"We declare war upon you—excuse me for using such an expression—in the peaceful field of trade. We challenge you to compete in peaceful things, such as the production of radios and televisions and vacuum cleaners—any kind of cleaners.

"We declare such a war. We will win over the United States. The threat to the United States is not the ICBM, but in the field of peaceful production. We are relentless in this, and it will prove the superiority of our system."

"We want to win over the United States, not in arms, but in the production of commodities," Khrushchev said. "We want to win in housing, construction, goods, more food, improvements, services rendered to the people.

"You have a higher standard of living in the United States. After all, you started yours earlier than ours. But we will win. We will outstrip the United States. And it will be this that will convince the people of the world that we are right."

About Hungary, Khrushchev was asked if he would proceed differently, in the light of the Soviet Union's good relations with two other countries (Yugoslavia and Poland) which went unscathed when they bucked its rule.

"It could have been different," Khrushchev replied. "But the situation there developed otherwise. Reactionary cutthroats threatened to deprive the progressive people of their gains. We intervened at the request of the government of Hungary. This has been a lesson to reaction. There is an old Russian proverb which says, 'Don't jump in the river without looking for the ford.'"

Khrushchev then quickly changed the subject. He picked up an ear of corn encased in clear plastic on his desk and spoke at some length in Russian, using the souvenir as a wand to emphasize his points. For the only time during the interview he referred to notes. He read portions of a speech by President Eisenhower of the previous week. He agreed with all of its calls for peace, he said, and when he came to that part where the President had given assurances that the United States will never be an aggressor, Khrushchev added that Russia would not be either.

"The President spoke of 'sacrifices,' and I'm afraid there will be varied interpretations of just what he meant," Khrushchev said. "I hope he wants to sacrifice in the work for peace. Let us come to an agreement right now and stop producing means of destruction. Mr. Hearst, convey this to your President."

The reason for the use of the corn memento became apparent. "I had a pleasant talk with President Eisenhower at Geneva," Khrushchev said. "As we stood in a great window admiring the view, he told me of his farm in America, and of the new breed of livestock that had been developed through hybridization. Let's compete in this field, instead of accumulating the means of destruction." Khrushchev said he had received this particular ear of corn from Roswell Garst, a friend of Henry Wallace and a corn specialist from Iowa who visited Russia not long before. "How much nicer," Khrushchev continued, "is it to speak of corn than of arms. I gave Mr. Garst a better ear of corn than he gave me," he added with something of a twinkle in his eye. "You needn't think you are ahead of us in corn either."

Khrushchev was obviously moved when Conniff asked him, "What has the Communist Party meant to you in your forty years of service?" He replied, "For me, the Communist Party is good because it expresses my hopes. Our Party, guided by the precepts of Lenin, has achieved colossal progress. It extends its fruits to all peoples. We want to see people made happy, irrespective of their nationality and the color of their skin. We want to see them receive the results of their work. Humanity will acknowledge the correctness of our view."

Hearst asked him to define his several references to ruling classes and working classes in the United States, and Khrushchev responded with a smile, "Ruling circles are ruling circles, and working classes are working classes. It's the same all over the world. It's the same in any language."

Then Hearst said, "But the working class in the United States is the majority and their voting power makes them the ruling class."

"Quite right, Mr. Hearst," Khrushchev said. "It's true your working class is in the majority, but it doesn't have the means of production in its hands. It doesn't own the radio, the press, the television. The rich monopolies control these things. This control of the cinema, books, etc. . . . they exert all means of moral pressures on the people. They threaten them with force, compel them to vote to retain them in power, in office. It is certainly a very clever democracy you have in the United States," Khrushchev said, "but your working class will find its strength in time. Patience is needed there. The conclusion you draw is wrong."

He picked up his ornate blue-handled letter opener, long as a stiletto, and wagged it at Hearst. "When the time comes," he said, "when the United States worker will say, 'I am the boss, I create all the values, and I will vote in the interest of myself and other members of the working class,' don't be afraid.

"We who will be in over-all charge then will tell the leaders of the working class of the United States, Mr. Hearst, that you were not a bad capitalist at all."

Hearst said, "Gee, thanks."

The big surprise of the session, curiously enough, came when we raised the question of religion. It turned out that Khrushchev had very decided views on the subject, which he proceeded to air with some heat. Indeed, it apparently roused stronger feelings in him than any other subject we discussed.

Moreover, we discovered more world-wide interest in this part of our interview than any other. We later cabled his remarks on religion as a "sidebar" to our main story on the burning topics of the hour. Somewhat to our surprise, we were to discover in the days following our homecoming that the "sidebar" apparently had sunk deeper in readers' consciousness than the main articles. It made headlines, and evoked tremendous response from people all over the world.

It was Considine who raised the question. "Mr. First Secretary," he said, "you have made several references to God, the human soul, and spiritual freedom under communism. How is it that any man who might believe in all those things is denied advancement in the Communist Party?"

"Because the situation is incompatible," Khrushchev replied. "We are atheists. Certainly we use the name of God, as in 'God's truth.' But it is only a habit. We could just as easily say, 'I give you my word.'

"We are atheists, but we have a tolerant attitude toward all people. There is no contradiction in this attitude. But if the acceptance of religion is intermingled with political activity that works against the Communist Party, that is different.

"If they intrude on political activity, that is against our constitution. We are not going to fight for God's body. We don't fight for a coffin so that other coffins will cover the globe. That's what the Crusades were fought for."

Hearst pointed out that there had never been a great country or civilization which hadn't believed in God, "or some kind of a Supreme Being."

Khrushchev shrugged and said contemptuously, "Let them believe what they want. It doesn't prevent us from coexisting."

Hearst persisted.

"That is the intrinsic difference between us," he said. "When we give our word we think it is a pledge to God, but in your case the pledge remains on paper only. I hope there can be a common meeting ground between us on this some day."

This one evidently stung. A dull brick color crept upward from Khrushchev's bull-like neck and slowly mottled the oval face. "We Communists, the Soviet politicians, are atheists," he said with some heat. "We set high value on our pledges, our word, and we never break them. We Communists are fighting actively to prevent another war. We are doing everything possible in order that there will be no new war."

The translator had hardly begun to read this back when Khrushchev abruptly intruded. He waggled the letter opener like a maestro directing the climax of a symphony.

"That is where the discrepancy lies," he said. "Such people seek to present things as if their activities really proceed from divine commands. Whereas, in actual fact, they contradict the very principles of humanity and, consequently, the whole of human society."

We were stunned by the vehemence of the man. Three hours of conversation had not prepared us for this sudden outburst. Khrushchev ripped into a denunciation of priests throwing holy water on weapons, priests who helped enslave colonial peoples, priests who "left the Gospel for the people and took the riches for themselves." Gone was his jaunty aplomb; in its stead was pure, unalloyed hatred.

"I recall a story I once heard," Khrushchev said in a quieter tone of voice, "about robbers who killed and robbed a man. Among the loot they found a chunk of fresh ham. After a time, the robbers decided to take a rest and eat the ham. They had started distributing it among themselves when one of them asked what day of the week it was. He was told it was Wednesday or Friday—I can't remember the exact day named in the story. He declared he couldn't eat the ham, for the Orthodox Church prohibited meat on Wednesdays and Fridays.

"You see how it is," he cried triumphantly. "The robbers

killed a man, took his life and everything he had, but did not eat the ham taken in the loot for fear of committing a sin!

"Don't the deeds of certain Western statesmen remind one of the sacreligious people mentioned in the story? For they, shielding themselves with the name of God, quite often do things which bring death to thousands and millions of people."

Evidently Khrushchev felt a lot better. The buoyancy returned to his voice, and again he was the genial Communist overlord being patient with three Americans who stubbornly insisted on believing in the old truths and ancient values.

"Is that enough?" he asked us.

It was indeed. We folded our notebooks and rose.

The long interview was drawing to a close. Not once had any of the two white or green telephones in the office rung. Middle-aged women stenographers had come and gone in hour shifts.

Khrushchev, as fresh as when he started, bounced to his feet. For ten more minutes or so we chatted idly about the Russian Olympic team, the new Soviet jet planes, and presents from visiting Communists which littered his desk, including an ivory figure of Gandhi and a golden head of Lenin.

Pleased as a boy, he showed us through a microscope a human hair engraved with this legend: "The Armenian people send warm greetings to the Communist Party of the Soviet Union."

We had heard much about Khrushchev's drinking, although we were inclined to doubt some of these rumors, and were impressed by his vigor. We asked him how he kept in shape. Despite his bulk, Khrushchev moves about with the agility of a good blocking back. The innocent question provided him with an ideological opportunity, and he snapped at it as a trout snares a fly.

"I live honestly," he said. "I devote my time to doing my best for the Party. I try my hardest to help the people. I work for peace and not war, and that's what keeps me healthy."

Khrushchev pointed to a model of the TU-104 on his desk

and asked if we had seen the colossal TU-114, the huge new Russian prop-jet, designed to carry up to 220 passengers, which the Soviet Union then hoped to put in world airline competition.

We told him that we had not seen it but that we would like to.

Khrushchev snapped his fingers. "I will have a word with Academician Tupolev." Tupolev was the designer of both the planes. We told Khrushchev that our trip in the 104 from Prague to Moscow indicated that Tupolev was a very good designer indeed.

The Communist Party leader's lower lip came out a truculent half inch or so.

"Yes, but your people would not let the TU-104 land in New York," he said aggressively, "when it took our United Nations delegation there a short time ago."

"That's nothing," Hearst said. "The New York Port Authority wouldn't let our own jet land there the day it set a transcontinental record. This was no discrimination against Russia. It's just that the Port Authority felt that the noise vibration would break windows in the area of Idlewild Airport."

Khrushchev considered the explanation as it was translated to him. Then he said, "You must have very bad windows in your country. Ours don't break." There was pride in his voice.

"If you want to show us the TU-114, why not order Academician Tupolev to send us back to New York in it?" Considine asked him.

Khrushchev shook his head, grinned his gold-tooth smile, bowed briefly, and said, "As yet we have only a prototype of this plane. Let us not kid ourselves. It has not completed the tests necessary before going into production. With the plane in that condition we would not think of endangering the life of such a distinguished capitalist as William Randolph Hearst."

We tarried in his outer office after bidding him farewell, and, on our way to the elevator, saw him once again. Minus any semblance of a guard, and jaunty in a sable-collared overcoat and a Russian *shapka* atop his all but nude pate, the number one Communist bounced off to a late lunch.

It was midafternoon when we returned to the hotel, tired from hours of note-taking and give-and-take, but stimulated by the experience and ready for work. Hearst went to work on his Sunday column. Considine and Conniff organized their notes, and Considine worked for about seven straight hours at his typewriter. Hearst finished his piece, and it was dispatched to London for transmission to New York. Hearst was able to speak to the New York office, and told them enough to start the promotion of the interview story to come.

The *New York Mirror* next morning, Saturday, November 23, 1957, prominently carried this announcement:

KHRUSHCHEV SPEAKS

For three hours and 35 minutes—in one of the most significant interviews of our times—the dominant figure of Soviet Russia has answered the questions of three famous newsmen. . . .

No subject was out of bounds, no holds barred as William Randolph Hearst, Jr., Frank Conniff and Bob Considine explored Khrushchev's views on war, peace, coexistence, science, satellites, missiles, nuclear power and the probable directions of Soviet policy.

All of which might sound exciting, except that the paper had no story. At midnight, Friday, Moscow time, Fliegers took our accounts of the interview to the Telegraph Building and handed them over to the slatternly Russian woman behind the high desk. She had gone through the usual routine of stamping the time at which the stories were delivered, and then had taken the armful of pages through the little door that leads to the censor's office.

They had not been returned. For twelve excruciating hours the censor maintained a terrible silence.

Our phone at the hotel suddenly could no longer reach the outside world, there was no chance to dictate the stories to Paris or London. We had made contact with the Czech couple who operated Press Wireless in Prague (and did it magnificently) but our phone calls even within the sphere of Soviet influence were stopped, too. We were blacked out.

Plainly, not a word was to be released until Khrushchev himself had an opportunity to read the stories.

Near noon Saturday, it appeared we would be forced to cable New York that the censors had decided to bury the interview. Fliegers slashed through as much red-tape as possible, in a land where no official has a known telephone number and there are no telephone books. But at several crucial points he ran into a blank wall.

Then at noon on the dot, Moscow time (4 A.M. Saturday, New York time), the stories were released and sent to New York without comment. Not one word had been changed, and there were many words—words that were to give the world a fresh view of a remarkable man and what he stood for.

For reasons we have never quite understood, it was arranged for us to interview on the following morning the man Khrushchev had handpicked to replace his friend Zhukov, Soviet Defense Minister Marshal Rodion Y. Malinovsky. Perhaps it was Khrushchev's idea; certainly it had to have his approval. It remains the only extensive interview that Malinovsky has ever given.

Malinovsky met us at his office. He was a man whose thick gray hair was combed straight back from his bulldog face without a parting. His eyebrows were black and expressive. He gave each of us a bone-crushing handshake, shook hands with a

major general and major—interpreters from the outer office—
and with his chunky girl stenographer. Malinovsky then took
his place at the head of the familiar conference table and indicated he was ready.

He wore nine rows of ribbons beneath the dangling gold
star of the Order of Lenin. The single Marshal's star on each
thickset shoulder was the size of a sheriff's badge. A painting of
Lenin reading *Pravda* looked down from one wall. On other
walls were large, flaming paintings of Russian arms in triumph
and torment on land and sea.

The Marshal has a deep voice and it was with an air of complete authority that he gave his blunt estimate of Russian military thinking at this sensitive hour in relations between two
great powers.

At the same time, we couldn't help remembering Stalin's
outburst: "Malinovsky, an old woman could operate tanks
better than you."

During much of the interview, we got an amplification of
threats which had been discreetly veiled by the First Secretary.

Considine asked him why Russia, while speaking so often of
peace, was investing a vast fortune in submarines, an offensive
weapon. He looked at us broodingly, and with his interpreter
only a few beats behind him, he said:

"The submarine is not only an offensive weapon. It is also
a defense weapon, and as long as we must keep our defenses
at a high level we are forced to build submarines on such levels.
It is a good weapon, a good weapon to use against United
States aircraft carriers. You mention submarines as an offensive
weapon. But how about the aircraft carrier? It is aggressive
and aggressive only.

"In order to provide for defense of the American continent
your airplanes could just as well operate from shore bases. Your

aircraft carriers plainly are meant to take your air force to far places." He paused, and said in a rather menacing tone, "The Mediterranean Sea for instance. It is difficult to see how carriers can defend American shores while steaming through the Mediterranean.

"We cannot exclude their coming to the Black Sea, so we build submarines. They have become the most modern weapon with which to drown any American aircraft carriers that appear in our waters. Your Navy does not seem to understand that they are already obsolete.

"I am familiar with your interservice fights in that respect, between your navy and your air force."

"Western military men consider political influence upon their affairs hampers them," Conniff said. "Why isn't the same feeling not valid in the case of the Red Army?"

Malinovsky seemed surprised. "The Communist Party is the ruling party of the U.S.S.R. and it influences all fields," he said, spelling it out. "I would say it would be the same thing as the control your Republican Party has over your military at present."

The mouse-quiet major general, seated several chairs down the table, opened a bottle of Russian beer with a loud bang and served the Marshal a glass which he barely touched.

"You do not understand," he continued. "Many Soviet military units have their own Communist Party organizations, just as nonmilitary organizations have their units. I reject the suggestion given by capitalistic countries that an army must be out of politics.

"The armed forces of the Soviet Union are a practical instrument of the Communist Party, an extension of the teachings of Lenin and Marx. It bespeaks unity. Our practice has proved correct."

Thus spoke the well-disciplined Communist military leader. The subject was evidently closed.

Hearst asked, "Is the rocket doing the same to the plane as the tank did to the horse?"

"Further development of the rocket makes action of the plane, the bomber, ever weaker," Malinovsky replied, obviously relieved to get on less dangerous ground. "It is a simple thing, where we are concerned. If you want to bomb a certain target you send your bombers. We defend. There are many obstacles for the bombers en route. Many bombers will suffer before they reach the target. Maybe only a few will reach their objective. The longer the distance, the smaller the number that will get through. There may be cases when not a single bomber will reach its destination.

"Our rockets can easily reach bombers. They can't stop our antiaircraft rocket because its speed is great. It can reach its bomber in a short time and accurately. Thus it has a very great advantage over the bomber. In time, it will put your bomber out of business."

He gave the matter further thought. "It is a good analogy that you present," he said to Hearst. "The tank has indeed taken the place of the horse."

But there is not much fun in patting a tank, Hearst quipped. Old cavalryman Malinovsky nodded. "The horse is a living thing that stands much closer to man than a tank."

Malinovsky turned to the Korean war, after denying Russia had contributed arms to Communist forces in Vietnam.

"The United Nations was but a small decoration, a badge, for the American military in Korea," he said to Hearst, who had asked him how Russia, a member of that organization, had aided the side which the United Nations had declared overwhelmingly to be in the wrong. "American prisoners of war taken by North Koreans spoke of this," Malinovsky said. "The emblem was but a mask, so to speak. Your General Dean spoke of this, I understand.

"Certainly we helped the North Koreans. We sold them some arms in much the same proportions as America provided arms for Syngman Rhee. But remember this: we did not fight there. No Red Army troops or pilots were there. But you were there."

"But you should have been there, too, as a member of the UN," Hearst insisted.

"We aided the North Koreans because they were fighting for their independence and liberty," Malinovsky replied stonily.

"We use the same words in our country about Southern Korea," Hearst said, "but they mean something totally different."

"Different meanings, indeed!" Malinovsky said. "We are Communist, you are capitalist. You have your ideas, we have ours.

"But I tell you this much: many American generals are very often sorry that they have no ideal to plant in the heart of the American soldier, so he will be willing to die for that ideal. You are jealous of us for this. The Communist soldier, the Red Army soldier, has such an ideal in his heart. He has it because he considers the ideal of the commander his own ideal.

"Your generals in Korea were sorry that Americans were not fighting willingly. We couldn't tell them why this was so, but I will tell you why. There is a difference between us. We have an advantage over you. We have an ideal for which we are prepared to die. You have not."

"But we do have such an ideal," Hearst said, "and have proved many times that we are willing to defend it far away from home; the ideal of fighting for a cause, as we did in World War I and when we fought together against Hitler."

The Marshal reminisced briefly over his long career, which began at the lowest rank when he joined Czar Nicholas' forces in 1914. He was a member of the Russian expeditionary forces in France in 1916–17, and recalled meeting many American soldiers.

"I had quite a number of good friends among them," he said. "We met as friends. I have the very best recollections about meeting them. They were mighty good boys!"

He said he met no American generals during World War II —unlike Zhukov, who was a personal friend of General Eisenhower.

Though his long career took him into the cavalry and a series of command schools, he retained his interest in the foot soldier. "No war can be won without the soldier," he said. "By no means could certain victory be achieved if there was no soldier to win it. His significance in modern war is very great—perhaps even greater than it used to be."

Malinovsky expressed doubt that Russia would ever depend upon the professional army, as has been suggested in the United States. "That depends on taste. If American military leaders consider it wise, perhaps they're more competent than we. Up to now, in America, United States wars have been fought by your army, not by the American people. The army went to Europe, Asia, and so forth.

"We don't think they alone conduct wars. Wars are conducted by the whole of a people. We don't think such a limited army would be suitable. It would be a step backward to the time of Frederick the Great or Swiss Landsknecht."

When asked why the Russians had such a large standing army, he stated that reductions in the Red Army had brought it down to the level of American forces. "We couldn't feel safe if we had a smaller force," he contended.

"We've run into a lot of proverbs since we've been talking

to Russian leaders," Hearst said to him. "Here's an old American one: Which came first, the chicken or the egg?"

It took some time for this to sink in. When it did, Malinovsky
gruffed, "Ha!"

"Our allies say we must stay big," Hearst continued, "in
order to protect them from this big, bad bear Marshal Malinovsky, and you in turn stay big because we are big. That's the old
chicken and egg story all over."

Malinovsky touched his rainbowed chest.

"This big, bad bear never went to the American continent,
never threatened your homes. But you have been here. During
our civil war, a whole corps of Americans fought against us. We
have some basis to be afraid of your army."

"Are you forgetting we sent you billions of dollars of aid in
World War II?" Hearst asked.

"Of course you did," Malinovsky agreed. "But we have no
Soviet naval bases around America, though there are a number
of American bases around the Soviet Union."

He told a lengthy story about two farmers, friends, who had
a falling out. One surrounded the farm of the other with servants
armed with sticks.

"We are the surrounded farm," he concluded. "We must be
careful. We must take every precaution. But you know of our
peaceful character. This may sound strange coming from a
military man, but all Soviet people, including military, hate
war."

"Historically, armies have had to follow political dictates,"
Hearst said. "Now, whenever a Socialist or Communist group
tries to take over in government you immediately send Russian
hardware. So they ask us for help."

Malinovsky countered with some rather odd logic. "It is bad
where there is a gap between military and politics," he said.

"Perhaps that's the case in the United States. Our case is different. If our Soviet army doesn't like war, it means that our Soviet government doesn't like war. And the Soviet government means the Soviet people. The views of the people entirely coincide with the point of view of the government.

"So there can't be a case where our government would start a war because it would be contrary to the wishes of the people."

The Marshal's beer was flat when he finished.

To us, as we made ready to leave Russia, there was no question as to who was boss. If there had been a summit meeting called at that time, protocol would have prevented President Eisenhower from meeting Khrushchev on equal terms, because Khrushchev had not yet become Premier. As at Geneva, Eisenhower would have had to do his business with Premier Bulganin. But now it had been made humiliatingly clear to Bulganin that he was but an official greeter. The head of the military, the stiff-as-starch Bolshevik, Malinovsky, was also obviously a puppet on Khrushchev's strings.

A snowstorm lashed the airport as we walked an icy path toward the beat-up twin-engined plane that was to take us to Warsaw. Leaning against the raw wind we made it to the steps and into the crate. It taxied slowly and clumsily out to the head of the runway, creaking with a heavy snow crust which had gathered on it as it sat on the ramp exposed to the Moscow winter.

Hearst and Conniff had been through this particular kind of departure before, but to Considine it seemed sheer madness to attempt a take-off in a plane so poorly serviced. Presently, what appeared to be a gas truck drove up next to us. Hoses were pulled out, and the truck crew began squirting hot water all over the plane.

"But it will freeze," Considine said. "We'll be a hunk of ice."

It didn't have a chance to freeze. We were suddenly off—up and away. We were glad to leave, but glad, too, that we had gone, and helped shed a little more light on a man whose opinions and decisions affected the lives of virtually every human being on earth.

CHAPTER 6

The men around Khrushchev

In order to understand the inner workings of Khrushchev's Russia, it is necessary to probe not only the character and career of the head man himself but to assess the personalities and roles of the Communist stalwarts who serve under him, who provide the bedrock of his support within the party, who carry out his policies in the Red empire, and from among whom his successor may well arise. You can be sure that Khrushchev has this last possibility in particular firmly in mind, and makes sure that none of his cohorts allow their ambitions to get out of hand. There is no doubt that Nikita Khrushchev has fastened a stranglehold on the Communist party apparatus and the government administration of the Soviet Union. And yet, even this old campaigner must keep an eye cocked on the party machinery, lest any opponent or cabal of opponents undermines him as he travels blithely about the world to summit conferences and state visits. Secure as he appears to be, Khrushchev surely knows from past experience that the Party's internal ferment must be carefully channeled and controlled, the nests of resistance sealed off, the responsible jobs entrusted to proven lieutenants.

But who among the men around him are the ones who really matter? What manner of men are they? No man—not even an absolute dictator like Stalin—can run the Communist empire alone. He needs advisers and assistants whom he can at least trust partially to bring him information and carry out his orders.

Under Stalin, the Politburo—later reconstructed and renamed the Presidium of the Central Committee—functioned like the inner sanctum of a Byzantine court. A few favored advisers jockeyed constantly for position, and they had constant reason, especially in the last days, to tremble in fear for their lives.

When Stalin died, Malenkov and his colleagues increased the functions and importance of the Presidium. Malenkov had come to admire efficiency as head of Stalin's personal secretariat. It was he who gave the Presidium its character of a "company board." When Khrushchev took over, he did not change this. He simply shook up the personnel of the board, putting in his own men. Mikhail A. Suslov and Alexei I. Kirichenko, for instance, were made Presidium members in 1955, Suslov rising from the secretariat of the Central Committee, where he had wielded great influence for years.

Khrushchev may be compared in some ways to a chairman of the board, but he is a chairman who owns all the stock. His position reminds me of the story that J. D. Gortatowsky likes to tell of William Randolph Hearst, Sr. It seems that at a board meeting, a vote was taken on a particularly controversial issue, and one by one every board member voted in the negative. Mr. Hearst was the last to be recorded. He voted aye.

Gortatowsky, who was chairing the meeting, computed the tally instantly. "The ayes have it," he said, "unanimously."

The Presidium nevertheless does not always give Khrushchev his way. One Eastern European diplomat, in a position to know, has claimed that the Presidium turned its leader down on at least one occasion. Khrushchev once wanted to give Ekaterina Furtseva, an old friend and a staunch supporter of his in the Presidium during the "anti-party" fight, an *Osobniak,* a private villa in Moscow.

This raised something of a furore in apartment-scarce Moscow. The Presidium, in polite but firm tones, told Khrushchev that he shouldn't do a thing like that. He, somewhat abashed, agreed with the verdict. Furtseva returned to her former apartment.

Probably the most capable and talented of the Presidium members, and the man closest to Khrushchev himself, is Anastas Ivanovich Mikoyan, the swarthy, energetic Armenian who is a powerful force in guiding the Russian economy. Mikoyan has been a Presidium figure since 1935, preceding Khrushchev by four years upon the loftiest ledge of communism. Before that, Mikoyan has a long record, going back into the Bolshevik dark ages, of supporting Stalin in his conflicts with his party foes. It gives one a start to read, some thirty years later, that Mikoyan played a role, if a relatively small one, in Stalin's showdown with Leon Trotsky.

Mikoyan has the respect and the grudging esteem of Western observers in Moscow, if only for surviving the brutal Stalin years. Now, with his bushy black hair, scrunched-in nose, Charlie Chaplin moustache, and flashing smile, he is a familiar figure of Moscow's "cocktail diplomacy."

But Mikoyan has gone as far as he can in the Russian firmament and knows it. An Armenian is essentially a territorial, an outlander in the essentially Russian government. Khrushchev can get by with his Ukrainian accent, but an Armenian is almost a foreigner. At any rate, Mikoyan is no direct threat to the top man, and knowledge of this on both sides makes for calm relations between them.

Khrushchev needs Mikoyan's wide talents, especially in view

of the pressing economic problems that still beset Russia. Mikoyan, in return, feels free to criticize the boss on technical matters. He is known to have expressed skepticism to some American visitors about Khrushchev's agricultural schemes. At the same time, he cautioned them not to make the criticism public because it would be "misinterpreted and give the wrong impression about our relations."

We chatted several times with Mikoyan on our Moscow trips but never had a formal interview. As luck would have it, our best shot at this energetic little man came in Karachi, Pakistan, in 1956, where Randolph Hearst and Conniff were able to buttonhole him at the inauguration of President Mirza.

Good timing plays an important, if not quite all-important, role in journalism. The two reporters had come to Pakistan from India to hear the other side of the Kashmir dispute. Much to their delight, they were informed on their arrival that they had flown in on a truly historic occasion. The very next day, March 23, Pakistan was to celebrate its first Freedom Day, inaugurate a new President, and whoop it up in colorful ceremonies to mark the end of British rule.

Karachi is hot, dusty, and uncomfortable, and the midday sun has been known to keep even Englishmen indoors. The Freedom Day ceremonies were therefore held early in the morning. President Mirza was sworn in at 6:45 A.M.—an hour when Harry Truman is just starting his morning walk. At 8:00 A.M. began the ceremonial parade.

With its connotations of an empire lost, this was a truly symbolic spectacle. The well-drilled infantry, the lithe cavalrymen astride their beautiful horses, the jet planes swarming overhead, provided an ironic footnote to an era. Comrade Mikoyan sat on the edge of the field with other distinguished guests. One can only imagine what the old Bolshevik thought of this blend of the last vestiges of empire with heady Asian nationalism. One can only be sure about how he felt. He felt damned hot. He was wearing the full ceremonial gear of the hated imperialists: striped pants, stiff shirt, Ascot tie, and stove-pipe hat. Sweat streamed from every pore, and he mopped his brow frequently with a large white handkerchief.

Mikoyan greeted Conniff and Randolph Hearst cordially enough. Conniff mumbled introductions and achieved the desired effect: Mikoyan thought Randolph was the Hearst who had had the interviews with Khrushchev, Bulganin, et al. It's not exactly deception, you must understand, just the forethought of a great publisher in naming two of his journalist sons "Randolph."

Mikoyan became even more cordial, even effusive. He kept repeating what a great job Hearst and his party had done in their Khrushchev interviews. Very objective, and all that. He was so complimentary that Conniff began to get embarrassed, and Hearst began to get suspicious.

"If they liked the interview all that much," he hissed to Conniff, "why did we ever print it?"

Mikoyan did give us one news story. He told us how he had "associated himself" with Khrushchev's famous attack on Stalinism a month earlier. News of Khrushchev's speech before the Twentieth Congress had only leaked to the Western world a few days before we talked to him.

"I not only associate myself with comrade Khrushchev's remarks," he said with some pride, "but I was directly connected with them. But I was not connected with their publication at the present time."

We told him that the bitter onslaught on Stalin had baffled the Western world. We asked him to explain the change after so many years of glorifying the Soviet dictator.

"There should be nothing surprising in that," he said, with the familiar bland look of amazement of the Communist bureaucrat when confronted by an obvious *non sequitur*.

"It is a form of Communist self-criticism," he went on. "Is it surprising that we should attempt to see a man's historical role in perspective? What we are trying to show the Russian people is a true role played by Stalin. Is there anything surprising in that?"

Another influential man around Khrushchev is Mikhail Suslov. He deserves special mention because he is the occasional favorite of London and Washington experts who like to imagine new intrigues against the leader.

He is a tall, bony man of sixty, who wears a pince-nez and bears a striking facial resemblence to Eamon De Valera. He is the undisputed "theoretician" of the Party, who advises just how far the leaders can stray from the teachings of Marx and Lenin without wrecking the party line.

Suslov's influence, especially within the Party is big. He occupied a choice position in the Central Committee Secretariat for many years, where he performed many dark and dirty chores for Stalin. His name always seems to pop up in dusty old accounts of the Stalin-Tito split. The ultimatum to Belgrade reading Tito out of Communist society bore his name. When the Cominform met to declare doctrinal war on the Yugoslav comrades, Suslov was one of the Russian delegates.

Recent Soviet group pictures, which usually give dependable indication of any individual's place in the hierarchy, fail to show Suslov in any prominent role. Mikoyan, Frol Kozlov, and even old President Klimenti Voroshilov are shown hugging the spotlight with their irrepressible leader, but the party tactician stays in the background.

These pictures may be deceptive as an index of his rank, for Suslov has been concentrating on organizational and theoretical work. Important Communist delegations are generally greeted by him in the name of the Party. In recent years he has attended the annual congresses of the Italian, French, and Chinese Communist Parties, and he delivered the "report" at the tenth anniversary of the Chinese Communist government in Peiping in October, 1959, another significant assignment in view of party dynamics.

Party position being the key factor in a Communist's rank, these duties indicate Suslov is extremely influential—and also a possible source of jeopardy, if ever Khrushchev should let down his guard. Because of his unsavory errands for Stalin, he has usually been regarded as a Stalinist remnant. Yet he owes his present position to Khrushchev, and voted for him in the showdown of 1957, when he might have expected to rally around the Stalinist stalwarts opposing the First Secretary.

One student of internal Kremlin affairs goes so far as to give Suslov credit for providing the theoretical basis for the entire Malenkov-Khrushchev program of the post-Stalin years. Dr. B. S. Gilani, who teaches political science and Asian history at John Carroll University, was for many years a member of the Nehru government of India. He is a Catholic, and the only Papal Knight in India, and his Vatican contacts have helped give him access to much inside information on the Kremlin. His theory is that as early as 1953, Suslov and Pyotr Pospelov, another Marxist-Leninist scholar, based a key study on a secret report from Nikolai G. Ignatov, an expert in political intelligence, who has since himself become a member of the Presidium.

Ignatov's report claimed that communism was losing its adherents all over the world, and that the morale of the Party outside Russia was so low that even in a showdown with the West, no help could be expected from foreign Communists. Suslov and Pospelov, according to Gilani, came up with some

simple remedies, which can be readily recognized as the bare
bones of the present Khrushchev formula. Essentially, the Party
was to revert to the old Leninist technique of "one step backward and two steps forward."

That is, they would go easier on the Russian people, and pay
more attention to their needs and grievances while relaxing
somewhat in demands upon them. In line with this, they would
soften their aggressive international line, and propose "peaceful
international relations" with other countries. And meanwhile,
they would go ahead and strengthen Russia's military might.

Whether or not Khrushchev owes his best gambits to Suslov,
the latter is evidently bright and capable, and a man worth
watching if only for the high standing he enjoys in the Party.

Should Khrushchev depart from life in the next few years
(and he is now sixty-six, it is likely that the post-Stalin pattern
of selecting his successor will be followed. That is, for a time, his
power is likely to be divided between two men: one will become
Premier, the other First Secretary of the Party. Then the struggle to see who emerges as the undisputed leader will inevitably
begin. The eventual winner may not be either of the original
heirs.

Observers who make this prognosis are even willing to
nominate their candidate for Khrushchev's successor as Premier.
The heavy favorite is Frol Kozlov, presently a First Deputy
Premier. Until a few months ago the same observers were also
prepared to nominate a successor to Khrushchev in the party
post of First Secretary: Alexei Kirichenko, whose career roughly
parallels that of Khrushchev.

Alexei I. Kirichenko, a Ukrainian in his early fifties, has been
described as "burly, curly, and surly." He came to know Khrushchev in the thirties, when Stalin sent Khrushchev into the
Ukraine to wipe out the last traces of Trotskyism.

A former mechanic and tractor driver on a Ukrainian *Sovk-*

hoz (state farm), Kirichenko was charged by Khrushchev with cleaning out Ukrainian industry, liquidating unreliable types, and putting the fear of Stalin in others to increase production.

During the war, when Khrushchev was a political commissar in the armed forces, he took Kirichenko along as a kind of private watchdog.

The two men reputedly worked especially closely at Stalingrad during the siege. It has later been suggested that the defenders of Stalingrad fought so well because they feared the execution squads of Khrushchev and Kirichenko even more than German guns.

After the war Kirichenko assisted Khrushchev in the bloody job of cleaning up the Ukraine, many of whose inhabitants had greeted the Wehrmacht as liberators. History might have been different had German policy in this hotbed of nationalism been more enlightened. The infamous SS took over, however, and instituted measures of repression that made the dissidents prefer their Kremlin masters. Many Ukrainian nationalists, nevertheless, took the opportunity to settle old scores with especially hated Communist bureaucrats. Red executioners were executed themselves. Anticommunist organizations were formed. There was even an attempt to break up the *Kolkhoz* and *Sovkhoz* systems and return the land to individual farmers. Strangely enough, it was the Germans who opposed this; their generals and *Gauleiters* felt the Soviet system was "more efficient and easier to handle" (this is a direct quote from a report by a German intelligence officer).

Kirichenko's official position was "Secretary in charge of cadres," that is, personnel, and he was associated with the Ukraine in the years after the war, charged with maintaining party discipline. He was also looked on as a personal protégé of Khrushchev.

At the 1959 conventions of secret-police bosses in the Soviet

Union, for instance, the main address was delivered by Comrade Kirichenko, representing N.S. Khrushchev, which suggests a very close relationship between the First Secretary and his fellow Ukrainian.

But the path to Communist glory is bumpy and tortuous. Early in 1960 Khrushchev turned on his protégé and demoted him to the relatively obscure position of First Secretary of the Communist Party in the Rostov district. He was also stripped of his Presidium membership and his post in the party secretariat. Apparently Kirichenko acted in a way to embarrass Khrushchev during the latter's frequent absences from Moscow. Either Kirichenko threw his weight around beyond limits set by his party boss, or botched key assignments. Whatever the cause of the split, Khrushchev showed no hesitancy about exiling him to the provinces. The top party job in Rostov rates high, but it is far from the eminence Kirichenko once enjoyed in the capital. Khrushchev may bring him back after a period of penance, but such rehabilitation is rare.

The fact that certain party figures are now considered possible successors to Khrushchev does not mean that they are especially eminent in Russia right now.

But the reason for the prediction above that Kozlov might become Premier is based on the theory that a man like Kozlov is one upon whom most of the other important figures could agree as an interim Premier. Distrustful of each other, they would agree upon Kozlov and then it would be up to him to keep the job. Malenkov started his office under similar conditions and could not make it stick. Whether Kozlov could do any better remains to be seen.

Kozlov, who made a fair impression during his 1959 American tour as a sort of cut-rate Khrushchev, is not as widely known as that international ambassador of Communist good will, Mikoyan. An interesting fact about him is that he spent some time in Communist concentration camps. He was put there by Stalin and later rescued by Khrushchev. This strange interlude probably occurred between 1940 and 1944, when there is a gap in his official biography.

One of Kozlov's early actions, according to East European sources, was to seek revenge. His opportunity did not arrive until 1949, when he was dispatched to Leningrad to liquidate the remnants of the Zhdanov group. In the middle 1940s, Andrei Zhdanov was considered Stalin's most likely successor, and Zhdanov apparently also considered himself the most likely to succeed.

Zhdanov died, but his group continued and established a more or less independent fief in Leningrad, where he had been all-powerful. Kozlov accepted the task of wiping out this group with especial pleasure, since the man who had ordered Kozlov's own arrest a decade before, Abakumov, was a member of the Leningrad faction. He had been Beria's number two man in the secret police and was instrumental in building the wartime *smersh,* "death to spies," counter-espionage and terror organization.

While rubbing out the Zhdanov remnants, including Abakumov, Kozlov incidentally made some strongly anti-Semitic speeches. This, unfortunately, is not likely to make a man unpopular with the party hierarchy. Kozlov proved handy to Khrushchev again during the downgrading of Malenkov, when he helped link the latter to the "plots" of the Leningrad faction.

He is a Great Russian, which means he does not belong to one of the minorities. He makes a nice appearance, dresses neatly, and has an agreeable speaking manner. Like Kirichenko, he is in his early fifties, and in the opinion of many observers, would make a good front man while the "heavies" in the back room decided who would be boss.

Reporters covering the visit of Vice-President Nixon to Russia in 1959 had a chance to notice how closely Kozlov has modeled himself on the Khrushchev pattern. His behavior at the ceremonies for Nixon's departure, which will be described in a later chapter, turned out to be especially memorable, displaying the same blend of affability and bluster which his boss has put to such effective use for five years.

Mikoyan and Suslov and Kozlov. This trio would seem to occupy the highest level next to that reserved for Khrushchev himself. Behind the top three, however, are several other men-on-the-make, even now terribly important in the Soviet setup—notably Aristov and Ignatov—and perhaps destined for greater glory in the shake-up sure to follow Khrushchev's death through purge or natural causes.

Who are these key lieutenants in the mighty bureaucratic army of Russia? They represent many diverse specialties, nationalities, and fields of endeavor.

Averky B. Aristov, for instance, is an industrial specialist who has been called the Henry Ford of Russia. He has been given most of the credit for the production of Soviet rockets and sputniks. The recent portion of his career can be charted right along the path of Russian progress in rocketry.

During the war Aristov was political boss of the Urals, Stalin's mountain industrial fortress. That is presumably where the first captive German scientists from Peenemunde and their V-1 and V-2 rockets were brought. He could also be found in Sverdlovsk, where the big Russian rockets were put into assembly-line production. From 1944 to 1950, he appeared as first Party Secretary at Krasnoyar, where one of the Soviet testing ranges is supposed to be located.

After Stalin's death, Aristov ran into serious difficulty. He was dropped from the Presidium when the new tribunes trimmed it from a bloated panel of twenty-five men to a serviceable one of ten members. He was also removed from his post as Party Secretary.

Furthermore, he split with Malenkov over what was to be the postwar emphasis in Russian industry. Malenkov wanted to increase the production of consumer goods. Aristov favored producing heavy machinery and war matériel, and to hell with shoes and overcoats.

In 1954 Aristov was sent to a place where he could appreciate the advantage of an overcoat: Khaborovsk. Khrushchev rescued him from his frozen oblivion and put him back in the Presidium. He is now fifty-seven and at present appears to be close to Khrushchev, who has used him for many confidential missions.

During the fifty-nine years of his life, heavy-set, shifty-eyed Nikolai G. Ignatov has had an up-and-down career. The son of a worker, he started from the bottom. He joined Trotsky's revolutionary army, then switched to Communist "organizing" —which is a Soviet euphemism for liquidating political enemies. Ignatov next became a member of the feared O.G.P.U., the secret police.

He was sent to liquidate the Basmacho movement, which had been agitating for independence in Soviet Turkestan. It was one of the first Red liquidations of a minority nation, later followed by genocide carried out against the Tartars and other Oriental tribes.

Having collected enough heads to prove his efficiency and loyalty, Ignatov was called back to Moscow to go through a series of "courses" given by the Central Committee. These are called "Leninist-Marxist Training Courses," but they are actually a system of brainwashing, where promising men undergo what could be called permanent mass hypnosis. They usually emerge as semifanatic servants of the party boss—Stalin then, Khrushchev later.

After graduation from this curious course, advance in the party hierarchy is generally rapid. Ignatov immediately became First Secretary of first one and then another regional party committee and was elevated to the Presidium in 1952. After Stalin's death, however, Malenkov decided to oust him, presumably because he had been too intensely loyal to Stalin. He was demoted to party work in Leningrad, then dropped even from that.

But Ignatov got his revenge against Malenkov, for he was drawn into the Khrushchev cabal that overthrew the Premier. And as a reward, Khrushchev allowed Ignatov to regain his place on the Presidium.

Today, Ignatov is in charge of party discipline and organization. He is believed to be as loyal to Khrushchev as he once was to Stalin, and is said to act as a sort of special watchdog for Khrushchev's interests against Kremlin and party intrigue.

A formerly high-ranking figure in Red councils is Nikolai I. Belyaev, known as the uncrowned King of Kazakhstan. (Once Serge Fliegers tried to send that description of him by cable from Moscow. The Soviet censor put a big black line through the word "King" and left the phrase, "Belyaev is the uncrowned of Kazakhstan," taking out a word offensive to true Bolsheviks but allowing the implication to remain.) The title is tribute to the work he did for Khrushchev's agricultural experiments in that province several years ago.

Belyaev was a troubleshooter for Khrushchev, a man whose methods were said to be nonetheless effective for being utterly ruthless. He joined the Communist Party in 1921, at the age of eighteen. He fought in the Red Army under Trotsky, then helped liquidate the Trotskyites for Stalin.

By Stalin's cruel code, the liquidators were usually liquidated in their turn, but Belyaev managed to lie low through the purge years. Not until after the war did he reappear in an important position, as Secretary of the Altai Krai committee in Central Asia.

His first really crucial job came in December, 1957. Khrushchev had gambled his prestige on the production of a bumper crop in the "Virgin Lands" of Kazakhstan. The gamble had failed, the crop had been miserable, and another bad year would open Khrushchev to serious and perhaps dangerous criticism.

He sent Belyaev to Kazakhstan. It is too much to suppose that Belyaev's fervor influenced the weather, but it did influence or frighten the *kolkhoz* members. In 1958, their Herculean labor from the dawn's early light until deep into the twilight brought in one of the finest harvests Russia ever had.

But in 1959, the peasants of Kazakhstan, even with the grim-faced Belyaev hovering over them, failed to duplicate their performance of the year before. The harvest was off considerably and Belyaev was publicly blamed for it by Khrushchev in a public dressing-down. The press repeated the party leader's blast, and Belyaev's career went into eclipse. Whether he can rehabilitate himself and regain his previous high rank is questionable.

Two other Presidium members deserve special mention because of their power and influence, although neither, for varying reasons, has any chance of becoming Khrushchev's successor.

The first of these is Leonid I. Brezhnev, a hatchet man. His particular hatchet work has been carried out within the armed services. During the war, he was one of the hated "political generals" who sat in rear-echlon headquarters and issued orders to "fight until death" to the front-line troops. During the defense of Nuorossisk, and later as head of the Eighteenth Army, poker-faced Brezhnev is said to have ordered hundreds of on-the-spot executions of "politically unreliable" soldiers and officers.

Khrushchev rescued Brezhnev from temporary eclipse and appointed him political supervisor of the Soviet Navy. Later he became top party watchdog over the Ministry of Defense. When things grew edgy in the Virgin Lands area, Khrushchev named him boss of Kazakhstan, a job he wrestled with for two years. In 1958, he was supplanted by Belyaev.

Brezhnev, now fifty-four, is heartily disliked by his Presidium colleagues. He, nonetheless, has his uses to Khrushchev, and derives considerable power from that fact.

The only woman member of the Presidium, Ekaterina A. Furtseva, cannot be considered a glamor girl by Western standards, but there is a group of Soviet students who claim she is something of a *femme fatale* of Kremlin intrigues. It is hard to imagine that relations between the motherly Madam Furtseva and Nikita Khrushchev could be anything but businesslike, yet a few historians contend she owes her present prominence to a youthful liaison with the rising party leader. Her career has indeed zoomed along with Khrushchev's, and he unquestionably trusts her and counts on her support at critical moments.

Furtseva first met the dynamic little man from the Ukraine in 1937, when she was studying chemistry at Moscow's Lomonosov Institute. She is said to have become, not long after, the protégée of Nikolai Bulganin when he was party boss of the Moscow district. Bulganin appointed her propaganda chief in his branch.

During World War II, she quickly rose to become Secretary of the *raion,* or "district." She also managed to get a part-time job in charge of political agitation in the armed services, which permitted her to continue her association with Nikita Khrushchev.

Furtseva is supposed to have been a great help to Khrushchev in the "anti-party" clash of 1957, through alleged influence with Dmitri Shepilov and Marshal Zhukov. At any rate, she has always come down hard on the side of her old Ukrainian friend.

Furtseva was born in 1910, and is better looking and dresses better than the average feminine Communist. Her husband, Vladimir Firyubin, has occupied several top diplomatic posts, among them Ambassador to Yugoslavia. He returned to Moscow in 1959 and became Vice-Minister of Foreign Affairs, dealing mostly with the inter-Red-bloc matters.

Furtseva also deals with Soviet relations in the satellite nations, and has done public-relations work among the Communists in Western Europe. A few years ago she visited France for the Bastille Day celebration in company with her Presidium colleague, Mikhail Pervukhin. She displayed her independence by abandoning the sour-faced Pervukhin at the Russian Embassy, and going out with some young French Communists. She danced in the streets and had a jolly good time.

Three older Presidium types, Voroshilov, Kuusinen, and Shvernik, are thought by some to have slight advisory influence on the strong-willed Khrushchev. Their positions are largely ceremonial—old Marshal Voroshilov is nominally head of state —and they usually play figurehead roles. One little-written-about but interesting Kremlin figure is Nuritdin Mukhitdinov, an Asian Moslem. While on tours through the Middle East and Asia, Mukhitdinov adheres closely to the precepts of Mohammedanism, praying toward Mecca five times daily and ostentatiously unfurling his prayer rug. He is known to have been in New Delhi only a few days before President Eisenhower's visit in 1959, and then departed for Indonesia, where he may have played a role in setting up Khrushchev's visit to Southeast Asia in the spring of 1960.

Whatever one's estimate of Khrushchev's underlings, good or bad, capable or incompetent, it's possible to develop a grudging respect for them, if you come in contact with almost any of the cowed proconsuls of the empire in the satellite countries. They make the Russian cadres shine by comparison. For instance, consider the audience which the Hearst team had with East German Communist leader Walter Ulbricht in April, 1958. Ulbricht is a frightened little party hack who looks like Ben Turpin with Comrade Lenin's goatee, and makes no impression whatever.

We went to interview this cut-rate Red leader in the wake of an interview with Konrad Adenauer. Cars were still being searched in those days as they entered the East sector from West Berlin. The driver of the car just ahead of us, as we passed through the Brandenburg Gate, was stopped and forced to get out and open his baggage for inspection. But we, accompanied by Jeremy Main of INS Berlin, were permitted to proceed quickly after a green-coated East German policeman had queried our chauffeur. Apparently we were expected.

The first pause behind Berlin's Iron Curtain was at Joseph Goebbels' old Propaganda Ministry, now commanded by Ulbrich's publicity man, a fat and resolutely hospitable German Communist named Kurt Blecha. Blecha had a gold-toothed smile and a girl interpreter with a streak in her black hair to match. She called him *Chef*.

When Goebbels was in charge of the same building the decor was fairly posh. Now it was immersed in the dim brownout which appears to be high fashion all over the Communist world.

Blecha had an unnerving suggestion at the start. He said, "Why don't you stay a month or two and have a good look around East Germany?" When there was absolutely no reply, he looked nervously at his watch and snapped, "Mr. Ulbricht will now see you at Central Committee headquarters." He led us through the chilled building to the street. His girl told Conniff and Considine, in her officious English, "The two *chefs* will go

in the first car." Blecha and Hearst climbed into the back seat
of a Zim, a Russian-built Buick, circa 1941. Conniff and Considine rode in a shabbier car, and the little procession made its
way across the ravaged, empty, listless city.

"Look at the two *chefs* up there," Conniff nodded at the heads
in the rear window of the Zim ahead. "Probably cooking up
a new *soufflé*."

You could blast a shotgun down some of the streets of this
shopworn showcase of Khrushchev's empire and never pink a
soul. The tiles were already beginning to peel off the facings of
the mile or two of buildings the Russians had ordered built on
both sides of Stalinallee, whose occasional arcades still reveal
the awesome vomit of Mars.

The scene in Ulbricht's conference room resembled a Communist courtroom decorated for a propaganda trial. Two large
conference tables were arranged into a T. Cameras and lights
were in place as we entered. Plainly, Khrushchev's German
stooges regarded the interview as potential "proof" that they
and their government warranted recognition in the West.

The top German Communist stood at the top of the T. He
was a short man who squints uncertainly through rimless glasses
as if momentarily expecting to be slapped. His gray business
suit was of the shapeless cut that Khrushchev tacitly endorsed before meeting an Italian tailor. His tie was tomato red with two
diagonal yellow stripes. On both tables were microphones, plat-
ters of cigars and cigarettes, and open bottles of seltzer water.
The Red *fuehrer* was all but lost in the room. To his left and
down the side of the T stretched a number of his associates. One,
an owlish little man, grinned sheepishly at Conniff and Considine, who had covered his exposure years earlier in the American Communist Party, and his later flight from the country. It
was Gerhard Eisler.

Ulbricht came around his table, followed by the others, and all shook hands with us with great pumping motions. The newsreel cameras whirred. Ulbricht and his team took their places again. He cleared his throat and in his high-pitched voice delivered a statement in German. When he finished, a towering, red-haired German girl interpreter, leaned between Hearst and Conniff like a falling coat rack and said on Ulbricht's behalf, "I have received certain questions from you, and have been pleased to answer them. You will now receive my answers."

With this, one of the Communist small fry handed each of us a twenty-four-page document. Ulbricht beamed as if the interview was over.

It wasn't. A few questions produced an absolutely unintelligible harangue against the West. As it progressed, the lights began to go out. Even the cameramen recognized the gathering catastrophe. Ulbricht bumbled on and on, finally comparing himself to Abraham Lincoln.

Hearst stopped him at that point. "Just a moment," he said. "I thought Abraham Lincoln was on *our* side."

Eisler burst out laughing, which didn't do Ulbricht's cause much good. Somehow, he got his speech under way again, plunging into a roundhouse attack on the Adenauer government. He complained that West Germany was equipped with atomic weapons, whereas East Germany was defenseless and asked only for peace.

"That's odd," Conniff said. "Khrushchev himself told us that the Red Army has the best equipment in the world, including the latest atomic weapons. The Red Army is here in East Germany. . . ."

"I don't believe . . . it is not true . . . that there are atomic weapons in East Germany," Ulbricht protested.

There was a pause.

"Are you calling Comrade Khrushchev a liar?" Considine asked quietly.

There was a fluttering of hands, a whitening of cheeks, an almost pitiable confusion of protests and denials, as if the room were "bugged," which it might well have been.

And then, as if to punctuate the interview, the last camera light blinked out.

CHAPTER 7

Khrushchev and Red China

At the present moment, it would seem that more holds Russian and Chinese communism together than tends to tear it apart. They need each other, and will continue to need each other for some time to come. But Red China is an ally with ideas of its own, run by a tough-fibred man who considers himself the senior statesman of world communism. This and other differences in the fields of ideology, human nature, and power politics are latent weaknesses in the house of International Communism. And as the gales and storms of the approaching years shake the ground upon which it is built, these structural stresses will take on greater significance.

The first person we can recall predicting this rift in the alliance between Russia, and its possible consequences, was that grand old man of Western statesmanship, Sir Winston Churchill. What makes his foresight so astonishing is that it goes all the way back to 1955, when the link between the nations never seemed stronger.

The occasion of Sir Winston's remarks was a visit we paid

him following our first visit to Russia in 1955. He sipped a whisky-and-soda and puffed on one of his familiar cigars as we discussed our recent experiences. He questioned us on all angles of the new Russian leadership. We told him, among other things, how Khrushchev had offered to act as intermediary between China and the West over the then-explosive issue of the Formosa Strait. Sir Winston said that he looked for developing tensions within the Russian-Chinese alliance to ease the pressure on the West.

"I'm not talking about the immediate future," he said, "I'm talking about thirty or even forty or fifty years hence. That's not too long a time as history goes. It seems reasonable to me that friction with its Chinese ally might ultimately turn Russia toward the West. And if Russia ever does turn toward the West, we should be ready to receive her."

At that time the theory was fashionable that we should rather try to wean Red China from Russia; and Sir Winston was the first one we had heard who put it the other way around.

During our visit to Moscow with Vice-President Nixon in 1959, we asked several top-ranking Western diplomats, competent authorities of the Soviet Union about the state of the alliance with China. To our amazement, the Moscow experts questioned only the thirty-to-fifty-year span of the estimate by Churchill. They claimed that the Russians were indeed concerned about Red China, not as of some distant date in an uncertain future, but as of right now.

Friction is already developing in Chinese-Soviet relations, according to these experts, and it is bound to increase. There are 4,000 miles of open border between the two allies, and the Russians know that the booming Chinese birth rate sooner or later will require more space. The population pressure north-northwestward into Siberia is even now being felt, according to these experts.

They point to the fact that 40 per cent of the latest Soviet expansion program is being invested in Siberia. The reason: not simply to develop the resources of the area, but also to fill the land before the Chinese move in. The Russians fear that the Red Chinese will first drift into the Siberian spaces as casual laborers, much like our "wetbacks" from Mexico. Then would come the building of Chinese-populated areas, so that large areas of Siberia would become Chinese-dominated.

And on the personal level, the Russian and Chinese temperaments simply do not mix. The Chinese are frankly contemptuous of the Russians, believing that their own long cultural and historical background puts them many degrees above the sweaty citizens of Russia.

This veiled dislike is apparent when Chinese Communist delegations invade the Soviet Union. In contrast to Americans and Russians, who seem to hit it off personally, regardless of ideological differences, the cold, impassive Orientals and their effervescent Russian comrades have a prefabricated personality clash.

These Chinese Communists, peering down their noses at primitive Russia, are proudly aware of China's own centuries-old culture and historical position in Asia. What few Americans realize is that Chinese power has run in cycles through the centuries and that a particularly low ebb in the eighteenth and nineteenth centuries coincided with the expansionist surge of the Western nations. The British, French, and to a limited extent, Americans moved into an area ripe for the taking. But this mighty giant would not remain forever prostrate. As Napoleon said ominously, "Let China sleep. She will eat us all when she wakes."

Yet generations of Americans have swallowed stereotypes of the Chinese, thinking of them only as laundrymen, jugglers, and waiters—people who all in all were not to be taken very seriously. But they are now being taken very seriously all over the world. It is doubtful if many non-Chinese Asians, more familiar with the nation's past, have ever succumbed to the illusion that China would remain forever helpless. Chinese Communist leaders are no more inclined to show any humility toward their Russian elders than the aloof students and training missions they send to Moscow. On the theoretical level, Mao Tse-tung has dubbed himself senior statesman in the Communist world. Now and again the memory must rankle of how lightly Stalin treated his chances of defeating Chiang. For once in his life, Stalin admitted that he was wrong and somebody else was right.

"It is true we also have made mistakes," he told a Yugoslav delegation during a temporary *rapprochement* with this unruly satellite in the late forties. "For instance, after the war we invited the Chinese comrades to come to Moscow, and we discussed the situation in China. We told them bluntly we considered the uprising in China had no prospects, that the Chinese Communists should reach a *modus vivendi* with Chiang Kai-shek, and that they should join the Chiang Kai-shek government and dissolve their army.

"The Chinese comrades agreed here in Moscow with the views of their Soviet comrades, but went back to China and acted quite otherwise. They mustered their forces, organized their armies, and now, as you see, they are beating Chiang Kai-shek's army.

It is not unlikely their future historians will deem the Korean war the turning point in Red China's relationship with the rest of the world—Communist as well as Western. Mao and his ambitious cohorts would pose no threat to N.S. Khrushchev if China had not emerged with tremendous stature from the test at arms against UN troops. The American forces and their UN allies covered themselves with glory in that bitter conflict, but

Red China gained credit for the courage of its troops, and prestige from the stalemate which resulted.

It may seem curious, but it is significant that Chiang Kai-shek's Nationalists on Formosa were deeply and favorably impressed by the performance of Chinese Communist troops in Korea. When Conniff came to Formosa from Korea in the spring of 1951, Chiang's officers could barely suppress their pride in the Chinese army which had fought the United States and its allies to a standstill.

"Pretty good troops, aren't they?" they'd say with just a hint of malice. "You're finding out they're pretty good, isn't that true?" It was only too true. They were Chinese fighting men, and in one sense it mattered little that they happened to be Communists.

Mao's legions have been on the prowl ever since, periodically bringing the Formosa Strait cauldron to a boil, moving ruthlessly into Tibet and violating the borders of India, and generally menacing their neighbors. It is just possible Khrushchev may sometimes wish we had put his upstart ally in its place when the opportunity arose.

This is the word a keen observer of Asian politics used to describe Red China's entrance into the Korean war: an "opportunity." When we talked with him on Formosa in the spring of 1956, Karl Rankin, Ambassador to Nationalist China, did not attempt to define what the UN's conduct should have been. He drily remarked, however, that it was an "opportunity" to deal with rampant Chinese expansion that Mao might not provide again.

A decade after its outbreak, the Korean war still smolders with controversy and it is still impossible for most Americans to view it objectively. Korea was an emotional experience which left living scar tissue on the memory of anyone who came close to the crucible. Even the name evokes a chord of sadness, a tremor of regret, a pang of melancholy induced by the feeling of unfulfillment. The enigmatic figure of General Douglas Mac-Arthur automatically closes ranks to one side or the other of the recurrent debate, and argument about the man obscures evaluation of his policies. His advocacy of more extended warfare against China becomes mixed up in his conflict with President Truman and the question of a general's responsibility to his commander-in-chief.

An extended discussion of the Korean controversy has no place here. We will say only that a more decisive military setback for Communist China might well have cowed some of Mao's obstreperousness since. At the same time, the risks which our nation faced in that period are well summed up in a candid remark which former President Truman once made to Conniff.

"Frank," he said, "World War III could have started in Korea if we handled it wrong. Just a spark in the wrong place and the whole world could have been at war, and atomic war at that."

We had a chance to view the positive side of the Russian Chinese alliance during our visit to Moscow in 1957. In particular, we saw how Mao provided welcome support to Khrushchev in keeping the satellite countries in line.

Mao's presence was conspicuous in Moscow during the fortieth anniversary of the October revolution. At the glittering celebration in St. George's Hall in the Kremlin, he clearly outshone the Kadars, the Gomulkas, the Ho Chi-minhs, and other princes of the proletariat. As we related earlier, Mao and Khrushchev entered the stalls of the Bolshoi after *Swan Lake* had begun, and took seats one row behind us. When the audience spotted his beaming moon face, they gave Mao a rousing reception. The Russians evidently liked the gesture of the two leaders joining them on the orchestra floor instead of closeting themselves in the Royal Box above, where only Mikoyan now sat in lonely Bolshevik splendor.

The warm and respectful reception given him unquestionably pleased Mao. At any rate, he took the lead in signing a 30,000-word Manifesto of Principles which the Russian Communists released with great fanfare at the height of the celebration. He also paid effusive tribute to his Soviet hosts.

The Yugoslavs, alone among the Communist bloc, refrained from signing this rambling compendium of clichés. Tito had already given warning of his intentions when he canceled his scheduled appearance at the celebration, pleading a backache— one of the first diplomatic backaches in history. When Serge Fliegers asked the Yugoslav Ambassador why his country had failed to go along, he shrugged his shoulders. "Because we didn't agree with it," he said. "That's all. We didn't agree with it."

This gesture of independence touched off a savage ideological debate the following spring. Mao exceeded all others in the fury of his denunciations of the Communist country which failed to follow Moscow's lead. His performance must have given profound satisfaction to Khrushchev. For, while Tito is apparently capable of brushing off the vituperation of his supposed masters, the other satellites are more impressed by these blasts and tend to watch their step.

Since 1957, however, there have been developments in China, well calculated to alarm a Communist ally whose present policy is peaceful coexistence. India and Burma, neutral nations which hoped to soothe the tiger, now feel the thrust of Chinese imperialism at their borders. Indonesia, which once seemed impressed with the blandishments of the Reds, is now threatened and harassed for its repressive policies against a large Chinese population whose loyalty seems to turn toward China. Throughout Southeast Asia, as a matter of fact, agitators from Red China are at work among the clannish communities of alien Chinese.

Some observers believe Khrushchev is even now seeking a *rapprochement* with the West, against the inevitable day when his ambitious Chinese neighbor becomes a nuclear power. When the latter happens, the balance of strength in the Communist empire will be destroyed. Peiping, with its seemingly infinite reserves of manpower, could conceivably become the capital of world communism. One can surmise that at present there is little reason for the Soviet Union to help its Asian ally gain such frightening power. The U.S.S.R. has been at the top of the Marxist mountain for many years, and this is one aspect of the *status quo* which the Kremlin wants to keep unchanged.

Khrushchev seems to be trying to build a bridge of understanding back to the West—always based on the premise that Russia would not disgorge any of the areas conquered by the Red Army in World War II. At present Khrushchev is at a climax in his long diplomatic campaign for big-power talks. Whether his protestations of "peace and friendship" will survive the tough bargaining that looms ahead is moot.

In both Moscow and Peiping it is recognized that the two big Communist nations are at separate stages of their so-called Marxist development. The Kremlin must take a tolerant view of some Red Chinese excesses, in view of its own checkered past, and the Red Chinese are evidently loath to accept much paternal advice from the older member of the Communist family. This variation in historical development together with a marked difference in national temperament, could well be the wedge that splits the two powers apart.

At any rate, an unprecedented event took place late in 1959 which illuminates current frictions in the Communist camp. A Soviet diplomat at Geneva summoned several Western reporters to an informal press conference and, obviously acting on instructions from the Kremlin, he made known Moscow's discomfort over deteriorating relations between Peiping and New Delhi. The diplomat plainly disassociated the Kremlin from the hard line of the Chinese. He implied that Mao's government was acting independently and had disregarded the advice of the Russians. This underlined Sir Winston Churchill's prediction four years before, that Soviet Russia might look toward Europe for help and understanding in dealing with Red China.

And it underlines also a prediction made to us by another venerable figure of Western diplomacy. Chancellor Adenauer, in an interview in April, 1958, forcefully emphasized the future threat of Communist China to the Kremlin's long-term plans.

"Mark my words," he said, wagging his finger like an elderly schoolmaster, "the problem of Red China is the decisive problem for the Soviet Union. It will decisively affect Russian policy, if not tomorrow, then in ten years. Russia would be quite happy if she had nothing to fear on her eastern borders."

He called attention to Red China's enormous yearly birth rate of nearly 12 million and compared Russia's 208 million population with China's 600 million.

"Red China must unload this population somewhere, and she can only unload in the direction of the Soviet Union," the Chancellor said. "This will turn out to be the Achilles heel of Soviet Russia."

CHAPTER 8

Mr. Nixon goes to Russia

The Hearst team's third trip to the Soviet Union was in 1959, as members of the corps of reporters that covered the tour of Vice-President Richard M. Nixon. Our part in this historic visit began with an informal interlude. Nixon invited Hearst, Conniff, and Considine to lunch with him in Washington. He wanted a reporters' view of Khrushchev, in addition to the reports given to him by the State Department.

"Watch out for him," Nixon was advised. "He's tough as nails, smart, and has a surprising sense of humor. He's an able politician. He's never easy to tag in an argument and never at a loss for the right statistic. He has a wealth of information of all sorts at his fingertips. You'd better bone up on figures for trade, agriculture, mining, natural resources, and every other subject you come across."

Nixon was plainly impressed.

"Anything else?" he asked.

"Yes," Considine said. "Bone up on American proverbs. He'll have a Russian proverb for every possible topic, and he

187

believes that these proverbs not only sum up all his arguments, but win them for him. You'd better get yourself some proverbs of your own, preferably from Lincoln or Franklin, or people like that."

"Well, I'll be damned," Nixon said, and made a note on the back of an envelope.

In the days leading up to his departure, the Vice President and those who were to accompany him either aboard the brand-new government jet or on the press plane—Pan American's first 707s—were subjected to a foretaste of Soviet bureaucracy.

Obstacles of every shape, size, and description were suddenly strewn in the Vice President's path. Only two weeks before the scheduled date of departure, the United States Embassy in Moscow was informed that Nixon would not be permitted to leave the U.S.S.R. via Siberia as planned. He had wanted to return home by way of Alaska. Furthermore, his requests for Kremlin approval to visit particular places he wanted to see, together with inquiries about the type of aircraft he would be allotted inside the borders of the Soviet Union, went unanswered.

The visas of the newsmen were still being held up by the Soviet Embassy in Washington a week before departure. No word had come from the Russians on censorship restrictions, or on the use of phones, cables, and radio circuits. Nixon did not know whether he would be permitted to bring along an interpreter, nor whether a joint statement would be issued after his interview with Khrushchev. The Vice President told Hearst that it was his intention not to release any part of his talk with Khrushchev unless the Russian Premier also gave out his own version of what transpired.

At the last possible minute, more or less, the whole project took shape and substance. Nixon and his party, including his wife, the President's brother Milton Eisenhower, Vice-Admiral

Hyman Rickover, head of our nuclear submarine program, and George V. Allen, head of the United States Information Agency, flew to Moscow overnight from Washington on July 22 and 23 with a fuel stop at Iceland. The bigger press plane flew non-stop from New York to Moscow in eight hours and forty-five minutes, the first such flight.

Khrushchev himself arrived at the airport from Poland only twenty minutes before Nixon's plane landed, but did not wait for Nixon. Officially, Nixon was paying a visit to his opposite number, Deputy Premier Frol Koslov, and the latter was assigned to greet the American Vice President.

Koslov and his subordinate dignitaries, as well as the press delegation, were in position and waiting expectantly, but otherwise there were scarcely two hundred persons at the airport as the Nixons stepped down from their plane into the brilliant sunshine, as Soviet and American flags whipped in the brisk breeze. Muscovites had read in that day's *Pravda* that Nixon would arrive, but the arrival hour was not given, and the obscurity of the item itself tacitly instructed the people to stay away.

The first of Nixon's brushes with Soviet methods began early Friday morning, July 24. Rested from his trip, he ventured out of Spaso House for a walk, accompanied by a Secret Service man. The latter brought along a home movie camera. The press, including the Hearst team, unfortunately missed the incident that followed.

Apparently Nixon and his companion soon found themselves window-shopping at Moscow's Danilovsky "open market." Nixon stepped inside and sought out the manager. He was recognized in short order, and all work in the place halted. Several of the Russian marketmen could speak English, and served as voluntary interpreters as he chatted with the employees and shoppers, asking them questions, inquiring about prices and the like. The Secret Service man took some pictures. Nixon signed autographs.

The crowd warmed to Nixon's informal manner. Eventually, one booth-keeper remarked, "We know your American Exhibition in Sokolniki Park will be outstanding. But we are sorry to say we have no tickets for admission." The man's dejected tone and somewhat ragged appearance touched Nixon.

"How many of you would like to go to the Exhibition?" Nixon asked. There was an excited buzz, and one of the English-speaking Russians finally spoke up and said, "There are two hundred of us who wish to go."

"How much are the tickets?" Nixon asked.

"One ruble each."

He reached in his pocket, then laughed. He had no Russian money. "You have any Russian money on you?" he asked the Secret Service man. The latter took out a 100 ruble note.

But the crowd around the Americans suddenly laughed and shook their heads. A Russian explained that they had the money to buy the tickets, but that there were just no tickets to be bought. Russian authorities had confined the ticket sale to 30,000 a day, although in the opinion of the American builders of the Exhibition, its grounds and exhibits could handle twice that number.

"I see," Nixon said. "Well, something ought to be done about that. Don't worry; I'll see to it personally that there are tickets for everyone here in the market."

The Russians applauded. *"Mir vo vsem mire!"* ("Peace for the whole world!") Nixon called out as he left the place. There was more applause.

But the next day's *Moscow News,* a tabloid published in the English language whose essential purpose seems to be to needle foreign visitors, carried a bitter and distorted account of the scene by one of the market employees. According to this story, Nixon set up the entire scene and brought along "photographers" to take pictures which would be sent back to the capitalistic press. These would supposedly depict Nixon giving money to "poor" Russian workers. It was even charged that the "photographers" took pictures only of the more ragged shoppers.

This ridiculous falsification made Nixon madder than anything else that happened during his stay.

That day of his visit to the Danilovsky market proved to be the busiest of his eleven-day stay. And certainly the most hectic.

Unaware that the visit to the market would become an "incident," Nixon returned to Spaso House, had breakfast, and, accompanied by the press representatives, was driven to the Kremlin. Here he exchanged a few perfunctory greetings in the office of Klimenti E. Voroshilov, the puppet president, and then he was led into Khrushchev's office.

Khrushchev stood his ground in the middle of the room and sized up Nixon with a characteristic visual frisk as the taller man approached. Khrushchev wore a baggy gray suit, with a decoration dangling from the right lapel, to which Nixon's dark, well-tailored business suit was in marked contrast.

They shook hands, and Khrushchev waved him to a chair. But he himself remained standing. He bounced over to his desk and returned with a sphere the size of a baseball.

"What's that?" Nixon asked.

Khrushchev looked at him, and at last replied proudly, "Our Sputnik."

Plainly, Khrushchev was determined that all subsequent talk with the Vice President would proceed from acceptance of this point of Soviet superiority.

After half an hour's conversation, which Nixon was somehow able to keep general, the two left the Kremlin in Khru-

shchev's Zis (actually, at this stage of Soviet history called a
Zil—the *l* for Lenin where the *s* had stood for Stalin). Behind
police guards from both nations they were sped to a preview of
the American Exhibition especially arranged for Khrushchev.
What followed made headlines around the world.

To get the best coverage of the scene, the Hearst team had
split up, and, like the other American newsmen, were scattered
at strategic points around the exhibition grounds. And so it
happened that Considine was present at the beginning of the
noisy brace of debates which established the vigorous, conten-
tious atmosphere of the remainder of the visit.

Khrushchev and Nixon stepped out of their limousine and
were joined by other Russian dignitaries. One of these was
Aanastas Mikoyan. Khrushchev, by now wearing a white, light-
weight summer hat, called for Mikoyan to join him, and introduced the Soviet trade specialist to the Vice President.

"Oh, yes," Nixon said, shaking hands, "I met Mr. Mikoyan
when he was in Washington." He then added to Khrushchev
(while an interpreter buzzed quietly in the Premier's ear), "In
the United States, we have great respect for Mr. Mikoyan's
ability as a trader. Everybody in our country recognizes Ar-
menians as the greatest of traders."

It was an opening Khrushchev had apparently been waiting
for. "Then your country has forgotten how to trade," he
snapped, "because Mikoyan could not make a single trade while
he was there."

Nixon's amiable smile subsided as the translation came
through. He saw Considine and John Daly of the American
Broadcasting Company standing nearby.

"Maybe I shouldn't have gotten into that," he said to them
quietly. Then, recovering his mood of affable hospitality, he
ushered Khrushchev and his party—Voroshilov, Mikoyan, Kozlov, and Yuri Zhukov—to the grounds.

The first stop was the exhibit of R.C.A.'s closed-circuit color TV and Ampex video tape. Nixon's only intention was to display to the Russian leader what he believed would be an exhibit of great interest, not only the color monitor showing them on camera, but also the running of the color tape immediately after the live performance.

Khrushchev had other ideas. He noticed a patently enthusiastic audience of Russians looking down on him from a gallery on all four sides of the small, brightly lighted studio. He was sure also that the program would be seen in the United States. As far as he was concerned, this was no time to bandy small talk about United States electronic ingenuity.

Nixon attempted to describe the color TV and the video tape system. Khrushchev was not interested. He said abruptly that the Soviet Union possessed such boons, if they could be called that. He then launched into an unexpected and heated dissertation on America's foreign bases, claimed that Russia was pulling its own troops out of occupied territories, and accused the United States of fomenting trouble in Berlin.

Surprised, and fully aware of the dangers of making off-the-cuff remarks on policy matters, Nixon tried to steer the conversation back to the topic of color TV. But Khrushchev would not hear him. He interrupted, and, to occasional sharp applause from adherents in the galleries, took the offensive again. America, he said, was dragging its feet in the matter of trading with Russia, cultural exchanges, and general recognition of the Soviet Union as an equal. He began waving his finger under Nixon's nose.

Nixon repeatedly sought to reply, but each time he was rebuffed. He stood in public, indeed before a TV camera, with the rough little Premier pounding out pronouncements more suited for a high-level summit meeting than a trade fair.

Nixon finally made a bold decision. He jabbed a finger under

Khrushchev's chin and said, quite sharply, "Now just a moment. You're trying to dominate this talk. From the way
you're trying to dominate it, you would've made a good
lawyer."

Khrushchev sputtered a denial, but Nixon had his footing
now. He lectured the older man pointedly on the danger of
issuing "ultimatums." He advised him to dismiss from his mind
any idea that when and if there was ever a top-level conference
he, Khrushchev, would find that he could have his own way.
"You don't know everything," he added bluntly.

"Who is giving ultimatums?" Khrushchev shouted.

Nixon answered that this was hardly the time and the place
to get into such a debate.

"Since you raised the question while people are listening,"
said Khrushchev, waving his arm at the TV cameras, "why
not now?" The Russians in the galleries applauded loudly. Then
he calmed down somewhat and apologized for having raised
his voice and for being inhospitable.

Nixon turned to an interpreter and smiled. "Tell him not to
worry," he said. "Tell him I've been insulted by experts."

Khrushchev then returned to the fray. Would this exchange
be broadcast in the United States?

Nixon assured him that it would.

"It will be edited so that it will hardly be recognizable," Khrushchev said flatly.

"It will be played just as it has been done here," Nixon said.
"I give you my word on that." He made the statement without
authority, but with the sure instinct that the networks would
be delighted to televise such an exchange.

"But will it be shown to the Russian people?" he asked
Khrushchev. The scattering of Americans in the gallery now
had their chance to applaud.

Khrushchev waved the challenge aside. "Of course," he

said. "If you show it, we'll show it. But I have reason to worry about how much of it you will show. You suppress."

Nixon blazed. "We suppress! Listen, for every word you print in your papers from a speech by our President, we print a hundred words of your speeches." There was another rattle of applause from the Americans overhead.

"So you will show it all?" Khrushchev asked.

"Of course we will," Nixon said, restraining his anger.

Khrushchev grinned under the hat he had worn through the entire exchange.

"Shake," he said. He raised his right hand over his head and brought it down resoundingly into Nixon's outstretched hand.

They watched part of the tape, then marched arm in arm through thickets of reporters and cameramen to the Pepsi-Cola exhibit, where the once-hard-drinking Premier downed a soft drink, and proceeded on to the model American home.

There, outside the railed-off kitchen, Khrushchev renewed his attack on United States policies, as if stung by Nixon's retaliatory efforts at the R.C.A. exhibit. It started with a mild exchange over American productivity but Khrushchev was soon vigorously accusing Nixon of calling him a dictator. While tempers had mounted, Nixon had interrupted one long Khrushchev harangue with the pointed observation that, "in our Senate we would call you a filibusterer." A few minutes later Khrushchev interrupted a prolonged Nixon statement by saying to the crowd, "Who is filibustering now?"

The angry exchange about dictatorship emerged from a misunderstanding by Khrushchev of a Nixon statement that no major power should try to "dictate" to any other nation "from a position of strength." Khrushchev would not listen to the Vice President's efforts to correct this misunderstanding, but accused Nixon of threatening him. Before Nixon could reply, Khrushchev continued angrily:

"We will answer your threats with threats. We have means at our disposal which can have very bad consequences for you."

Nixon was at the end of his patience. He poked Khrushchev in the chest.

"We have, too," he said.

Khrushchev would not be topped.

"But ours are better," he said.

And so it went for nearly an hour. When they emerged and Khrushchev saw the crowd of Russians outside the model house, his moon face was suddenly wreathed in a knowing smile. "Meet some Soviet 'slaves,' " he said jovially to Nixon. They plowed a furrow through the crowd and Khrushchev's mood brightened as he progressed.

Hearst had witnessed the foregoing exchange from the crowd surrounding the house. Nixon spotted him and beckoned him over. He started to introduce Hearst to Khrushchev, but the Premier immediately recognized him.

"Ah, my capitalist friend," he said, shaking hands. "The American newspaper monopolist."

Within one hour of their heated exchange, Nixon was impressed by another side of Khrushchev. The Premier, as versatile as a chameleon racing across a patchwork quilt, proved a gracious, attentive host at a luncheon in honor of the Nixons.

Before sundown, however, Khrushchev made a brief effort to rejoin the issue. He appeared at the formal raising of the American flag at the fair, late that day. He still apparently had more he wanted to say—certainly more than was contained in the bland speech he had prepared for the occasion.

As Nixon delivered his own talk, and an interpreter relayed it in Russian to Khrushchev, the Premier took sudden exception to some assertion in it. He shifted in his chair near the speaker's lectern and called out something in Russian to Nixon.

Nixon stopped his speech just long enough to turn to

Khrushchev, look at him impatiently, and bark, "I have the floor! You can speak when your time comes."

It was the parting thrust of a day which had seen Nixon venture forth into the streets of Moscow with credentials which President Eisenhower had defined as "really an exchange of visits between Mr. Kozlov and Mr. Nixon. It is a good-will gesture, and we wanted to have a prominent American to officiate at the opening of our exhibit."

But it had developed into something quite different. Khrushchev had come face to face with the highest-ranking American official he had confronted since taking over. He evidently proposed to test that American to the limit. What he forgot, or perhaps never knew, was that he had picked on a modern master of politics.

Meanwhile, the other Americans in Moscow were meeting with the same baffling combination of conciliation and bluster, cooperation and hostility. Even as Khrushchev was toasting the Nixons and peace on earth, and calling for more exchanges between the two peoples, over 150 American books were removed—at Russian demand—from the book exhibit at the United States Fair. Most of them contained critical references to communism, but others were not concerned with this subject or with the Soviet Union.

A single roll of tape made of the debate in front of the R.C.A. cameras was shipped out immediately, but all the other film taken that Friday by both newsreel and still-photographers was impounded. It had already been loaded in the hold of the Pan American press plane, which was returning to New York to be put in regular service, when Russian customs men and police came aboard and gave Pan Am President Juan Trippe, who was returning with the plane, his choice of surrendering either the film or his passport. The film was taken off and returned to the press room in the Hotel Ukraina where, regardless of the anguished cries of the cameramen, it remained for forty-eight hours.

At the Telegraph Office, resident American correspondents groaned at the strange double standard imposed by the censors. Whatever these regular reporters wrote or attempted to transmit by radio was rigidly scanned as never before. Their stories and scripts were returned to them with all but the innocuous or complimentary gruffly stricken out. But the newsmen traveling with Nixon were permitted to send out the frankest kind of criticism, and no limitations were placed on what they broadcast.

Some American correspondents hoped wistfully that this unprecedented leniency might prove contagious, and might become regular procedure after the visiting newsmen departed. They were soon disillusioned. Hearst and Conniff remained briefly in Moscow after Nixon flew to Warsaw en route to Washington. A story Conniff filed a few hours after Nixon's departure arrived in New York so cut and garbled that it consisted of hardly half-a-dozen incoherent sentences. Editor Milton Kaplan cabled back, "Received your byline. Please send story."

Khrushchev, always a man full of surprises, abruptly revised the plans for his formal talk with Nixon. The Vice President had presumed it would be a quiet exchange of views behind closed doors. His main concern was whether Khrushchev might unilaterally release his interpretation of what was said.

On Saturday afternoon, July 25, Khrushchev sent word to Nixon that he wished the Vice President and Mrs. Nixon to spend the night as guests of himself and his wife. The Nixons instantly accepted and had just finished packing when the Khrushchevs arrived at Spaso House for a state dinner. The Nixons left shortly thereafter, expecting to be taken to the large home the Khrushchevs have in Lenin Hills, not far from the University. Instead, the Russian chauffeur sped them to Khrushchev's *dacha,* set in a pleasant area of woods and lakes about thirty miles outside Moscow. Here a large staff of servants greeted them and showed them to their quarters.

No, a major-domo informed them, the Khrushchevs would not be there. They would come tomorrow. The puzzled American couple were forced to turn down a huge dinner the staff had prepared for them, and turned in.

Khrushchev and his wife arrived at 1 P.M. Sunday, at the head of a virtual expeditionary force. With them were Mikoyan and his wife, Mr. and Mrs. Kozlov, and assorted interpreters, aides, and advisers. Bringing up the rear came United States Ambassador Llewellyn Thompson and the President's brother, Dr. Milton Eisenhower. The Nixons met the congregation at the front door.

"Were you comfortable?" Khrushchev asked briskly.

The Nixons politely maintained they had never had a more comfortable night.

"You know, it's hard to believe that this place is only a half an hour outside of Moscow," Nixon said. "It takes our President two hours or more to drive to his retreat at Camp David."

Khrushchev snorted. "If you drive two hours from Moscow," he said, "you can shoot a bear."

The Premier clapped for service and issued orders to his classless servants. The entire party, he announced, would now go for a boat ride on the nearby lakes and the river which connected them. He led his guests to a pier where three motor launches were manned and ready, their motors already turning. He helped Nixon into his own launch, and the little flotilla cast off.

On eight occasions during the two-hour ride, Khrushchev ordered his launch stopped. Each time, dozens of bathers swam out from shore.

"Are you captive people?" he shouted to the swimmers as they treaded water or held onto the side of the launch. This was apparently his answer, for Nixon's benefit, to the Senate endorsement of Captive Nations Week.

Each covey of bathers loudly called back, *"Nyet! Nyet! Mir i druzhba!"* ("No! No! Peace and friendship!")

Khrushchev would then order the launch to proceed to the next obviously planned stop.

At the last stop, Nixon turned to the Premier and said, "You know, Mr. Khrushchev, I must admire you. This is the eighth time you've stopped at the right place. You never miss a chance to make propaganda, do you?"

Khrushchev looked at him as if in surprise.

"No, no, I never make propaganda," he said, staring earnestly at the Vice President. "I make only truth."

The long-awaited "formal talk" turned out to be an out-of-doors luncheon that lasted from 3 P.M. until darkness fell. Khrushchev urged all guests, including the wives, to express their views. But the discussion was largely a monologue by the host.

In the course of the almost endless meal, Nixon and Khrushchev agreed not to make any specific report about the meeting. Very few newsmen were present at this bucolic retreat, and only a few crumbs of information were later released.

"I had a very constructive and full discussion with Mr. Khrushchev on some of the problems we have between our two countries," Nixon reported the following day. "I would say we had some differences. I would say it was not a case of his convincing me on major points at issue or of my convincing him.

"But there is one point on which we did agree—that difference between nations must be settled at the conference table and not on the battlefield."

"The discussions at all times were calm," Nixon's press officer Herbert Klein told newsmen after the meeting. Klein went to some pains to point out that the truculence shown by both principals at times on Friday was not as significant as it seemed. He recalled one particular exchange from the luncheon meeting. Khrushchev had expressed surprise that the press had described the debate as stormy.

"Were you offended?" he asked Nixon.

"Never," Nixon answered, looking at the other guests. "Mr. Khrushchev and I have some real and honest differences, but we are alike in this respect: we both come from humble families and both have a practice of speaking directly and not beating around the bush."

"Good," Khrushchev responded heartily. "I agree."

It was the last Nixon and Khrushchev were to see of each other on that trip. Nixon went off on a gruelling swing through Leningrad to Novosibirsk in Siberia, then doubled back to Sverdlovsk in the Urals, and returned to Moscow for his telecast and press conference. The Hearst team, with the other representatives of the press, followed him by plane across the vast reaches of the Soviet Union.

Nixon saw to it that the Russian people heard him speak of peace as often as their leader did. The Vice President carried the cry of "Mir i druzhba!" into Novosibirsk ("The Chicago of Siberia") and Sverdlovsk ("The Pittsburgh of the Urals"), cities only recently opened to Western visitors. The farther he got from Moscow, the warmer was his reception. But no day passed wherein he was not reminded that he was in a militantly regulated country. Wherever Nixon went, "workers," as pompous Yuri Zhukov invariably called them, constantly emerged from the crowds to ask such simple workingmen's questions as, "When will the United States cease atomic tests, which imperil the peoples of the world with fall-outs of strontium 90?"

As head of the Soviet Commission on Cultural Exchanges with Foreign Nations, our old acquaintance Zhukov, whom we had first met in 1955 when he was editor of *Pravda*, played a large role in the Nixon visit. He was apparently in charge of marshaling and rehearsing these "spontaneous" hecklers, a sorry enough indictment in itself. This was only the beginning, however. Zhukov took it upon himself to needle Nixon personally during their long automobile trips across the Russian countryside, when the Vice President, aware of the danger of any false step, and badly in need of rest, wanted only to relax and conserve his stamina. Zhukov's thrusts were not lost on other Americans in a position to hear them. He may have emerged from the Nixon visit with enhanced status in the Soviet Union, but he won the undying contempt of his Western visitors.

Nixon had an answer for all questions, however ill-natured. But none of these well-rehearsed hecklers seemed trained in the art of debate. Their job was simply to propound questions already raised dozens of times before by Khrushchev in speeches castigating the United States. There was seldom an exchange of views between Nixon and these remote-controlled mouthpieces. The "workers" would merely go on to another memorized question, leaving Nixon's reply to the previous query unchallenged.

In Novosibirsk, while inspecting a heavy machinery plant, Nixon noticed many banners and slogans strung from the ceiling of the massive building. Before Yuri Zhukov could present the inevitable "worker," Nixon singled out one of his own and, through the interpreter, asked him what one particular banner said.

"Let Us Develop Socialist Competition to Complete Our Seven-Year Plan Ahead of Schedule," the man read.

"Do you think that gets more production out of you people?" Nixon asked seriously.

The worker smiled and said, with a shrug, "It is propaganda."

Nixon took him to task in a mock way.

"No, it is not," he said, in a severe tone. "Mr. Khrushchev says there is no propaganda in this country—only truth."

Nixon picked up able allies when this program of heckling reached its peak at a machinery plant in Sverdlovsk.

A foreman, identified as Nikolai Spravtsen, confronted Nixon and almost bawled, "Look at the lovely sky! Do you see any Iron Curtain keeping you from getting through?"

Getting fed up, Nixon replied toughly, "Yes, I can. Let's take radio, for instance. We can listen to your broadcasts. But you can't listen to ours because your government jams them."

The man went on to another subject, and so did Nixon, who interrupted him.

"Mr. Khrushchev says many things that we don't like, see? Such as his statement that our grandchildren will live under communism. But those things are printed in our country and are heard on our radio. We expect our people to listen, to read, and make up their own minds as to whether this is a fair prediction." He looked around the modern plant and continued, "We believe sincerely that you've made great progress in the Soviet Union. But we also believe that you would make greater progress if you had, or were permitted to have, a full exchange of ideas."

The foreman grew quite indignant, and not quite coherent.

"What you say about our progress is correct. But how you say it is a dirty slander."

Milton Eisenhower, one of those accompanying Nixon on his cross-country tour, stepped in with the famous remark of Voltaire:

" 'I disagree with what you say,' " he told the big foreman, " 'but will defend to the death your right to say it.' "

"What about your rocket bases?" a mechanic yelled at Nixon.

Testy Vice-Admiral Hyman Rickover, another member of the Nixon party, fielded that one.

"What about your rockets?" he demanded. Then he walked over to the man and said, "You're a politician, not a worker. I don't want to talk to politicians."

The man denied he was a politician.

"All right, then, are you a Communist?"

"No, I'm just a candidate for party membership," he answered.

"All the same thing," Rickover said crisply. "I don't want to talk to party members either. I want to talk to the people, if we can find them."

Nixon returned to Moscow late Friday, July 31, and spent the next day working on his television speech for that evening. For reasons never explained, on Saturday Khrushchev also returned to Moscow, from a trip to the Ukraine. It had been announced that he would not return to the capital until after the Vice President had gone. But he did return, and made a spectacular appearance at the airport. Whether he had come back to be sure to see Nixon on TV that evening, or to create diversionary news cannot be known.

It is perhaps significant that the newsmen covering Nixon's visit had arrived ahead of the Vice President, and were available to record what turned into a one-man show. At any rate, the American Embassy received a last-minute call that the Premier was on the way to the airport to inspect the two United States jets parked there—Nixon's plane and the Trans World Airlines 707 which had been flown in to carry the press home.

In the TWA jet, the pudgy Premier looked around and asked, "How many passengers?"

"It can seat one hundred," he was told by Gordon Gilmore, a vice president of the line.

Khrushchev dismissed the 5-million-dollar plans with a wave. "Our jets seat more," he said.

But the plush jet being used by the Nixon party plainly impressed him. "Very good," he said. "The finishings are excellent. Good taste. Practical."

He spotted a Russian photographer. "Take plenty of pictures," he ordered. "We can learn something from this plane."

The famed Russian aeronautical engineer and designer, Academician Tupolev, jovially referred to as "Russia's only capitalist," was also nearby. "Make some notes," Khrushchev shouted to him. "Sketch some of these designs." When Tupolev looked a bit uncertain, Khrushchev asked, with feigned wonder on his face, "You engineers always steal from each other, don't you?"

Khrushchev was obviously in a clowning mood. When a crew member showed him the galley icebox the Premier poked a hand inside and pulled out a bottle of American vodka.

"What's this?" he asked, screwing up his nose as if the bottle gave off a bad smell. Then he put it back.

Would he have a drink? Certainly, he would have a drink. "But I want American whisky," he insisted. "If I'm on American property, I will drink the whisky of the country." He was poured a bourbon-and-water highball. He took a sip, made a face, and tried to dig the ice cubes out of the glass. "The trouble with Americans," he complained, "is that when they give you a drink, they give you more ice than whisky."

Then, seriously and gallantly, he stood and toasted the President, the Vice President, and Ambassador Thompson, the latter of whom reached the airport just in time to greet the irrepressible Premier.

Then a reporter asked him a big question, one that was already being debated hotly back across the Atlantic.

"Mr. Khrushchev, would you like to fly to the United States in a plane like this?"

"This one or some other one," Khrushchev instantly answered.

"When?"

"When the time is ripe—in good time," Khrushchev replied.

Nixon quietly enlisted the technical help of John Daly in advance of his unprecedented appearance on Soviet TV and radio on the last night of his visit. It was a wise precaution. Just before air time, two of the three studio television cameras suffered power losses and other ailments. Under Daly's handling, the remaining camera did all the work and was moved around in a manner which kept the "picture" from becoming static.

The speech, which reached an audience estimated at ten million, was perhaps the high point of Nixon's visit. The ground rules forbade the presence of reporters in the studio— perhaps out of fear that they might applaud and thus lend audible approval to some of the touchy points Nixon raised. The Hearst team, after securing a copy of the text, watched the first part of the talk in a darkened room off the Intourist Service Bureau in the National, then heard the remainder on the radio upstairs while beginning their stories.

The Vice President appeared dressed in a dark suit, with a gray tie. He spoke seated at a desk beside his State Department translator, Alexander Akalovsky, who gave a running translation of his address.

The subject of his speech was peace, the favorite subject of the

free-wheeling Premier of the Soviet Union. But while discussing peace he was able to reply to most of the questions and
criticisms, honest or rehearsed, that had been put to him during
his travels. He began by making clear just what he meant by the
elusive term.

"The American people and the Russian people are as one in
their desire for peace," he said, "and our desire for peace is not
because either of us is weak. On the contrary, each of us is
strong and respects the strength the other possesses.

"This means that if we are to have peace it must be a just
peace based on mutual respect rather than the peace of surrender or dictation by either side. Putting it bluntly, both of
our peoples want peace, but both of us also possess great
strength, and much as we want peace, neither of us can or will
tolerate being pushed around."

He recalled one worker, apparently a real one rather than a
party stooge, whom he had met in Novosibersk. "My heart
went out to him," Nixon said, "as he told me that he had been
wounded in World War II and that his father and mother had
been killed by bombs. But then he said, 'I don't believe when
you say America is for peace.'

"Nothing he could have said could have astonished and
saddened me more.

"... I say tonight, if you doubt that the American government and the American people are as dedicated to peace as you
are, look at our record and you can reach only one conclusion,
that only aggressor nations have anything to fear from the
United States of America."

The Vice President then went on to quote facts and figures
in answering the attacks made by Khrushchev and his cohorts
on this country. He started by explaining why America felt it
necessary to maintain military bases around the world as a
deterrent to Communist aggression. "Let us look at the record,"

he said. "We disarmed rapidly after World War II. Then came a series of events which threatened our friends abroad as well as ourselves. The Berlin blockade and the war in Korea are typical of the actions which led the United States and our allies to rearm. . . .

"We must also remember that these events occurred before the Twentieth Party Congress changed the line to the one Mr. Khrushchev enunciated again in his speech at Dnepropetrovsk, that communism will now try to achieve its international objectives by peaceful means rather than by force. I could cite statement after statement made by previous leaders of the U.S.S.R. which advocated and threatened the use of force against non-Communist countries. . . .

"Some may ask, why don't we get rid of the bases, since the Soviet government declares today that it has only peaceful intentions? The answer is that whenever the fear and suspicion that caused us and our allies to take measures for collective self-defense are removed, the reason for our maintaining bases will be removed. In other words, the only possible solution of this problem lies in mutual rather than unilateral action leading to disarmament."

Nixon dealt with equal forthrightness on the problem of atomic tests. "That question," he said, "is not whether we both should enter into an agreement to stop tests, but whether that agreement is one that will make sure that the tests actually are stopped.

"That is why we say that if both sides honestly want to stop tests, we must first agree to set up inspection procedures in both of our countries which will make certain that the agreement is not violated. We believe this position is the only one that gives assurance of accomplishing the objective of stopping tests rather than just signing an agreement to do so."

He went on to specify several occasions on which the Soviet

Union had vetoed Western proposals on disarmament and preserving the peace, from the Baruch plan for international control of atomic energy in 1946 to the open-skies aerial inspection plan of President Eisenhower. He then touched on another sensitive issue:

"Let us put a stop to the jamming of broadcasts," he said, "so that the Soviet people may hear broadcasts from our country just as the American people can hear forty hours of broadcasts a day from the Soviet Union. And let us have a freer flow of newspapers and magazines, so that the Soviet people can buy American newspapers and magazines here just as we Americans purchased one and a half million Soviet publications in the last year alone."

And he made a stirring appeal for peace and friendship in a real sense:

"Let us expand the concept of open skies. What the world also needs are open cities, open minds, and open hearts.

"Let us have peaceful competition not only in producing the best factories but in producing better lives for our people.

"Let us cooperate in our exploration of outer space. As a worker told me in Novosibersk, 'Let us go to the moon together.'

"Let our aim be not victory over other people, but the victory of all mankind over hunger, want, misery, and disease."

It was obvious Nixon scored a resounding success with his television address, if only because Kozlov was sent to the airport to see Nixon off for Warsaw and to get in the last word—or words, some twenty minutes of them. He rang all the familiar charges about American bases, the cold war, and so forth, while 5,000 Muscovites gawked from the airport apron and the windows in the administration building. During this tirade the First Deputy Premier was subjected to some jet-age upstaging by his American guests. The TWA jet plane carrying the Nixon

press party took off ahead of the Vice President's, and in the
midst of one of Kozlov's impassioned outbursts it roared overhead at full throttle, greasy spumes of smoke pluming from its
four burners. The heads of the crowd swiveled away from the
speaker and focused on the spectacular vision above. It didn't
seem to please the speaker at all.

This eleventh-hour assault upon a departing guest seemed a
calculated insult. Old Moscow hands like Harrison Salisbury
took it in stride, however. "Never be surprised by anything
these people do," he said. And the minute Kozlov concluded, he
proved the reporter's point by breaking out in a wide smile and
pounding the Vice President jovially on the back. Then, as the
Nixon plane taxied out for a run-off, Kozlov, "The Little K,"
as he was privately dubbed, attempted to swap repartee with
remaining newsmen in imitation of his master. He obviously
lacked the deft touch and sharpness of his model, but he tried
hard. The laughter was a little forced but most of the reporters
were at least partially disarmed by his amiable attitude.

Hearst and Conniff, who remained in Moscow after Nixon's
departure, were able to witness the final scene of the historic
visit. The entire crowd, including Kozlov, remained at the field
while the Nixon Air Force jet rolled out for a take-off. The
next stop was Warsaw, a two-hour trip requiring a small fuel
load. The Russian Tupelov jets are fine, sturdy planes but they
eat up most of the runway and climb slowly after becoming airborne. The Nixon pilots decided to "turn it on" for the
spectators. They got the plane in the air after an unbelievably
short run and started climbing at a terrifying angle. When the
Boeing aircraft streaked over the administration building, it was
already hundreds of feet up and still climbing at 45 degrees or
better. Some show. The noise, the smoke, and the speed were
a parting message to the Russians that the United States of
America still had a few technological tricks up her sleeve.

CHAPTER 9

A view of the new Soviet

The Hearst team found Moscow in 1959 a far different place than the dreary city which they had visited in 1955 and 1957. For one thing, the Nixon tour took place during the summer, when Moscow wears its most charming and colorful dress. The earlier visits were made in November and January, when the city wore the mourning weeds of winter.

But the whole atmosphere of the country had changed. Khrushchev's Russia is a livelier place than the frightened, suspicious nation of Stalin's day, and a far more relaxed place than in the tense days of the interregnum following Stalin's death. It is still a dictatorship, but a dictatorship with a difference.

Perhaps the first thing that struck the eye of the 1959 visitor to Moscow was the number of other Americans there. The American Tourist was there in thousands, patiently thumbing through guidebooks, and listening quietly while Intourist guides described monuments of the capital in stiff schoolroom English. Elderly couples, many of them trying the latest fashion in tourism, having "done" London, Paris, and Rome, checked in at the registration desk at the American Embassy in droves, inquiring after their mail from home. In well-cut cotton dresses, brightly hued bandanas, and dark glasses, the good-looking models, dancers, and attendants from the American exposition gave additional color to a city unaccustomed to such festivity.

In 1955, when Hearst, Conniff, and Smith invaded Moscow, we lived a restricted, almost monastic life, in our expensive proletarian pad at the National. Fact is, we had no other choice. We were conducted to the few sources of diversion with punctilious decorum by the Intourist agency, which saw to it that culture in large doses was always at our disposal, but had no suggestions at all to appease any livelier human instincts.

"I've seen more ballet here in two weeks than in the rest of my life put together," grumbled Hearst one disenchanted evening. "What I'd like now is a dark, smoky night club with Joe E. Lewis about to come on for a couple of hours."

Joe E. Lewis didn't make it to Moscow in 1959, and the ballet was still the hottest show in town, but by both night and day the city offered to her visitors far more entertainment. And more provision was made for the simple creature comforts of life.

Four years earlier we had spent twelve hours on the night train to Leningrad from Moscow, the three of us and our Intourist interpreter jammed into one small compartment. When we accompanied Vice-President Nixon to Leningrad we came up from Moscow in one of the new Soviet jets in exactly one hour. The flight was smooth and easy, and Aeroflot hostesses served tea and fruit in marked contrast to the sandwiches of congealed fat we tried to swallow on the earlier trip.

These were but the most superficial evidences of a process of evolution which appears to be slowly but definitely reshaping the social structure of Communist Russia. Most observers hold the strong-willed Premier responsible for the change.

It remains a tightly run dictatorship, with personal freedom, economics, and political activity kept on short reins. But the country is now more relaxed and informal in comparison with the oppressive, police-state atmosphere which prevailed in 1955. Stalin had been dead for two years, but the grip of Stalinism was still hard on the land. MVD boss Lavrenti Beria had been liquidated a few months after Stalin's death, but the average Soviet citizen still lived in dread of the brutal methods of the secret police.

Consumers goods were rare. The emphasis was heavy on the making of armaments and on the so-called "production of the means of production"—heavy machinery. Housing, the most pressing need of a compliant people, ranked low in priority.

What a difference a few years make when a determined and ambitious leader like N. S. Khrushchev takes over. The change was already apparent in November, 1957, but it was not until the latest visit that its full impact hit us. Russia is enjoying a mild boom comparable to the prosperity of America and Western Europe, and the spirits of the Russian people reflect this upward material spiral.

The people seem better fed and better clothed than before. Unfortunately, this phrase became a cliché used to describe the material progress of the Russian people. Smith had attended the Big Four Foreign Ministers conference at Moscow in 1947, and Hearst and Conniff in 1955 quizzed this Russian veteran—the conference had lasted a full week—to sum up the changes, if any, in eight years. Smith took a puff on his United States commissary cigar, sipped his vodka, and offered his considered opinion.

"They seem better fed and better clothed," he said.

Two years later it was Hearst's and Conniff's turn. Considine implored them to sum up the changes since 1955. Conniff puffed on his commissary cigar, Hearst sipped his vodka, and then both replied in unison:

"They seem better fed and better clothed."

In 1959 Considine ran into trouble finding someone to ask him about the changes over the intervening two years. He kept his cigar and vodka ready but practically everyone in Moscow had themselves been there before. He finally found a young college graduate working part time at United Press, who was innocent enough to put the question to him.

"They seem better fed and better clothed," he said. It was a moment to treasure.

The truth of the matter is that the Russian people did seem to be making progress toward acquisition of material benefits. Better clothed and better fed they certainly were.

Premier Khrushchev has cleverly managed to keep his rocket program going full blast, to maintain Soviet armed forces at a high level, and still provide a reasonable amount of consumer goods for the masses. In 1955, it was impossible to purchase certain items even if your pockets bulged with rubles. In 1959 some of those items—radios, for instance—were on hand in such quantities that old-fashioned capitalist sales were conducted to move them off the shelves.

In 1959, television masts were in bloom atop Moscow roofs, testimony to the number of sets Russian industry had been able to provide for the people. Recognizing TV as a prime medium of propaganda, the Soviet leadership encourages the purchase of sets, and makes it easy in some instances by adopting the free-enterprise tactic of installment payments. It is rumored, however, that if you fall behind on your payments, they don't repossess the set, they repossess *you*.

Housing and other new construction go on at a fast clip, al-

though it will be many years, if ever, before the Soviet masses
are accommodated in a manner considered acceptable in the
West. Unfortunately, housing still carries a *B* ranking in Communist priorities, even with the increase in over-all construction. Only recently, some Western observers believe, the program had to be curtailed to divert materials urgently needed
by the rocket and other arms programs.

Anyone who has lingered near a Soviet housing project, must
wonder how they get anything accomplished. A few men seem to
be puttering around a skeletal frame, and there are usually a
few pieces of rusty machinery on the premises. But where are
the teeming multitudes, the cranes, the tractors, and noise and
scurry of a construction project as we know it? We were told
by those in the know not to be deceived by appearances.

"Their building methods are different from ours," we were
informed. "They work a lot at night, for one thing. And there's
plenty of people there, don't worry. They have to use lots of
manpower to make up for their scarcity in the right kind of
machinery."

The huge housing project on the road to Vnukovo airport,
meant to hold several million Muscovites, always seemed
devoid of activity. Yet an American Embassy official who lived
near the complex said he was constantly astonished at new
buildings that seemed to go up overnight. And in 1959, when
we arrived in Moscow, nobody, but nobody, seemed to be
working very hard on a pedestrian underpass on Gorki Street.
But when we returned from the Nixon tour through Siberia a
week later, the underpass had been cut through! By gnomes,
elves, or old Trotskyites, we suppose.

But even more than material prosperity, the relationship of
ordinary Russians with Westerners chiefly show the differences
that Khrushchev has wrought.

The people are more relaxed and responsive. They no longer

seem to shun social contacts with non-Russians. While much has been added, something even more important has been removed from their daily life, and this appears to be fear of the secret police.

A few years ago there was no fraternization with Communist bureaucrats of any rank. Leonid Khortakov, for instance, accompanied us for three weeks in 1955 as its Intourist guide and never once lunched or dined with us, except when we were on the road. Day after day we would return to the hotel and invite Leonid to join us for lunch in the dining room. He courteously but insistently refused.

Four years later Leonid not only lunched with his old Hearst friends but played host himself. He gave a big lunch for us at the National. He behaved, it must be admitted, in the fashion of a circumspect young man returning a social obligation, for some months previously we had entertained Leonid in New York, when he was in the United States with a trade mission.

The appearance of social amenities is only one phase of a process manifest in all facets of Soviet life. And so far has this evolution gone that experienced American observers of Soviet affairs believe it would be impossible for the Communist leaders to halt the trend even if they so desired. These observers assert that the Kremlin brass has no such desire, but that in fact they are enjoying these changes themselves.

Khrushchev, Mikoyan, and other party leaders are grateful to have survived the worst years of the Stalin terror. They have no nostalgia for the Beria reign of terror, when even the party apparatus was threatened by the secret police.

For the Hearst team, this lifting of the human Iron Curtain brought some excellent, if embarrassing, dividends. Alex Rogow, manager of the Intourist Bureau at the National Hotel during our 1955 visit, was in charge of arrangements for the Siberian tour. Rogow seemed to recall his old friend Hearst as the last of the big-time spenders. In 1955 the dollar-ruble exchange rate was rigged at an artificial four-to-one—embassy experts figured that in a free market the rate would have been sixteen-to-one—and it was not until several years later that the prevalent ten-to-one tourist rate went into effect. So, just as in capitalist countries, Rogow was going to take good care of a client who had paid through the nose to swell the Intourist coffers.

At the airport in Leningrad, first stop of the tour, Hans Tuch (pronounced *Tuck,* and inevitably nicknamed "Friar"), press attaché of the American Embassy, stepped out on the runway apron to read off the billeting assignments. "All correspondents on the first press plane will stay at the Europa Hotel," he announced, "with these three exceptions: Hearst, Considine, and Conniff. They will stay at the Astoria."

This was just dandy. The Astoria is a first-class hotel, and we were assured of separate rooms and baths. The Europa is a flea-bag in which the correspondents were stashed as many as four and six to a room, and the sanitary facilities are best not described.

While we were basking in a heady glow of satisfaction, the stentorian voice of "Friar" Tuch could be heard repeating the announcement, ". . . With these three exceptions: Hearst, Considine, and Conniff."

"This is plain segregation," muttered one disgruntled newsman, who had paid exactly the same Intourist fare as the favored few. "These Russians haven't heard of the Supreme Court decision."

"Friar" Tuch must have liked the phrase, or something, because he bellowed it out for a third and fourth time. By this time, we wanted to crawl under the pavement. With a great effort, however, we concealed our shame and consented to stop at the Astoria.

Our shame grew easier to stifle with each successive halt. The correspondents upon reaching Novosibersk and Sverdlovsk swore great oaths as they were bundled four, five, and six to a room. But Mr. Rogow would give his old friend Hearst a large, dirty, imperialistic wink and a private room and bath.

How did all this happen?

How has a state, entangled in a stifling police regime, managed to emerge even partially from these self-perpetuating bonds?

If Khrushchev is responsible, and many Westerners believe he is, he deserves tribute for shrewdness and even for vision. His "New Russia" represents a more formidable challenge to the West than outmoded, reactionary Stalinism. But in addition to shrewdness and vision, the chunky politician has one advantage that any statesman, ancient or modern, might envy.

He has been lucky.

After becoming top dog in 1955, Khrushchev allowed his name to become identified with several risky gambles, and as of early 1960 they seemed to be paying off. The "Virgin Lands" experiment, for instance—in which tens of thousands of Soviet young people were transported to a Siberian strip never before successfully farmed—drew scornful comments from Western experts when first announced.

The experts were not laughing a few years later. Although still claiming that the mean rainfall of the area will not support good crops over a period of years, they have had to admit that the yield has so far proved worth the effort.

At the same time, Premier Khrushchev has made gestures to ingratiate himself with the touchy Russian intellectuals by permitting them "liberties" never tolerated in the Stalin era. They are now at "liberty," for instance, to view Impressionist and modern paintings which had gathered dust in Soviet cellars because of the disapproval of Stalin. Whole rooms full of French masterpieces—picked up for a pittance in prerevolutionary days by two astute Russian businessmen, Ivan Morosov and Sergei Shoukin—are now on display for the first time in the Pushkin gallery in Moscow and the Hermitage in Leningrad.

Khrushchev also keeps a wary eye on his feuding writers, and in May, 1955, intruded at the Third Congress of Soviet Writers Union to insist that the "angels of reconciliation" descend on the battlefield. Five years later it even seemed quite possible that Dr. Boris Pasternak, whose *Dr. Zhivago* aroused a storm of controversy, would be readmitted to the Writers Union. Apparently, Premier Khrushchev thought the whole Pasternak controversy had been allowed to get out of hand, and that it should be quietly smoothed over. It is noteworthy that Pasternak was never officially punished, or made to humiliate himself publicly. His appearance at the concert of the New York Philharmonic Orchestra in Moscow late in 1959, and his backstage visit to conductor Leonard Bernstein, indicated that the "angels of reconciliation" were at work.

The Soviet Union, in fact, seems to be evolving, in many ways, into a general approximation of a bourgeois state. Bourgeois values once derided by revolutionary theorists—love of home and family, respect for parents and for individual dignity —are now being stressed in domestic propaganda.

Reporters traveling with Vice-President Nixon whiled away the hours on jet hops to Siberia reading Soviet English-language publications. One smartly illustrated magazine featured a long pro-and-con article, titled "Is Romantic Love Possible?" In its tone and implications, it demonstrated the drift of Soviet life toward characteristically Western values.

No, said one side, Romantic Love is not for Leninist-Marxists —it is not scientific and has no place in dialectical materialism. One picture showed a young worker, fist raised in the air, his face distorted by high emotion. The caption under this fledgling

commissar carried the imperious demand: "Love Must Be
Organized According to Plan." The intentional parody of
Stalinist puritanism could hardly be missed.

Another faction argued that Romantic Love was in full con-
sonance with party principles. When Ivan at the lathe and
Natasha at the bench discover that something besides interest
in the Gorki Machine Works is drawing them together, it does
not constitute deviation deserving of report to the factory commissar. Should emotion ripen into passion, Communist young
men and women can fall into each other's arms with the bless-
ings of Karl Marx, Friedrich Engels, Nikolai Lenin, and Nikita
Khrushchev.

It should be remembered that nothing is said, done, or written
in an official Soviet publication except for a purpose. Both sides
of the question had been represented in the article; but also
on hand was a "theoretrician" who thereupon laid down the
new Party line on Romantic Love. The Party line, it appeared,
recognized the existence of the sublime passion.

The theoretician gently explained how the erroneous idea had
arisen that love was bourgeois and reactionary. In the early
days of the revolution, the Bolshevik leaders had been forced
to concentrate so intently on their duties that they had created
the impression that there was no room for the emotional side of
life. Their work perforce had been their all, and dedication
to duty and sacrifice of personal wishes had dominated their
lives.

But the impression this gave was misleading, the theoretician
went on. There was Krupskaya, the great Lenin's devoted wife:
Could there be anything more inspiring than their great Love
Idyll? And the other early leaders, dedicated as they were to the
rugged work of revolution, all were sustained by the tender love
and support of their respective spouses.

But love was indeed reactionary in the bad old days before
the revolution, the writer further explained, because the serious

class cleavage engendered by monopolist-capitalist imperialism debased honest emotions. Tender young working girls were victimized by the richer elements, and the affections of young workingmen hadn't a chance. (One member of the Hearst team, recalling when his best girl had been snatched up by a raccoon-coated rake driving a Pierce-Arrow, nodded his head in agreement.) Now all had been changed. The end of the class war in Russia gave everybody a fair shake.

The discussion of Love-at-the-lathe and Passion-behind-the-plow illustrates the controversy going on in Nikita Khrushchev's "New Russia." Evidently somebody in the Kremlin likes the idea of dealing with down-to-earth topics, of coming to grips with the problems and experiences of ordinary Russian men and women. N. S. Khrushchev's greatest contribution to Marxist theory may be that he has tried to align doctrinaire principles with the everyday life of his people.

It is in common, everyday conversation with Westerners that the Russian of today most strikingly differs from the Soviet citizen of the pre-Khrushchev era. The conversation remains in a narrow and cautious orbit, to be sure. The talk of the "New Russian" is still far more limited than the all-out release of opinions, judgment, and personal prejudices so characteristic of Americans.

We heard no discussion of political problems in 1959, nor anything about the political leadership. One rising young government official, however, did say to Hearst, in the course of a conversation, "You Americans don't believe the old man's stuff about your grandchildren being brought up under communism, do you? We don't believe it ourselves, so we hope you're not taken in."

And a university student told Eileen Kingsbury Smith, daughter of our own Joe, while she was working at the American Exposition, "We young people are dissatisfied with the way things are being run. I want to be a doctor, but I have no choice. They tell me I'm going to be an engineer, and that's what I'm studying to be whether I want to or not."

The Nixon visit may have done much to break down some of the conversational and social barriers between ordinary Russian citizens and Americans. For one thing, Mr. Nixon and his party were the first Americans allowed to visit certain hitherto forbidden areas of the Soviet Union, and they were the first Americans that many Russians had ever seen. Furthermore, the sizable party of American correspondents and officials were thrown into intimate daily contact with their Communist opposite numbers, and these contacts, you can be sure, were very illuminating on both sides.

The young, vivacious, and often very pretty Intourist girl guides assigned to the Nixon entourage made a particularly deep impression on the travelers. They were often very intelligent and outspoken, and gave the correspondents some fairly penetrating insights into the opinions and feelings of young people in the Soviet Union. Moreover, not only would they join the correspondents for dinner and dancing, but made no bones about the fact that they were enjoying themselves thoroughly. Each evening before dinner they would hustle off to the nearest available washroom, no matter how small, to have a shower, and change into their best summer dresses.

In the provinces, Leningrad, Novosibersk, and Sverdlovsk, as well as in Moscow, the dance band specialized in nostalgic American swing tunes dating back to the Goodman-Dorsey-Miller era. The girls loved the beat, and knew the arrangements of "In the Mood," "Jersey Bounce," and "Little Brown Jug" by heart. In fact, one of the oddest paradoxes in modern Russian life is the jazz mania sweeping Soviet youth, while their Communist elders forbid it.

"Of course we play your jazz music all the time," one of the young Intourist guides told us, as a Soviet trumpeter hit a hot riff. "You should come to our homes and see our dancing parties."

Well, then, how come, we asked, the government frowns on it, and Yuri Zhukov resolutely refuses such American jazz musicians as Benny Goodman and Count Basie to appear in Russia?

The answer we received shows how we sometimes forget the human equation in our preoccupation with doctrinaire political problems.

"How old is comrade Zhukov?" asked Miss Intourist.

"Oh, about fifty or fifty-five," we said. "Somewhere around there."

"I thought so. Does he have any children?"

We had no information on that point.

"Well, I'll bet he has," said Miss Intourist with conviction. "And I'll bet he's just mean enough not to want them to listen to jazz, just like my father. He shuts the radio or phonograph off the minute he catches me listening to a jazz record."

We who remembered our own fathers switching the radio dial in great anger from the broadcasts of Duke Ellington, Fletcher Henderson, and Don Redman from the Cotton Club and Connie's Inn, and whose own attitudes toward rock-and-roll was markedly similar, began to think it was a small world, after all.

"You've got to remember," said Miss Intourist, "that our government is run by old men just like my father. They don't know what's going on with us younger people. So they think they're protecting us from something they don't like. It won't last forever."

Jazz is, in fact, seeping in through every crevice in the Iron Curtain, and the Yuri Zhukovs and other bureaucratic hacks who try to shut it out are largely wasting their time on a hope-

less task. In the satellites, for instance, the authorities have all
but stopped making the effort to control the kind of music their
young people want to hear. A few years ago, we asked Alexis
Johnson, then United States Minister to Czechoslovakia, to
name the most subversive ideas then agitating the satellite nations.

"Jazz and Poland," he said.

The glow of Poland has since dimmed, but the influence of
jazz grows progressively stronger. The State Department may
one day have to tell Yuri Zhukov and his ilk that the exchange
program must be a two-way street, and that we can't permit the
Russians to dictate our contributions indefinitely. But, in Miss
Intourist's comment was the implied promise that the coming
Russian generation would take care of the matter themselves.
Her remarks also suggest strongly that Russian leaders of the
future may have ideas about politics at variance with those of
their elders—just as Khrushchev and his team brought to the
Communist state methods vastly different from those of Josef
Stalin.

Hearst, it might be added, brought with him to Moscow in
1959, a portable phonograph and about twenty long-playing
jazz records. He kept the windows of his National suite open
and the solid sound wafted into Manezhnaya Square and blasted
against the walls of the Kremlin hour after hour. When he departed, he distributed the discs among his young Russian friends,
establishing himself as a combination Santa Claus and imperial-
ist agent.

Nikita Khrushchev's rise to power has been so dazzling, and
so stridently has the Communist press whooped up his triumphs,
that Westerners are sometimes prone to overlook the less glittering aspects of his "New Russia."

The man has problems. Big problems. Political, economic, and
ideological problems. Problems that could intensify, despite

Khrushchev's shimmering successes. Recent Soviet accomplishments in the jet and sputnik fields, for example, have been so spectacular that they tend to overshadow many failures in other areas.

For forty years the Russians have been talking plans—the first was announced in 1920. Their constant boast is that everything is organized "according to plan." Yet their plans for building heavy industry never included a railroad network, a highway system, or the urban housing that should go with an expanding industrial base. After forty years, there is still only one double-track railroad across Siberia, and the highway complex is skeletal by Western standards. They dragoon peasants to the towns and cities to work in their factories—then fail to provide housing for them.

Premier Khrushchev, that inveterate gambler, has recently come forward with a seven-year plan designed to lift Russian living standards to the current American level. But economists who have studied the man and his operations believe he has only a rudimentary knowledge of the subject. He has too much faith, they say, in "economics by decree" and the power method, both of which bypass economic realities.

One reform which has already turned a little sour is the decentralization program. This sweeping measure was enacted in order to eliminate red tape which snarled Soviet plans in Moscow bureaucracy. Under it, more initiative and more power was entrusted to local Communist leaders. Anastas Mikoyan especially favored the reform—he claimed that key projects often died in the waste baskets of Moscow officials.

In theory, decisions were to be made on a regional basis. But the bureaucrats who grumpily left their beloved Moscow for the provinces soon developed a disease called "localism," which has provoked harsh tirades by the Premier.

"Localism" is the term of opprobrium used when the regional

brass put the interests of their own territory ahead of those of
the nation. They may prefer to establish a good regional record
by hoarding needed materials rather than to integrate their needs
with their neighbors', and the exchanges of their resources may
have no reference to the over-all plan.

Agriculture also causes recurrent nightmares. Statistics in
1959 show that some 43 per cent of the available labor force
was required to till the fields and harvest crops, as compared
with the 8 per cent needed in America. The complexities of
the agricultural problems in Russia are beyond the scope of this
book; suffice it to say that backward and uncoordinated methods
seriously diminish efficiency of production and provoke repeated
crises.

Partly at least because of the Russian triumphs in science,
some of us are inclined to think of Russia as a smoothly func-
tioning state run with push-button precision. It is hardly that.
It is instead a nation of 200 million people, many of them
very backward in their ways, painfully seeking to rival the industrial might of the United States.

Russia's leaders are at grips with problems of production,
food supply, and industrial expansion—problems which would
create migraines for the most gifted geniuses of American production. And it must be remembered that not the same men
run the big factories, the farms, the food shops, the bus lines
and taxicabs, the schools and the subways, the railroads and
the airlines, the ballet and motion pictures and television, and,
of course, the ballot box. The men who run "New Russia" must
toil over the intricacies of jet aircraft construction, ride herd
on platoons of space scientists, and must lavish Russia's resources on plant expansion designed to keep communism's war
potential on a par with that of the West. They must somehow
find the means, despite the urgent claims of domestic needs, to
supply arms and a rock-bottom industrial base to their Chinese

allies, who are long on boasts but short on bombs. And then
there is the problem of fitting the satellites into the Communist
economic blueprint.

And all this takes place in a nation which only entered the
industrial age forty years ago and which, after more than a
generation of privation, still lags far behind America in such
vital items of industrial economy as coal and iron and steel.

A lesser but nevertheless irritating problem in Khrushchev's
"New Russia" is the emergence of a new elite, proving that
under Communist dictatorship everyone is equal but, as on
Orwell's Animal Farm, some are more equal than others. Such
an elite group has always existed in the Communist state, but
only in the last few years has it become obvious to the outside
world.

Traditional privileges of birth and rank have long since been
done away with. But human nature being what it is, Soviet
Russia has its share of political favoritism and bureaucratic
boondoggling. The loftiest echelon of the Soviet "classless" society is a managerial elite, whose status is based on position in
the Communist bureaucracy and production structure. Plant
directors and managers, chief engineers and technicians, directors of state farms and tractor repair stations, *kolkhoz* chair-
men, high-ranking army officers, the literary and scientific in-
telligentsia—these comprise the upper crust. This class is leav-
ened by the celebrities of the opera and the ballet. Russians in
these categories live far better and higher than the masses of
workers beneath them.

Hard work and rugged competition, however, keep most of
these comrades toeing the line, and the regime applies the "in-
centive" motive of the capitalist system. In Russia today there
are so-called "millionaire factories" such as the Stalin plant in
Moscow, the sales revenues of which run into many millions of
rubles. There are also "millionaire *kolkhozes*" where superior

management and production bring rewarding bonuses to directors and workers alike.

Some observers feel that the "millionaire" Stalin factory gets preferential treatment in materials and first-class production techniques and that some "millionaire" farms owe their success to the good, rich earth of their particular areas.

How much are top executives and managers of such places paid? The chairman of a well-situated *kolkhoz* about eighteen miles from Moscow told us he makes 2,400 rubles a month, plus produce amounting to double the amount received by the average worker on his farm. He had a new small Pobeda car, a TV set, a radio, a Longine watch, and a telephone—eloquent testimony to the relative luxury available a man in such a position.

Such tangible evidence is significant because it is hard to estimate the dollar value of wages. The exchange rate of the ruble, for example, was artificially pegged, at four rubles to one dollar in 1959, but Western economists estimated the market rate at closer to twelve rubles to the dollar.

President Eisenhower became aware of this false exchange rate during his postwar visit to Russia. When Hearst saw him in the White House he told Hearst the answer he had given a *kolkhoz* worker who asked what a comparable worker in America would earn.

"I knew that the salary alone wouldn't tell the true difference," the President said. "So I translated it into what the American worker could buy with his pay. I told him that his opposite number in America would probably own his own home, a car, have his children at a university, attend the movies and theater regularly, and in general possess many of the good things of life."

The President smiled. "Marshal Zhukov was listening," he said, "and I could tell he didn't like this line of talk. So he turned on the worker and said, 'Stop bothering our guest with such silly questions.' "

Even workers in Russia have an elite—the *stakhanovites* (workers who invent labor-saving shortcuts), shock-workers (those who overfulfill their quotas by big margins), and brigadiers (foremen of collective farms whose squads make impressive performances).

The very cream of Russian "society," however, is represented by the artistic world—performers of the opera, and ballet, and theater who rise to the top by virtue of their talent and fame. Ballerinas, opera singers, conductors, movie producers, directors, and writers get the best apartments and are among the few people in Russia to dress well—though not fashionably by Western standards. They are household idols throughout the Soviet Union.

A stiff artistic price is often exacted from these beneficiaries of Soviet favor. Composers and writers in particular must hew to the current line and may be soundly reprimanded, or worse, by the Party for deviations. There appears to be one exception to this rule. Performing artists—the prima donnas, actors, and dancers—seem exempt from these restrictions.

The story is told of Kozlovsky, a top Russian tenor who got paid twenty-five times the stipulated state rate for each performance, that he rebelled against a proposed tour of the so-called "peoples' democracies." He complained that the pay wasn't enough and that the technical resources of many of the opera houses were beneath his standards.

For this show of temperament Kozlovsky drew the usual stern wigging in the party press. But nothing else happened. He was singing as usual next season and as popular as ever.

"The Russians are like the Westerners in that respect," said one diplomat. "They make allowance for the artistic temperament. As long as the fellow continues to perform satisfactorily, they'll let him get away with a lot of things."

To understand the grip that some performers hold on the affection of the people, one should consider Ulanova, prima ballerina of the Moscow Ballet and rated by many critics as the world's greatest.

Ulanova earns about 5,000 or 6,000 rubles a month, plus perquisites which include a decent apartment and a maid. In addition, her title, "People's Artist of the U.S.S.R.," brings in extra money, as do the Lenin (formerly Stalin) prizes she regularly wins. Finally, in addition to her basic salary, she receives a substantial bonus for each performance.

The members of the new elite ordinarily mind their manners in public. They could pose a serious domestic problem for Khrushchev if they ever made themselves conspicuous. The Premier's program has definitely bettered the material conditions of his subjects, but not by much, and comparisons would be odious.

For this group has been assuming privileges beyond the reach of the average Russian, and shows no eagerness to give them up. Party aristocrats live very nicely indeed, while tens of millions of their fellow Russians exist on a bare subsistence level. The aristocrats have the cars, the homes, the *dachas,* the good food and wines, the furs, and the fun and the travel. If the gulf between the elite and the people continues to widen at the present rate, the so-called classless society could, in a generation or two, become positively feudal. We know Khrushchev is worried about this very development, because he has time and again loosed his thunder at party functionaries who were abusing their privileges.

The Kremlin leaders seem to realize that they have taken Communist theory into a new stage and may never be able to return. Only a serious internal threat to their own regime or a showdown war with the free world would be likely to bring back the conditions prevailing in the Stalin years.

The Communist leaders themselves encourage the notion that, following the precepts of classical Marxism, the state is finally beginning to "wither away" and socialism approaching at last the promised land of pure communism. They point to several organizations which have been removed, in theory at least, from the strict supervision of the state and encouraged to operate on a "civilian" basis. These include the trade unions, the sports organizations, and to a limited degree, the police apparatus, where something called a "Volunteer Militia" has recently been introduced. But there is much shadow and very little substance to the "withering away" process. This implies these groups still have the same table of organization and an identical operating procedure as before. Their leaders are the same hacks reporting to the same "desks" in the Central Committee of the Party.

Nevertheless, sequence of historical change may be contrary to the order Marx envisioned. More precisely, socialism as practiced in Soviet Russia may not necessarily foreshadow pure communism, but may be progressing in reverse toward a bourgeois revolution denied it when the revolution leaped directly from feudal autocracy into the Leninist absolutist state.

One further evidence that bourgeois values are growing in Soviet Russia is that nepotism is rearing its unlovely head. Khrushchev himself, no less, has moved to take care of his own. His son-in-law, Alexei Ivanovich Adzhubei, has been established as editor of *Izvestia,* as a reward, no doubt, for his talent, brains, industry, and correct ideology. But we shall not labor this particular point.

"I don't think a discussion of how sons become editors through their family connections would lead to any fruitful conclusion," said William Randolph Hearst, Jr. "Let's just say it's a sign the Russians are in a decline."

CHAPTER 10

Mr. Khrushchev
comes to America

Nikita Khrushchev received a cool but correct greeting when, at the President's invitation, he arrived in the United States, at Andrews Air Force Base, Md., September 15, 1959. It was a type of reception that was to continue generally throughout the most-photographed visit ever made by a foreign dignitary to this country.

President Eisenhower himself was on hand at the well-guarded field, accepting the Soviet Foreign Office's almost indignant pronouncement that the Chairman of the Council of Ministers—a position equivalent to prime minister—was indeed also "head of state" and thereby entitled to the Presidential courtesy.

The Hearst team rolled out its ladies auxiliary for the arrival. Dorothy Kilgallen arrived at the field in a chartered Rolls Royce, and Ruth Montgomery from Hearst Headline Service's Washington Bureau was also on hand. Considine was using his height to see what he could over the heads of the crowd. Unfortunately there wasn't much to be seen through

the wire fence that the Air Force had erected in a successful
effort to keep the two chiefs of state from fraternizing with the
press.

Surprisingly trim-looking in his dark, Italian-tailored suit,
swinging a black Homburg in his left hand, Khrushchev came
down the ramp from his towering four-engined, eight-propel-
lered TU-104 to receive a crisp handshake from the President.
Eisenhower's features relaxed a bit when he was introduced to
the motherly-looking Mrs. Khrushchev and the diffident family
—pert Yulia, wistful Sergei, pretty blond Rada and her husband
Alexei Ivanovich Adzhubei, just then appointed editor of
Izvestia.

"How was the trip?" Eisenhower asked. (The turbo-prop,
largest passenger plane in the world, had flown nonstop from
Moscow against stiff headwinds in twelve hours and twenty
minutes.) The question was faithfully relayed by the Russian
interpreter Oleg Troyanovsky, our old Moscow acquaintance.

Khrushchev boomed back the proud answer: it was "very
pleasant."

The two leaders walked down a 125-foot red rug stretching
from the colossal plane to a small reviewing stand which faced
waiting honor guards and a band. It was flanked by a towering
stand for the press, the photographers, and the TV cameras.
Eisenhower's manner was that of a man who had undertaken
a difficult and even somewhat painful duty, but was determined
to see it completed successfully. He engaged in brief bursts of
conversation as he marched at Khrushchev's side, and helped
State Department protocol chief Wiley Buchanan introduce the
Premier to a welcoming committee that included Secretary of
State Herter, Gen. Twining, Chairman of the Joint Chiefs of
Staff, and the man who would serve as Khrushchev's harassed
guide during the visit, UN Ambassador Henry Cabot Lodge.

The principals traded polite barbs in their remarks.

The President's face was a mask of sobriety. "The political and social systems of our two countries differ greatly," he said in his prepared speech. "In our system the people themselves establish and control the government. . . . Although they have built and maintain strong security forces, it is clear that because our people do want peace and because they are the decisive influence in basic actions of our government, aggression by this nation is an impossibility. . . . I assure you that they have no ill will toward any other people, that they covet no territory, no additional power. Nor do they seek to interfere in the internal affairs of any other nation."

Khrushchev, who had held his Homburg over his bald head as protection against the burning sun during Eisenhower's remarks, clapped the lid squarely on his head and applauded. He then put on his glasses, pulled his own speech out of his pocket, and in half-shouted Russian had his own say:

"We have come to you with an open heart and good intentions. . . . We entertain no doubt that the splendid scientists, engineers, and workers of the United States of America who are engaged in the field of conquering Cosmos will also carry their flag to the Moon. The Soviet flag, as an old resident of the Moon, will welcome your pennant and they will live there together in peace and friendship as we both should live together on the Earth in peace and friendship, as should live in peace and friendship all peoples who inhabit our common Mother Earth—who so generously gives us her gifts."

The President and Mr. and Mrs. Khrushchev, crowded uncomfortably into a White House car, then drove the fourteen miles to the capital. The usually radiant Eisenhower smile was in eclipse. The ride was through crowds of generally silent spectators. It sometimes more closely resembled a funeral procession than the arrival in America of a man whose announced determination was to thaw the Cold War. There was occasional muted applause along the way, mostly from children who had been excused from school for the occasion. But it was plain that the customary affection in which the public held the President was being held in check, since any ovation might be construed as approval of the man at his side.

This was made pointedly clear when the President returned to his car after shepherding the Khrushchevs to the door of Blair House, the White House guest residence on Pennsylvania Avenue. The Russian couple remained in the open doorway, waving chubby hands at the President, as Eisenhower tipped his hat and stepped into the car. As it pulled away, the crowd cheered, giving vent to their pent-up feelings.

Khrushchev himself was briefly booed later in the day when he rode the less than 200 yards which separate Blair House from the White House. But there was scattered applause, too. The Russian Premier did not appear to take notice of either reaction. His face, through his first day in America, hardly changed expression. It was the countenance of a man shrewdly sizing up his hosts. If he felt any trace of awe at his surroundings, he concealed it very well.

The President and the Premier were alone, except for their interpreters, for only thirteen minutes. The remaining hour and three quarters was a seminar. Their talk was characterized by Press Secretary Hagerty as "preliminary" and "exploratory," but apparently it explored, in a preliminary way, such hard-core sources of dissension as Berlin, disarmament, nuclear tests, and inspection of atomic activities.

Their joint statement, phrased so as not to arouse hopes too high or to offend allies on either side, read:

"President Dwight D. Eisenhower and the Chairman of the Council of Ministers of the U.S.S.R., Nikita S. Khrushchev, met for nearly two hours this afternoon. They were accompanied by the Vice President, the foreign ministers and other advisers.

"The President and the Chairman reviewed the relationship between the two countries and exchanged views in general terms on international problems. They agreed on the general line of their further discussion, which will take place on all these subjects following the Chairman's return from his visit throughout the country.

"They plan to meet for this purpose at Camp David from Friday evening, September 25, until noon on September 27.

"The atmosphere of the talk was friendly and frank, with agreement that the discussions should continue in this spirit to seek ways to achieve a better understanding."

After their talk, Eisenhower bundled Khrushchev into a Marine Corps helicopter and, pursued aloft by the inevitable press in a sister copter, took him on an airborne sightseeing tour of the capital.

Khrushchev appeared completely at ease that night when, at what was supposed to be the first "white tie and tails" dinner of his life (he appeared in a business suit), he chomped away at a White House state dinner of melon with Prosciutto ham, curry soup, Crab Louis, roast young turkey with cornbread dressing, scalloped sweet potatoes with pineapple, French green beans *amandine,* tossed bibb lettuce with "Green Goddess" dressing, lime *glacé,* lady fingers, nuts, candies, and coffee.

Meanwhile, irate pickets from the slave states were kept 500 feet from the floodlit White House.

The President, resplendent in white tie and tails, raised his glass to Khrushchev to propose this pointed toast: "Now, today, it seems to me that our two countries have a very special obligation to the entire world. Because of our strength, because of our importance in the world, it is vital that we understand each other better. The Soviet Union and the United States must have a common purpose in developing the maximum of fact and truth, so that we may better lead, between us, this world into a better opportunity for peace and prosperity."

Khrushchev eagerly responded. "The United States and the Soviet Union are too powerful to permit quarreling among themselves," he said expansively. "If we were weak countries, then it would be another matter, because when the weak quarrel they are just scratching each other's faces, and it takes just a couple of days for a cosmetician to repair this mischief, and everything comes out right again. But if the United States and the Soviet Union quarrel, then not only our countries can suffer colossal damage, but the other countries of the world will also be involved in a world shambles."

He seemed ready to sit down, but reconsidered.

"Russians believe their Communist system to be superior," he went on. "Americans may believe the same of their system. But surely we should not bring the quarrel out into the arena of open struggle. It is better to let history judge which system is right."

After dinner, Khrushchev sought out Senate Democratic leader Lyndon Johnson, Senate Republican leader Everett M. Dirksen, and House Speaker Sam Rayburn and questioned them at some length on the workings of the two-party system. But his main target was the tall, affable chief of the Central Intelligence Agency, Allen Dulles.

Khrushchev asked questions about the gathering of intelligence abroad which the brother of the late Secretary of State was in no mood or position to answer. Khrushchev's easy fringe knowledge of United States operations in this field did, however, prompt Dulles to ask one question of his own:

"Perhaps you have seen some of our reports, Mr. Chairman?"

Khrushchev grinned knowingly. "We get much of our own

information from the same people as you do," he said. "Maybe we should share the expenses."

Guests at the White House function related later that Mr. Dulles was not too pleased by this sally.

The American people got their first good look at Khrushchev when he appeared next day at a nationally televised luncheon and news conference at the National Press Club.

For Khrushchev, it was a day that began on a note of informality. He appeared in shirtsleeves, shortly after 7 A.M., to take a breath of fresh air on the front steps of the somewhat severe Blair House. He grinned and waved at photographers and early risers scurrying to work. By 9:30 A.M. he was at the Department of Agriculture's research center at Beltsville, Md., yawning through a lengthy briefing on such new world wonders as weed control, and clucking at cows, pigs, sheep, and the center's special breed of small white turkey. "We have them bigger," he said, having ignored the explanation of the work that had gone into developing a meaty bird for the small family.

Before the Press Club luncheon, Khrushchev was guest of honor at a reception given in the club lounge by its president, William H. Lawrence of *The New York Times*. Hearst was present at this reception, and Khrushchev asked to see him. When the publisher stepped forward, the familiar exchange of "capitalist and monopolistic publisher" vs. "that's not true" was resumed. Hearst showed the Premier the front page of that day's *New York Journal-American* which featured a cartoon by Burris Jenkins, Jr., depicting Khrushchev as an enormously pleased man in the moon—a heavenly body his missilemen had hit the previous Sunday. Khrushchev shook with laughter.

"I never thought a few years ago that I'd ever be with you in the Kremlin or you'd ever be with us here," Hearst said.

Khrushchev wagged a finger at the monopolist newsman.

"There's an old Russian saying," he said, "which goes, 'two mountains never meet, but two people can.' "

Khrushchev moved on to the bar. With some misgiving he took a Scotch and soda offered him.

"How do you like it?" asked one young reporter whose total consumption through the years probably amounted to less than Khrushchev had spilled.

"Spoiled water," he said. "It's difficult to know whether it needs more soda or more Scotch."

The crowded room (this was the first time the conservative club had admitted women reporters to one of its luncheons) endured rather than enjoyed Khrushchev's prepared speech, which was placidly interpreted by Troyanovsky. The script featured such phrases as:

"We have come with a feeling of friendship for the American people and a sincere desire to bring about an improvement of the relations between our countries, to strengthen world peace. This is the main purpose of our visit. . . . I think that the President and I will concentrate in our talks on the question of ending the Cold War. . . .

"I can tell you, without anticipating what I intend to say before the General Assembly [of the UN], that I intend to concentrate on the problem of disarmament. The Soviet government intends to submit to the United Nations a proposal which, we hope, will play an important part in the solution of this, the most burning issue of our time. . . .

"The absence of a peace treaty [with Germany] poisons the relations among scores of states. . . . There is only one way out —to acknowledge that there exist two German states, i.e., recognize the *status quo* in the German question, and conclude a peace treaty with the two German states instead of further dallying with the elimination of the remnants of war. . . .

"All the goods exchanged by our two countries in a year,

figuratively speaking, can well be carried by two ships. And yet our states account for over a half of the world's industrial production. . . ."

Lawrence had given Soviet authorities and the State Department fair notice the night before that if there was any attempt to censor the written questions submitted to Khrushchev from the floor, he would end the meeting immediately after lunch. He also set the frank mood of the question-and-answer period by asking the Premier to confirm or deny a story that was popular in Washington at the time.

The story, Lawrence related, was that after Khrushchev made his speech attacking Stalin at the Twentieth Party Congress, a delegate sent an unsigned note to him asking, "What were *you* doing when Stalin was committing these crimes?"

"The story goes," Lawrence continued, "that you asked the person who sent you the question to stand up. Nobody stood up, so then you said, '*Now* you know what Khrushchev was doing.' "

Laughter filled the room. Khrushchev faced TV cameras that showed his anger all over the nation, seized the microphone, and said indignantly, "The author of this fable is someone who wanted to place me in a difficult position." He looked around the room sternly. "I notice that there was laughter here before I could reply," he said. "I consider this a provocative question. I deny any such malicious rumors, any such lies that do not conform to truth."

The next question was softer. Was it really coincidence that Soviet science shot the moon on the eve of his arrival in the United States, and would Russia lay claim to it?

Khrushchev relaxed and smiled. "It was a simple but pleasant coincidence," he said. "But to conclude that we will enter a claim is wrong. We represent different political systems. This thought of a claim reflects the capitalistic philosophy of private property. We don't think of 'my' moon. We think of 'our' moon. We look upon this not only as a great victory for our country, but a great triumph for all our countries." He was applauded.

"We have not come here to beg," he responded to a question about trade. "We have not come with a long hand to get into your pockets. We have pockets of our own. What we don't like is the discrimination in trade. We should be able to buy what we need, and you should sell what you should."

The Russians would not attempt to put a man on the moon until technical developments were perfected, he said in answer to another question. "We have no intention of now throwing a man at the moon," he chided his questioner. "We value human lives in the Soviet Union."

His face toughened when a question concerning anti-Semitism in the Soviet Union was read and translated. "There is no such thing in our country," he said with a trace of his earlier anger. "In our country a man's religion is not asked. We look upon a person as a person. We are made up of many nationalities. The Jews in the Soviet Union are no national problem. As a matter of fact, Jews were among the persons who took a foremost part in the launching of the moon rocket."

Would he explain the remark for which he was most famous— ". . . we will bury you"?

Yes, he had indeed said something like that, Khrushchev acknowledged, but the meaning of his statement had been distorted. What he had meant, he explained, was that the Communist system would one day produce such a high standard of living for people living under it that it would become apparent to the peoples of the world that this was the best system—and thus such systems as capitalism would be buried.

He looked around the room in amusement. "Why," he said, "naturally I did not have reference to a physical burying. This group here represents only a very very small percentage of the American people. But if I would try to bury even this little group, this roomful, one lifetime would hardly be enough."

But the question that followed produced the most shocking answer of the day. "How do you justify," he was asked bluntly, "your 'no interference with the affairs of foreign nations' with your crushing of the Hungarian revolt?"

The gold in Khrushchev's teeth glinted ominously. "Hungary has stuck in some people's throats like a dead rat," he barked, tense and tough. "It is unpleasant, but they can't spit it out. We've got a lot of dead cats we can throw at you, and they are fresher than any Hungarian dead rat."

He waved his chubby fist at the crowded Press Club dining room. "I've explained our position regarding Hungary a number of times, including to the people of Hungary," he said with heat. He then added proudly, "On my recent trip there I received a warm, enthusiastic response from the Hungarian people. We're marching together on one road, with one aim, one purpose.

"I have no intention of putting difficult questions to *you*. I've come here with an open heart, not in a mood to relive old difficulties. I've come here to remove stones in the path of better understanding. The main purpose of the visit is the improvement of relations." He wrenched himself away from the microphone. He was done with the subject, wanted to hear no more, his manner emphatically indicated.

The written nature of the questioning made it impossible to pursue the topic.

Here permit us a digression to suggest an explanation, though not a justification, of Khrushchev's twisted reasoning, and its rather ominous significance for American policy.

Khrushchev seems to be honestly baffled by the way Hungary has "stuck like a dead rat"—to use his own ugly phrase—in the throats of Western people. On his distorted scale of values, Soviet Russia was only acting the way a great power should in drastically eliminating a pressing menace. His study of what he calls "capitalist nations" leads him to believe that they would act similarly if confronted with a comparable challenge. So what, asks the Premier, is all the shouting about Hungary?

We will hazard the guess that Khrushchev expects the United States to take just such steps should it ever be confronted with a dangerous revolt in its own front yard. He hardly anticipates that we will sit idly by, for instance, should a Communist government take over in Panama. Nor does Khrushchev, with his pragmatic view of affairs, expect we would allow Cuba to become a Communist satellite before our very eyes, and undoubtedly views Mikoyan's recent triumph in making a trade agreement with that country with especial interest. He still has enough respect for us as a great power, however, to believe that we will act in our own best interests should a real crisis arise. Members of the Hearst team have watched the man in action long enough to believe that his hopes and plans are almost always realistically formed. In Latin America especially, Khrushchev will fish in troubled waters and hope for the best. A "Latin-American Hungary" would be a dandy dividend for the adroit campaign the Kremlin is presently waging. But if we were ever to stand back while the Panama Canal slipped into hostile hands, or while a Communist puppet government began to build rocket bases in Cuba, Khrushchev would, first of all, be very much surprised; then he would draw the conclusion that America's day as a great power was over. He would, we firmly believe, become a dangerous exponent of brinksmanship from that moment on, and nuclear war would be much more of a possibility than it is now, when Khrushchev still believes we will not shy from taking all measures, including unpopular ones, to safeguard our security.

New York was the next stop of Khrushchev's tour—New York the melting pot, haven of more articulate and more vigorously organized refugees from Communist oppression than any other city Khrushchev would visit.

This put the men charged with the Premier's safety on the spot. Personally, they may not have cared for the man; personally, they may have felt some sympathy with those—especially those who were refugees from Red slavery—who might wish revenge upon the head of the Communist state. But they were also fully aware that if any harm should come to Khrushchev, it might touch off World War III. So the Premier barged into New York, guarded as no visitor to that metropolis has ever been.

Ahead of his special train from Washington sped a pilot train whose unknowing passengers would have been the victims of any mines hidden on the tracks. The Pennsylvania Railroad stationed guards at one-mile intervals all along the 226 miles of track. The long streamliner slowed down, but did not halt, at the regular stops of Baltimore, Wilmington, or Philadelphia: the Secret Service informed Soviet security officers that they could not properly protect the Premier if the train tarried at these stations.

Khrushchev spent the entire four-hour trip seated at a table in his sun-splashed club car, the last on the train. He gazed curiously at samples of the industrial muscle of the United States—the big Martin missile plant, assembly plants of the big three automobile manufacturers, Bethlehem Steel's huge Sparrows Point plant, the E.I. du Pont de Nemours chemical complex, shipyards, and refineries. Frequently he waved to unprepared bystanders as the train whizzed past at speeds near 80 mph.

Despite the rigorous security precautions he had two unscheduled American visitors during the trip—Conniff and Considine. Upon boarding at Washington, they had taken seats in the Soviet section of the train, instead of the American press section. As the long train pulled out of the terminal, a barricade was set up to shut the American press off from the Russian section of the train.

News of the journalistic crime apparently leaked out. Every now and then a couple of American policemen would wander through the car in which Conniff and Considine sat, innocently looking out the window.

"I know they're back here somewhere," one of them would say. "Two big beefy guys."

When the coast was clear, and a small and heavily screened pool of photographers was permitted to advance on Khrushchev's car, Conniff and Considine joined them.

"Give me a camera," Conniff hissed to one of the photographers, when it appeared that he would be barred on the very threshold of the Khrushchev car. It turned out, he didn't need it. The very fact that he and Considine had started the trip as "Russians" sufficed, so far as the Russian secret police were concerned.

The United States policemen were hardly sharper. "I know they're back here somewhere," one kept insisting, as he passed within inches of Conniff and Considine.

"Yeah, I know," the other said. "Two big beefy guys."

Otherwise, the almost unnerving thoroughness of Khrushchev's protection was evident as soon as his train rolled into the caverns of Pennsylvania Station. A blight had settled on the terminal. The huge depot had been cut off from the seething mercantile area in which it sprawls. The big waiting room held only a fraction of its normal mass of people, and a good percentage of those it held were uniformed or plain clothes policemen. No taxi had been allowed near the station for the previous two hours.

Even so, Khrushchev was led through the dismal innards of the lower level to an official reception in a pipe-cluttered subterranean room. There he was met by Richard C. Patterson, former Department of Commerce official and United States Ambassador to Belgrade, then representing the City of New York. Despite introductions, Khrushchev insisted on calling him "Mr. Mayor." After a few perfunctory remarks he stepped into a big air-conditioned Cadillac, which nosed out a seldom-used exit of the station. There, one hundred motorcycle police were waiting. With a deafening roar they jockeyed their vehicles around the Khrushchev car and convoyed it up the incline to Seventh Avenue.

Khrushchev's first view of New York must have been startling. One of the busiest thoroughfares on earth had been swept clean of traffic. There were spectators, to be sure, but they stood motionless behind the police lines, and hardly a sound passed their lips. A few boos floated hollowly from their ranks, and from behind a police barricade three blocks away could be heard the thin cries of a protest group.

There was no ticker tape. Indeed, the only sign from on high was made by a skywriter. High against the deep blue dome of the sky he etched a perfect white cross. Nevertheless, the correspondent for Warsaw's *Tribunu Luda* cabled home that the huge symbolic crucifix was actually a *K*. Communist coverage of the visit was not notable for its truthfulness.

Mayor Wagner's luncheon for 1,000 business and civic leaders gave the Russian Premier an opportunity to display the versatility of his temperament to a representative "live" group and a huge TV audience. It was a virtuoso performance. Scarcely pausing for his interpreter, he ran the following gamut:

He had words of praise for Wagner, for Ambassador Lodge, and the President, who had said a few hours earlier at his news conference in Washington that he believed Khrushchev sincerely wanted peace. "He has to be a great man to invite *me* to this country," Khrushchev boomed in the course of his tribute to Eisenhower.

He went from there to poke fun at the capitalistic system: "But if this is the system you choose to live under, God be with you."

But then, out of the blue, he cried, "When our revolution took place, you forgot something. You sent your armies against us, to try to crush us. You and the French and the British. We requested you to return to your motherlands, or get kicked out. You returned. But it took you sixteen years after that to recognize [diplomatically] that something was going on in our country, something had been born without your permission and was developing according to its own will. If *now* you were to indulge in any such forceful measures in regard to us, well, I'm sure you're well aware of what this might lead to."

His manner made his implication plain.

But then the storm was over as suddenly as it began. "However," he said blandly, "having made your acquaintance, I'm certain you don't want any war between us. Therefore, let us conclude an agreement on how to preserve eternal peace."

Away from the cameras and reporters, he proved less amiable during a short visit at the home of Averell Harriman late that afternoon. Newsmen were not present to cover the event, but apparently he resented the fact that what he expected to be a sociable affair turned into a formal interrogation, with sharp questions being asked by Harriman's wealthy friends.

Hearst attended the posh dinner at the Economic Club that night at the Waldorf, where Khrushchev grew more openly fiery. He was asked from the floor of the packed main ballroom of the hotel, "Why aren't the Russian people allowed to listen to American broadcasts? Why isn't there free distribution of American newspapers, magazines, and periodicals? Why does the Soviet Union insist on censoring the dispatches of American correspondents?"

Khrushchev, after a moment of consideration, began:

"I am here at President Eisenhower's invitation, and, in turn, we have invited him to come to our country. We agreed that our discussions would not concern third countries, and that there would be no interference in the internal affairs of each other's nations."

He paused as if collecting his thoughts.

"Answer the question!" several in the audience shouted.

Khrushchev blazed.

"If you don't want to listen, all right!" he said angrily. "I am an old sparrow, and you cannot muddle me by your cries. You should show hospitality enough not to interrupt. If there is no desire to listen to me, I can go."

What amounted to the silence of a tomb descended on the room.

"No cries can do anything to offset or make the world forget the great achievements of our people," he said intensely. "What our people hear on the radio is of no concern to other nations. As a matter of fact," he said, looking out at that part of the banquet hall from which the heckling had come, "you also jam American voices sometimes. I am referring to the unfortunate fact that your great Negro singer Paul Robeson for some five to seven years was denied the right to go abroad. Why was his voice jammed?"

While he argued with the economists and their guests, a poignant human river of protest flowed up and down Park Avenue opposite the Waldorf. As it turned out, it was the biggest of the protests against Khrushchev—which never developed as fully as their sponsors had announced or would have wished. Still, the Park Avenue demonstration was impressive.

Considine was on the street with the demonstrators. The pickets were Hungarian and Ukrainian refugees, shouting, chanting, and singing. They carried placards with such messages as, "Khrushchev, the Butcher of the Ukraine," "6,000,000 Starved by Khrushchev in Famine He Planned and Supervised," and "Freedom for Hungary." A nice-looking old lady in an Eastern-European version of a Queen Mary hat handed out to passers-by little mourning cards engraved, "Don't have a crush on Khrush. It's you he wants to crush."

The pickets were held back behind wooden barricades, while mounted police loped back and forth before the barriers—fence-riding against the chance that one of the pickets might try to duck under or vault over and assault the skyscraper hotel.

The mood of the demonstrators would change from moment to moment. At times there would be silence. But then someone would start to chant, and the others would join in and the noise would rise to a climax. Or someone would lead the rest in a heartbreaking song from the old country—somehow more touchingly poignant than any of their other gestures of protest.

A patient but harassed police sergeant remonstrated with some of the demonstrators who got out of hand. The old lady in the Queen Mary hat threw her arms around him and kissed him. "Keep moving," he said gruffly, then smiled at her and added, ". . . please."

Next morning Khrushchev drove to Hyde Park to visit Eleanor Roosevelt and lay a wreath on the tomb of the late President. He seemed a bit startled when Mrs. Roosevelt confided to him (and a TV audience) that F.D.R. was not buried under the stone itself but well in front of it. "Franklin would have wanted to look up at the trees and the stars," she explained.

Khrushchev was plainly preoccupied with other thoughts. He cut short his lunch with Mrs. Roosevelt and her guests, and hurried back to the city. This was his day, as one commentator expressed it, "to put up or shut up"—his day to present his disarmament proposal to the UN.

The United States and British delegations to the UN were in no mood to permit Khrushchev to portray the Soviet Union as the sole champion of disarmament. In advance of the Premier's speech to the General Assembly, Secretary of State Herter made his first address before the world body. He declared that America would not yield in its insistence on proper inspection in any disarmament program. Without mentioning Khrushchev by name, he pointedly challenged him to enter into negotiations to prevent the arms race "from exploding into nuclear conflict."

British Foreign Minister Selwyn Lloyd presented an even more concrete program for disarmament. It involved a gradual but progressive schedule for the ending of atomic tests, cutbacks on the stockpiles of atomic weapons and an end to their further production, reduction of conventional arms and armies, and the creation of an international police force. Like the American proposal, the British plan stipulated adequate inspection and control to make sure everyone was living up to the agreement.

The Anglo-American proposals were intended to cushion the impact of what Khrushchev would come up with. But Khrushchev's plan had received so much advance publicity that even though it had been proposed twice before since the Bolshevik revolution, it still commanded the attention of the world.

He called upon all nations over the next four years to demobilize their armies, navies, and air forces; to stop atomic tests, destroy their weapons, and utilize the fissionable material in their atomic arsenals for medical and industrial research; to shut down such institutions as West Point, Annapolis, and the Air Force Academy; to return all war workers to peaceful pursuits and convert such missile centers as Cape Canaveral and Vandenberg Air Force Base into pure research laboratories for space exploration and travel.

He used large statistics freely to shore up his arguments. One hundred million persons, he told the delegates, were engaged directly or indirectly in preparing for war. One hundred billion dollars was being spent through the world on weapons, war research, and the training and maintenance of military forces. If this incredible amount of treasure and effort could be redirected into peaceful pursuits, he said, the earth would soon abound with new hospitals, schools, and housing. The money the great powers had spent on arms in the previous ten years, he added, could have built 150 million homes, educated the illiterates in all the countries of Asia, Latin America, and Africa. The constant threat of a war in which hundreds of millions of human beings might perish would disappear, he promised, for if his conditions were met, nations would have no means of fighting a war.

Some remembered a similar proposal advanced by the Russians at the League of Nations in 1927, and again in 1932 at the World Disarmament Conference in Geneva. On that occasion the champion of the plan, Maxim Litvinov, was gently chided by the Spanish delegate, the famous historian Salvador de Madariaga.

"Does Mr. Litvinov remember the fable about the animals' disarmament conference?" he asked. "When the animals had gathered, the lion looked at the eagle and said gravely, 'We must abolish talons.' The tiger looked at the elephant and said, 'We must abolish tusks.' The elephant looked at the tiger and said, 'We must abolish claws and jaws.'

"Thus each animal in turn proposed the abolition of the weapons he did not have, until at last the bear rose up and said in tones of sweet reasonableness: 'Comrades, let us abolish everything—everything but the great universal embrace.' "

But many hesitated to dismiss Khrushchev's proposals out of hand. Two who came quickly into print were Senator Hubert Humphrey, who said, "This cannot be dismissed as 'propaganda,'" and Adlai Stevenson, who warned, "The proposal must be taken seriously, however skeptical we might be."

Khrushchev did not confine his remarks to disarmament. In addition to a plea for the election of Red China to the UN (the continued isolation of that massive country is "inconceivable," he said), Khrushchev called for increased trade among nations, an end to the exploitation of oil and other natural resources of impoverished peoples, and increased exchanges of all types with the Soviet Union.

He was willing, he added, to negotiate on certain aspects of his "swords-into-plowshares" plan.

Representatives of Nationalist China, which Khrushchev fiercely called a "corpse," boycotted the session. But the Assembly as a whole applauded generously at the end of the Premier's one hour and ten minute declaration.

That night he attended a rather quiet dinner given by UN Secretary General Dag Hammarskjöld; and next morning, Saturday, September 19, he left New York by an Air Force jet transport (the same plane he had inspected at the Moscow airport in July). En route to Idlewild airport the Premier, bouncy and inquisitive as ever, suspected that his hosts might be giving him the "scenic view."

"Let us drive through your Harlem," he suggested slyly. And so the caravan swept through the astonished Negro section of the city. The trip seemed to do something for Khrushchev's spirits. He was in good fettle as he led his group aboard the hulking jet that would hasten them to adventures in the West.

CHAPTER 11

The proletarian prince
in the wild west

By coincidence or design, United States authorities, working with Los Angeles police, ordained that Khrushchev would alight from his plane virtually at the doorstep of the North American Aviation Corporation plant on the far side of the airport.

North American is the home of the F-86 fighter which won the jet war over Korea against Russian-built MIG-17s. It is also the birthplace of the design for the B-70, which will fly in 1962 or 1963 as the "last manned bomber." The B-70 will have a speed of three times that of sound and the range of the present B-52G, if not more.

Khrushchev could not have been less impressed.

However, he managed to perk up in time to be introduced to Hollywood at a memorable lunch.

The scene: the somewhat garish dining room on the Twentieth Century Fox lot.

The cast: a goodly proportion of the most famous and most glamorous stars of the motion picture capital, many of whom had schemed and politicked for weeks to get invited to what was the most fashionable event of the Hollywood social season.

The action : fast and unpredictable.

At the head table were a mixture of film executives, government officials, and Russian dignitaries. Khrushchev sat next to his host Spyros Skouras, President of Twentieth Century Fox. In the presence of this curiously scrambled audience Khrushchev chose to show America and the world some unrevealed facets of his personality.

During a speech by his host, Khrushchev began a series of sometimes ludicrous but often tense interruptions, although he was to grow peevish later when he himself was interrupted. The first of these intrusions came as Skouras was explaining to Khrushchev that the one-time Iron Curtain that divided Hollywood from the Soviet film industry was being at least slightly lifted.

"Let's hurry up about it!" Khrushchev shouted through interpreter Victor Sukhodrev, who had been straining Skouras' remarks into the Premier's ear. He stood up, ready to take issue with Skouras on the whole issue of film exchanges.

"Zhukov!" he shouted down the head table to the beefy cultural commissar whom he had brought in his entourage to America. "How many American films have we chosen to show in the Soviet Union lately?"

"Ten!" Zhukov shouted back.

"How many of ours have they chosen to show here?"

"Seven!" Zhukov roared triumphantly.

Skouras was not impressed. Things move slower in America, he tried to explain to his guest, because individual companies are permitted to make decisions on their own. "We are not guided by a central authority," he said. "We must check up on contracts individually—the contracts with your government."

"Dig into your own contracts!" Khrushchev thundered jovially. "We don't have to dig into ours."

"No wonder," Skouras commented. "Your country is the greatest monopoly the world has ever known.

"Here's something you don't understand about us," Skouras went on, lecturing at the top of Khrushchev's bald head. "Never in history have so many emigrated to one country and lived so happily. This is because of the free American system.

"I must tell you, Mr. Chairman, that I came myself from a very poor family, born in a small and obscure town in Greece. When we came to this country, my two brothers and I worked as humble busboys. But because of the American system of opportunity for all, now I am President of Twentieth Century Fox, an international organization employing 10,000 people. This has been the case with millions of other American citizens.

"You should remember, I think, that capitalism and private enterprise must not be criticized. It would be better for you to observe it, study it. Without it, there could not be an America as you see it today."

Khrushchev received the words through Sukhodrev and bided his time. Skouras went on unmolested, recalling American relief efforts in Russia after the revolution. He also urged Khrushchev to permit American films to be shown not only in the cities, but in the rural areas of the Soviet Union, "because these films will inspire your people to achieve their goal, which is to rise to the living standards of America. We hope you achieve this goal.

"Don't feel so bad about the so-called unemployment figures in our country, Mr. Chairman," Skouras advised his guest. "There is no cause to arouse Russian sympathy. We have no unemployment here."

Khrushchev stood up suddenly and seized the microphone.

"I am not to blame for commenting on your unemployment,"

he protested. "Your own State Department released figures on that. I'm only the reader, not the writer of such statistics."

Skouras wagged a finger at him. "Don't believe everything you read," he advised.

Khrushchev shrugged and said, "I cannot help but believe what your trade unions say."

Khrushchev began his own lengthy speech on a note of religion.

"My dear brother Greek," he said, looking down at Skouras. "I can call you brother because Russia took part in the war to liberate Greece. In the old days we took the Greek religion. We are friends and brothers before Christ.

"I, personally, am an atheist," Khrushchev told the suddenly hushed room. "But among our people we have representatives of all religions and people of no religion, too."

He put aside his notes.

"Ladies and gentlemen, I had planned to speak along other lines today," he said. "But my Greek brother has changed my thoughts." He looked down at Skouras once more, as if sizing him up for a fight.

"What were you in Greece?" he asked.

Skouras thought a moment, then solemnly and proudly answered, "I was seventeen." It confused many in the room, including Khrushchev.

But the Premier plunged on. "It has impressed me, your talk of working at an early age," he said. "This, however, is of no great surprise to me. I myself started working as soon as I could walk. Until the age of twelve I was a sheep herder—I tended little cows. Then I worked in a mine and then in a factory, then a mine again, then a machine plant. And let me say something about our own system. I was poor, too, and unknown, but through that system I am now the Prime Minister of the great Soviet state, with more than 200 million people. Don't apologize for, or be unduly proud of work. All work is worthy of respect. Work, as such, cannot be dirty. Only man's conscience can be dirty."

To the astonishment of everyone, Skouras suddenly stood up, took the microphone from Khrushchev's hands and said into it, "How many prime ministers in Russia?"

Khrushchev's eyes narrowed, and there was a trace of impatience in his face.

"How many presidents in the United States?" he asked. The tension in the room broke, and there was applause and laughter.

Still on his feet, Skouras bawled into the microphone, "We have 2 million presidents—presidents of American corporations . . . their stockholders!"

Red-faced with anger, Khrushchev got his microphone back and launched into a vigorous defense of the Soviet system and what it has done for the individual. "Now, Comrade Greek," he concluded, "is that not enough for you?"

"But that's still a monopoly," Skouras insisted.

"Ah!" Khrushchev answered, "but it's a people's monopoly. The rich men I have told you about possess nothing, really, but the pants they wear. . . ."

He was about to continue when Skouras put his arm around him and started to add fresh fuel to the debate. Many of the flabbergasted stars in the audience cried out "No! No!" Skouras scanned his audience, thought better of his intentions, and resumed his place at the head table.

"Let us keep these questions to ourselves," Khrushchev chided him. "There's an old Russian proverb which goes: 'You won't catch an old sparrow napping.' "

Khrushchev then launched into a soft-spoken tribute to the contribution American engineers and others had made to the industrialization of the Soviet Union. "For this we render our thanks and bow down to you," he said meekly. "You may be

proud as a teacher is proud when the pupil shows the fruit of
the teacher's labors."

He soon tired of his diet of humble pie. "Now, however, we
want to surpass you," he said. "We were not dumb pupils. When
Ford built the first automobile plant in Russia, we broke a lot
of machines because we had not learned to use them. Now we
have sent a rocket to outer space and planted our pennant on
the moon. Not bad for a pupil, eh?"

He urged the United States to continue living under capitalism. "But don't inflict it on us," he said with mock gravity.
"Don't try to help the sheep who have wandered from the fold.
Stop hoping that we will return to capitalism. Do you assume
our system will fail? Well, it won't!

"You may believe I am an ignorant man," he said. "That's
your privilege. But it is also my right to say that you in America
have not grown up to see and understand what has happened in
the world. When you don't understand, you think of fighting.
Shall we fight? That's the way it was once done. In the olden
days, men tore out each other's hair, ripped out parts of their
beards. But the vanquished would simply get a haircut or shave,
to even things off, or let the hair grow out again.

"But what of today? There's an old Russian proverb which
answers that question: 'When you lose your head, don't cry
over your hair.' That is why I say let's live in peace. Let time
judge which is the better system."

The room burst into applause. The reaction moved him.

"We love and esteem people of intellectual toil such as you,"
he said. "You require the best treatment, for you are like an
orchid. You require humidity, warmth, light."

He paused, and continued in a surprising vein. "I recall the
conversation I once had with an old czarist intellectual," he said.
"I was in Kuban, where we routed the White Guard. I lived in

a bourgeois intellectual household. I still had coal dust on my hands. But in time they saw I was not a cannibal. I was simply hungry and had no bread. I was a peasant. I was a human being.

"Sure, I was a Bolshevik. We were considered robbers. Yet, in time, there was respect for me in that household. We were crude and illiterate, many Bolsheviks, but we were honest. We wanted to learn how to administer the state, how to build a new society. They found it hard to believe that we could do this.

" 'What do you know about the ballet?' they would ask me, taunting me, showing up my ignorance. I didn't know what the word ballet meant, really. Did you eat it?

"But I would say to that or any other question of that nature, 'Wait. It will all come.' If the hostess of the house, who was a schoolteacher, had asked me, 'What will come?' I could not have answered. But I knew in my heart that something would come to me and to our movement one day, and that when it came it would be good."

It was an almost tender moment. But it was not to be prolonged.

"Forgive me," Khrushchev continued, pulling himself together. "I planned a short, tranquil speech here today." His voice rose. "But I cannot stand it when someone steps on my pet corn." He glared down at Skouras. "I always want to give a worthy response in defense of our country, our people, and our system."

Now he was sore all over again, and off on a thoroughly unexpected tangent, making blatant propaganda use of the security precautions taken for his safety.

"I cannot but express deep disappointment and surprise over something I have just learned here at the table," he said petulantly. "We in Russia have always regarded the United States as the last word in culture and refinement and progress. Now we find ourselves in a city where lives the cream of American arts. I, as Prime Minister, was given a definite program and a plan in advance of my arrival here.

"But just now I was told I could not go to Disneyland!"

He said it as if he had been denied permission to inhale the California air.

"What do you have there—rocket launching pads?" he brayed. He seemed serious and deeply hurt. "Your American security says it cannot guarantee my safety if I go there. Is there an epidemic of cholera there? Have gangsters taken control of the place? Your police are strong enough to lift up a bull. Surely they are strong enough to take care of gangsters if indeed gangsters have taken over Disneyland."

He shook his head back and forth and said with stubborn tenacity:

"I would very much like to see Disneyland. What must I do now?—commit suicide? This situation is inconceivable. I will never be able to find words to explain this to my people."

He waved his arms in an all-embracing gesture and shouted:

"Come to my country! I will guarantee that no one shows you anything but respect. No foreign guest will ever be harmed in the Soviet Union. I thought I could come to this country in peace. I thought I could come as a free man. Instead, I must sit in closed cars in the smothering heat under the sun.

"We have an old proverb which goes, 'Eat their bread and salt, but speak your own mind.' "

He took a breath and smiled.

"Forgive me if I have seemed hotheaded today," he asked, almost gently. "Perhaps the temperature here and my Greek friend warmed me up. If I have offended any of you I ask your forgiveness. Thank you, dear friends."

Khrushchev was led from the dais by Skouras, who introduced him to only one of the glamorous stars on hand—Marilyn

Monroe. The Premier declined an invitation to kiss her. ("Interesting," she said of him later.) Then the movie mogul escorted his guest to Sound Stage 8, to watch Frank Sinatra filming Hollywood's answer to the Bolshoi Ballet—*Can-Can*.

That night, to the utter dismay of the State Department, Khrushchev threatened to cut short his visit and return to the Soviet Union without engaging in the scheduled talks with the President.

He had no such intention, of course. But what had provoked him was a belligerent reference by Mayor Norris Poulson to his famous phrase, "we will bury you." He commented sternly that the Mayor should read the papers more carefully: he had explained the remark at length at the National Press Club in Washington, and mayors of Russian cities are expected to, and do, stay abreast of current events. He mentioned the possibility of a quick flight home, and rattled his missiles.

The next morning, however, found him in a better mood. He napped, joked, and pontificated his way from Los Angeles to San Francisco aboard an eighteen-car special train guarded both on land and in the air during its ten-hour trip up the California coast. Khrushchev left the train briefly at Santa Barbara and San Luis Obispo. He was to have inspected the terminal at San José, but was sound asleep when the train pulled in. It was a sleep he badly needed.

"I've had only one night's sleep since I landed in this country," he complained to Lodge early in the day. "Hammarskjöld let me go at ten o'clock the night he gave me a dinner in New York. That was my only night of real rest." Lodge urged him to get some sleep during the long Sunday train ride.

At the station platform in Santa Barbara, he grumbled to a handful of well-dressed spectators, "The security guard is keeping me from meeting the people . . . the workers."

"He's been an awful headache to us," a State Department

security man said as the train carried Khrushchev to the next stop. "But Mr. Lodge feels that it's better to be charged with overprotecting him than underprotecting him. That beef about not being able to go to Disneyland was phony, by the way. He didn't show the least interest in going there until the last moment, long after we could have made security arrangements there."

But the cause of so much national turmoil didn't seem to have a worry in the world as he strolled through the press cars just before the San Luis Obispo stop. The train lurched as he waddled through the reporter's dining car, which was crowded.

"Now the American reporters will say Khrushchev lurched because he was drinking," he announced.

In the Tavern Car Considine had arranged for a cold bottle of vodka to be served him. "No, thanks," Khrushchev told him, after thinking the matter over. "It's too hot for vodka."

"Cognac? . . . Scotch? . . . Bourbon? . . ."

He shook his head. "No, it's too hot."

He strolled on, then stopped at the sound of a voice speaking Russian. It was that of Harry Schwartz, whose penetrating analyses of Soviet affairs in *The New York Times* are world renowned. Schwartz was asking him for his autograph.

He identified himself and said, "Your country thinks I am a bad person, but the autograph would be for my children."

Khrushchev replied, "Stalin said we shouldn't hold children responsible for the sins of their parents. But," he added, as a kind of afterthought, "the sins of the parents should not be forgotten, either." He would not give his autograph.

That night he ran into what may well have been his worst experience of his trip. Top labor leaders pricked him with sharp questioning for more than three hours at a private dinner boycotted by George Meany, president of the AFL-CIO.

Details of what must have been a stormy session (no reporters were present) were given to the press late that night by the Premier's hosts, chiefly Walter Reuther, vice president of AFL-CIO and head of the United Auto Workers Union, and Joseph Curran, the national Maritime Union leader.

Reuther had the most to say. "I told him he should drop that old line about American labor unions being a part of the 'capitalistic cadre,' " he said. "I told him it wasn't doing his side any good. 'Nobody'll believe you,' I told him. 'Nobody believes that communism has a monopoly on working for the rights of workers.'

"I told him American labor unions and union leaders have had to fight communism and Communists in our movement. We've had to fight it and them because we found they often betrayed the best interests of the workers."

Khrushchev's dinner companions quoted the Premier as stating that there were no strikes in the Soviet Union "because there is no need to strike. All our workers know our government is working solely for them."

Curran reported that he then asked, "Has there ever been a situation wherein your trade unions differed from the Communist Party?" He got no answer from Khrushchev.

They asked him about the suppression of freedom fighters in Hungary, and he was quoted as replying:

"The Hungarian troubles were caused by hooligans and saboteurs. They attempted to make a counter-revolution. I was proud to suppress it. If I hadn't the Nazis would have taken over."

"What about Imre Nagy?" one of the labor chieftains asked.

"I wouldn't like Nagy named among the good Communists," Khrushchev was quoted as saying with a shrug.

He was pictured as growing quite angry when the subject of the jamming of the Voice of America was brought up.

"What do you like to eat?" he demanded of one of his hosts.

The somewhat startled man thought a moment and answered, "Roast beef."

"Well, I don't like roast beef!" Khrushchev half shouted. "You can have your roast beef. The Soviet Union will take borscht."

"But how do you personally decide what the people will have?" he was asked.

"I am the head of the dictatorship of the proletariat," Khrushchev replied proudly. "I am defending the workers' interests." Curran said Khrushchev pounded the table at this particular point.

He seems also to have danced the cancan during the memorable session. This extraordinary exercise emerged from his excoriation of American culture. He had been relating his experience at Twentieth Century Fox.

"We don't want this kind of trash in the Soviet Union," he said of the picture he had seen being filmed. "There should be a law against that sort of thing." Then, according to Reuther, Khrushchev bounced to his feet and performed a travesty of the French chorus-line dance, flipping the front of his coat and finishing with what is referred to in burlesque circles as a bump.

"Mikoyan had better control," Reuther said of Khrushchev in retrospect. "Mikoyan doesn't evade questions. Matter of fact, I told Khrushchev, 'an angry answer is not an adequate answer. We won't accept that sort of thing.' But we could never get him to answer any question of substance."

Curran reported one Khrushchev victory. "We got into the question of racial problems in labor," he said, "and Khrushchev had a lot of questions about discrimination and segregation. We didn't have any answers for him."

Khrushchev retired to the Royal Suite of the Hotel Mark Hopkins about 10:30 that night. A few minutes later he sent down a breakfast order for himself and his party, to be served promptly at 8 A.M. The hotel considered the order novel enough to release to the press:

Fresh California orange juice, yoghurt, creamed cottage cheese, boiled (not broiled) halved chicken with steamed rice (no salt), hearts of filet steaks (well done), crisp French fried potatoes, flower cabbage fried in oil with whites of raw eggs, new peas sautéed in butter, halved cucumbers (not peeled), fresh tomatoes (whole, not peeled), green and ripe olives, sliced Swiss cheese, white toast, *croissants,* brioches, sweet rolls, jelly, marmalade, coffee, tea, and milk.

Khrushchev's all but shattered illusions about American labor were briefly restored next day, September 21. He met the boss of the International Longshoremen's Union, Harry Bridges, for years under fire in United States courts as a Communist. About five hundred longshoremen helped Bridges welcome the undisputed boss of *all* Soviet labor at the union hall in San Francisco. They cheered him, shook hands with him, clapped him on the back. It was the warmest reception of Khrushchev's American tour.

Like almost everything else he did in San Francisco, Khrushchev switched plans to put the I.L.W.U. hall into his itinerary: it was not on his schedule. But he passed the hall early in the morning, during the course of a constitutional walk, saw it later from a cruise boat while surveying the Bay area, and asked that a visit be planned pronto.

Bridges and his wife were waiting for Khrushchev at the hall, along with several officials and associates of the left-wing union. Mrs. Bridges presented the dictator with a spray of red roses. When Khrushchev barged into the midst of the longshoremen, one of them clapped a longshoreman's brimmed white hat on his head. Many reached out to touch him, shake his hand, wish him well. The police had to push open a circle around him, when he took the microphone to speak, so that he could be seen as well as heard—for most of the longshoremen towered over him.

"Tovarisch! May I call you all comrades?" he called out. That won a big response.

"The main hope of workers in America is peace," Bridges told him.

"We in the Soviet Union do what we can to bring about peace," Khrushchev replied.

"I know," Bridges said. "So you are welcome, for that is the purpose of your trip: peace and the expansion of world trade, too."

"This is important and our objective," the Russian rejoined.

Not even the shock of seeing American photographers running amok when he visited a supermarket at nearby Stonestown later that day could take the edge off his pleasure. While the beefy little Bolshevik strolled through the place, pinching the tomatoes and thumping the melons, the photographers clambered up pyramids of canned goods, stood on the cashier's fingers, and used shopping carts as camera dollies. A lady shopper fainted near the meat counter. A not very bright cop bent over her inert form. "Do you suppose she fainted?" he asked a callous photographer. "She's either fainted or on sale," the latter replied.

Khrushchev was still warmed by the glow generated at the I.L.W.U. reception in his farewell speech to the city. He was even ready to forgive Mayor Poulson of Los Angeles.

"Mayor Poulson has a charming wife and fine children," he told a dinner group. "I enjoyed meeting them. Perhaps he had got out of bed on the wrong side that morning. We all make speeches we sometimes later regret.

"Christian teaching," the well-known atheist continued, "says forgive the trespasses of others, if they understand that they have trespassed. Mayor Poulson spoke from the mind, not the heart. I have invited him to visit the Soviet Union," he said magnanimously. "A man can drop an unfortunate phrase."

Reporters accompanying Khrushchev were now becoming convinced that he was a consummate actor. He could be by turns gay, sad, friendly, or downright furious, according to what would serve him best. At Los Angeles his outburst about Disneyland was designed to convince the Russians and other peoples around the world that he was caught in the toils of the American police state. He could invoke the scriptures and spread Christian teachings like a man of the cloth. He could play the clown. He could play the menacing war lord. He could play the homely Russian philosopher. He could play the suave politician.

By now, halfway through the tour, Khrushchev was showing impatience with play-acting and sight-seeing. He apparently was both tired of his travels and eager to get to what he considered the main business of his trip, the meetings with President Eisenhower at the latter's retreat at Camp David, Maryland.

It had been expected that the tall corn and the farming innovations in Iowa would intrigue the supposed agricultural expert. Khrushchev was plainly bored. He bustled through a packing plant and a farm-implement factory in Des Moines. His hosts were eager to explain; Khrushchev either did not listen or cut them short. During his visit to the packing house he apparently realized he was endangering his image as a leader devoutly interested in learning anything that would improve the lot of his people. He stopped suddenly and poked a stubby finger into a pile of livers, and later managed to down a hot dog, with mustard—"of course, I want mustard," he said with a conspicuous display of gustatory satisfaction.

The main event of Khrushchev's Iowa tour was his visit to

the farm of Roswell Garst near Coon Rapids. Khrushchev had met Garst in Moscow, and Garst seemed to the Russian the embodiment of a successful farmer in the best farming country in the most agriculturally productive nation in the world. But if Khrushchev was impressed, he managed largely to conceal it. He seemed to enjoy most the sight of his host Garst throwing silage at newsmen who pressed too close for his comfort and administering a kick in the shins to Harrison Salisbury, the quiet, unobtrusive, scholarly-looking Russian expert of *The New York Times*.

On the way east, he stopped at Pittsburgh, where he viewed such modern technological methods as automation at the Mesta machine plant, and where Pennsylvania's Governor David L. Lawrence spelled out for the dictator what unity means in America.

"We may seem a divided people to you," Lawrence told his guest. "We are not an employers' nation. We are not an employees' nation. Management and labor are free to test their strength, one against the other—as you have seen in the case of our steel strike. We are not a one-party nation. I don't belong to the President's political party. Everything I can do next year to bring about the election of the candidate of my own party, I will do. I will work against the candidate of the President's party.

"But we are immediately as one with our President in any time such as this. You have seen by now that wherever you have gone in the United States, politics stops at the water's edge. In his meetings with you, President Eisenhower will speak for a united country. Americans will follow him wherever he goes."

A full historical evaluation of the results of the Camp David meeting will have to await the passage of time and the test of deeds. But since, only a few months after the meeting, the

Soviets were invoking "The Spirit of Camp David" in an attempt to cow the United States from any decisive stand, a hard look is required at what is known of the talks.

During the three-day get-together at the Presidential lodge in the Catoctin mountains the two leaders conversed alone for only six and one-half hours. Additional conversations took place with Secretary of State Christian Herter, Foreign Minister Andrei Gromyko, and other aides in attendance. It had been made clear by President Eisenhower long before the talks, and it was repeated in the communiqué issued when they were completed, that "the talks were not undertaken to negotiate issues."

The communiqué is no more rewarding to the reader than such instruments of vagueness usually are: "The Chairman of the Council of Ministers of the U.S.S.R. and the President of the United States agreed that the question of general disarmament is the most important one facing the world today. Both Governments will make every effort to achieve a constructive solution of this problem. . . . In the course of the conversations an exchange of views took place on the question of Germany, including the question of a peace treaty with Germany, in which the positions of both sides were expounded. With respect to the specific Berlin question, an understanding was reached, subject to the approval of the other parties directly concerned, that negotiations would be reopened with a view to achieving a solution which would be in accordance with the interests of all concerned and in the interest of the maintenance of peace. . . . The Chairman of the Council of Ministers of the U.S.S.R. and the President of the United States agreed that all outstanding international questions should be settled not by the application of force but by peaceful means through negotiation. . . ."

Elaboration of the communiqué awaited a speech by Khrushchev after his return to Moscow and a news conference by

President Eisenhower. But in the meantime Khrushchev provided an answer to one question Americans had been asking since his arrival: his mind had not been materially changed by what he had seen on his tour. In fact, he devoted most of a forty-five minute nationwide TV address to extolling the progress his country had made under the leadership of the Communist Party. What he saw of the United States, he said, had not shaken his "faith that the political, economic and social system in the Soviet Union is the fairest and most progressive."

At his news conference the next day President Eisenhower revealed what was, for the West, the nub of the discussions: the Soviet leader had "stated emphatically that never had he any intention to give anything that was to be interpreted as duress or compulsion" against the stationing of Western forces in West Berlin. Khrushchev had, in effect, formally ended a threat to Berlin which he had initiated in November, 1958. He had at that time set a six-month time limit for settlement of the Berlin question, an ultimatum carrying an implied threat of trouble. Later he had extended the time limit to eighteen months. Now he denied he had ever handed out an ultimatum in the first place. But Eisenhower wanted him on the record, and demanded this assurance as a condition for a summit meeting.

What Khrushchev got out of his tour and the Camp David meetings was not spelled out by him in the same detail, but he did not leave the United States empty-handed. His concession on Berlin had removed one big stumbling block to the summit meeting the Soviet leader so ardently desired. Perhaps equally important, his visit had helped build up his position at home, and his image as a peace-maker in other parts of the world. He received a hero's welcome when his TU-114 turboprop airliner arrived in Moscow after a nonstop flight of 4,986 miles in ten hours and twenty-eight minutes. Like a country boy returned from the Big City he told the airport throng, "Okay, I've been in America, but Russia is better. It's good to be home."

Khrushchev's visit to this country climaxed the first half-decade of his rule, and forms a natural conclusion to this narrative. During this period we of the Hearst team had observed not only the rise of this bright, cocky little man to the apex of the party pyramid in the Soviet Union, but also his rise to international eminence as a world statesman. We had seen his capabilities applied not only to vanquishing his rivals for the Communist dictatorship, but also to clever maneuverings in the diplomatic arena. He, we are convinced, is largely responsible for the direction of the party line, with its emphasis on competition and coexistence; whether we like it or not, we seem to be forced to fight by the rules he has set down. In this account of our observations of Khrushchev, we have attempted to show the forces that have helped make him, the methods by which he operates, and the goals for which he strives. The coming months and years will see us negotiating closely and intensely with this man, and the future of the world will largely depend on our wisdom in these negotiations. But in all these negotiations, all these conferences, it is necessary to understand one thing clearly: that in Nikita Sergeyevitch Khrushchev, we have a clever, versatile, and dangerous opponent who will take our best effort and deepest understanding to handle. If this book contributes to that understanding, it will have more than fulfilled its purpose.

ABOUT THE AUTHORS

WILLIAM RANDOLPH HEARST, JR., began his journalistic career on April 12, 1928, when he went out on his first assignment for the *New York American* on the City Hall beat. In 1936 he was appointed publisher of the paper and continued in that capacity after the merger with the *New York Journal.* During World War II he served in the European theater as war correspondent and reported from the thick of the fighting in Africa, Italy, Normandy, and Germany. In 1955, he organized the Hearst Task Force and astounded the world with accounts of unprecedented interviews with top Soviet officials. For this feat he was named co-winner of the Pulitzer Prize in Journalism in 1956. In 1958 he was one of the winners of the coveted Overseas Press Club award for a similar Russian expedition. Among the numerous posts he holds is that of Editor-in-Chief of the Hearst newspapers.

BOB CONSIDINE is one of the world's most famous and respected reporters. From free-lance sports writing for the *Washington Post* in 1929 he rose to Sports Editor and soon caught the eye of William Randolph Hearst, who brought him to the *New York Mirror* as a sports columnist. He has served with distinction in almost every area of journalism, has written many popular books, and has won fame writing for and appearing on radio and television.

FRANK CONNIFF has risen from sports reporter on the *Danbury News Times* to National Editor of the Hearst newspapers. He has worked for Hearst papers since 1936 when he began as a reporter for the *New York Journal American.* Having served as a war correspondent during World War II, he afterward won wide popularity as a columnist. Mr. Conniff reported from the front lines during the Korean War and was one of the original members of the Hearst Task Force.